Ishbel

Lady Aberdeen in Ireland

Ishbel

Lady Aberdeen in Ireland

Maureen Keane

Colourpoint

Published by Colourpoint Books
© M Keane 1999

6 5 4 3 2 1

Designed by Colourpoint Books
Printed by ColourBooks

ISBN 1 898392 53 6

Extracts from *Lantern Slides* by Bonham-Carter and Pottle, published by Weidenfeld and Nicolson, are reproduced by kind permission of Orion Publishing Group Ltd. Colourpoint would also like to thank Lord Haddo for his time and courtesy when consulted about the photographs included in this book.

Cover: Ishbel Aberdeen, portrait hanging in Library of Haddo House.

Colourpoint Books
Unit D5, Ards Business Centre
Jubilee Road
NEWTOWNARDS
County Down
Northern Ireland
BT23 4YH

Tel: (01247) 820505
Fax: (01247) 821900
info@colourpoint.co.uk
www.colourpoint.co.uk

Maureen Keane lives in Dublin, the city in which she was born and educated. She graduated from University College, Dublin with an MA in English, and worked first as a teacher and then as a freelance journalist. She later obtained a PhD in English from NUI, Maynooth. *Ishbel* is her second book; her first, *Mrs SC Hall: a Literary Biography*, was published in 1997 and has been nominated for the Irish Times Literary Award.

Sincere thanks to the many people who helped in the preparation of this book, especially the staff in the libraries and archives where I worked. I am also deeply indebted to Frances Carruthers who shared with me the results of her academic research. Frances O'Shea who prepared the manuscript deserves a special thank you not only for her professional skill but for her patience and tolerance.
I am profoundly grateful to my editor Sheila Johnston for her help and encouragement. Without her this book would never have appeared in print. Finally, thank you to my husband David Keane for his continued support.

Maureen Keane
Dublin, April 1999

Contents

Introduction

ISHBEL, LADY ABERDEEN, ACCOMPANIED her husband to Ireland when he was appointed Viceroy there early in 1886. At first reluctant to live in Ireland she quickly became devoted to everything Irish. She admired native arts and crafts and founded an association to stimulate the growth of cottage industries. When the Aberdeens left Ireland after six months, her interest never flagged and she was responsible for an increase in sales of Irish goods.

Lord Aberdeen returned as Viceroy in 1906 and in the nine years which the couple spent in the country Ishbel worked tirelessly for many charitable causes. She was interested in education, housing, child welfare and town planning but her greatest interest was in the fight against disease, particularly tuberculosis. Through the efforts of the organisation which Lady Aberdeen founded, the Women's National Health Association, a country-wide campaign of preventive education was lauded, and rest homes and clinics were set up. Two sanatoria, one at Peamount outside Dublin, and one in Rossclere, County Antrim, were established, to treat sufferers from tuberculosis.

When Lady Aberdeen left with her husband in 1915, she did not abandon her many schemes, but retained an active interest in them up to the time of her death in 1939. Her work, however, is largely forgotten, and so is she, but it is about time that she be given due recognition. That is my purpose here.

When I prepared to write this account of Lady Aberdeen's connection with Ireland I had high hopes of discovering original material – letters, diaries, journals. Unfortunately most of Lady Aberdeen's journals were missing so I had to rely on secondary sources for much of the information I needed. Lord and Lady Aberdeen did, it is true, publish their memoirs, We Twa, but this was in 1925 and they, therefore, lacked the immediacy of a diary, and The Canadian Journal of Lady Aberdeen, published in 1898 is of little relevance here.

With regard to original letters to Lady Aberdeen I was more fortunate. Lord Haddo, great-grandson of Lady Aberdeen, kindly allowed me to use the archives in Haddo House in Aberdeenshire, and there I found some letters that shed some light on her character. These letters are from people who admired her, but contemporaries who did not admire her also recorded their views.

Important sources were the letters and diaries of Sir Horace Plunkett, whose earlier liking for Lady Aberdeen turned to distaste. Other contemporaries – Englishmen who worked in the Irish administration, wrote memoirs of their time in Ireland and were, in the main, highly critical of Lady Aberdeen's work and general behaviour. These I have quoted, and I find it revealing that female contemporaries who wrote their memoirs mentioned Lady Aberdeen with respect and affection.

This respect and affection was also expressed in anecdotal form to me by men and women whose parents, or connections, had had dealings with Lady Aberdeen. A particularly touching story, complete with photocopy of a letter from the Countess, was sent to me from an old woman in Scotland, and I have used it as the conclusion to my story for I believe it is extremely illuminating of Lady Aberdeen's personality. In the main, though, I have had to rely on newspaper and periodical accounts of Lady Aberdeen's work and activities in order to form my own assessment of her as a person. Here and there I have made assumptions but I have mostly based these on the internal evidence of Lady Aberdeen's speeches. I must confess too that I have indulged in a little speculation, but perhaps that is an indulgence allowed to the biographer who becomes closely attached to her subject. That also accounts for a certain defensive tone when I allude to attacks made on Lady Aberdeen by people who disliked her, her position, her politics and her personality.

An extremely useful source of information about the work of Lady Aberdeen's organisation to combat disease – the Women's National Health Association – was the collection of issues of the Association's magazine, *Sláinte*. This I was allowed to consult in Peamount Hospital, and it not only gave a picture of social conditions in Ireland, 1907 - 1915, but the editorials written by Lady Aberdeen herself provided an insight into her thinking.

For factual information about Lady Aberdeen's life and family I have relied heavily on the biography *A Bonnie Fechter* written by her daughter Lady Pentland, and for information about the Canadian years I have consulted Doris French's *Ishbel and the Empire*. I must emphasise that my work on Lady Aberdeen is concerned chiefly with her Irish activities so that only passing references could be made to other important areas of her life, notably her involvement with the International Council of Women.

It is my wish that what I have written about Ishbel, Lady Aberdeen, will bring her to public attention and that she may receive some of the respect and honour which I believe she deserves as a lover of Ireland and a devoted worker for the health and happiness of the Irish people.

Ishbel

Marchioness of Aberdeen and Temair
1857-1939

Born	**1857**	Daughter of Lord Tweedmouth.
Married	**1877**	John Gordon, Seventh Earl of Aberdeen. Founded Onward and Upward Association for education of maidservants. Active in charitable work.
	1886	Accompanied husband to Ireland as Vicereine. During Aberdeen's six month tenure as Viceroy became enthusiastic promoter of Irish industries. Continued to work for this cause after return to Britain. Took active part in Women's Liberal Federation and worked for various charities.
	1893	Organised Irish Village at Chicago World's Fair.
	1893-1898	During Lord Aberdeen's years as Governor-General of Canada, founded Victorian Order of Nurses. Elected first President of International Council of Women (and founded National Council of Women in Canada) in 1893 and held post until 1898. Re-elected President in 1904, held post until 1914. Organisation lapsed until 1920, but Lady Aberdeen elected President again in 1922 and remained in office until 1936.
	1906-1915	Lord Aberdeen Viceroy of Ireland. Lady Aberdeen founded Women's National Health Association, to fight tuberculosis in the country.
	1915-1939	Retained interest in Irish affairs and in International Council of Women until her death in 1939.

Preface

LORD ABERDEEN SERVED TWICE as Viceroy in Ireland. His first term in 1886 was a short one – six months – but his second term lasted from 1906 to 1915. The two periods of office could not have been more different. In 1886 Irish hopes were high for a limited amount of political independence – Home Rule – and Lord Aberdeen was known to be in favour of the measure. His wife, Ishbel, initially unhappy with the prospect of coming to Ireland, quickly found herself sharing Lord Aberdeen's political sentiments, and also developing a deep love of Ireland and all things Irish. She gave practical expression to her sympathies by encouraging the growth of Irish home industries and promoting the sale of Irish crafts abroad. Both Aberdeens were very popular and there was general regret when they left, following the defeat of Gladstone's Liberal government. Hopes for Home Rule were dashed in 1886 but when the Aberdeens returned in 1906 there was again a strong possibility that the long-held aim would be achieved. They had reason, therefore, to believe that they would be the last Viceregal couple before Home Rule, and that they would be even more popular than before. Lady Aberdeen, in particular saw her husband's term of office as a time when she could build on her earlier popularity and do even more for her adopted country.

What the Aberdeens did not fully grasp, were the changes that had taken place in Ireland since 1886. The Irish Parliamentary Party still campaigned at Westminster for limited powers of self-government, but public demand for Home Rule was not as strong as it had once been. A major social change had taken place in Ireland with the transfer to tenants of much of the land held previously by their landlords. This, while lessening the social standing of the landlords, engendered a new sense of pride and personal independence among their former tenants, a pride that was reinforced by a fresh awareness of Irish culture. The richness of the native language, music and dance was being recognised, due to the efforts of the Gaelic League, while the Gaelic Athletic Association promoted Irish games such as football and hurling. Literature in the English language drew on the Irish literary tradition and was greatly inspired by legends and folk tales. In this social and cultural climate there was little respect for the alien *mores* represented by the Viceregal establishment.

7

The agrarian unrest which had been a feature of Irish life during the first Aberdeen Viceroyalty had largely disappeared by the time they returned, but in the towns, and in Dublin particularly, there was serious discontent. Wages were low and working and living conditions were poor. Labour troubles resulted in strikes, the worst of which was the strike and lock-out in Dublin in 1913-14. The employers won that battle but the war went on under the leadership of the Union which had been founded in the workers' interest. An Ireland both socialist and republican began to be seen as preferable to one under a traditional form of government, even if that were home-based.

A direct challenge to the Irish Parliamentary Party's efforts to obtain Home Rule came from a movement known as Sinn Féin (Ourselves) which proposed that the elected Irish members should withdraw from Westminster and set up their own assembly in Dublin. Although Sinn Féin never posed any serious electoral challenge to the IPP, its propaganda affected popular thinking. A darker strand of thought lay below the Nationalist constitutional surface and this was the view of extreme nationalists who would resort to violence to achieve their aim of an Ireland that was completely independent.

The complexities of the Irish political situation during the second Aberdeen Viceroyalty were compounded by the attitude of those who totally opposed Home Rule. These, who wished to maintain the Union with Britain and the Empire – Unionists – were especially numerous and vociferous in Ulster, the northern province of the island. For historical reasons they wished to remain separate from an Ireland that was independent of Britain and declared their willingness to fight rather than be included. It was no bluff, as they showed when they assembled a fighting force, and smuggled in guns to arm it. A similar force was assembled in the rest of Ireland, principally in Dublin, and conflict between north and south of Ireland was averted only by the outbreak of war between Britain and Germany in August 1914.

This, then, was the Ireland in which Lord and Lady Aberdeen lived for nine years from 1906 to 1915. They were present, although they did not know it, in the years when Irish identity was vigorously asserting itself and British domination was coming to an end. An independent state was coming into being, and it was a state which had no place for a couple who, however well-intentioned and active in charitable work, were representative of the British Crown.

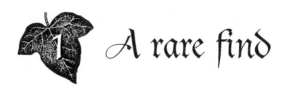

A rare find

O N SATURDAY FEBRUARY 27TH, 1886, *United Ireland*, a newspaper of Nationalist sympathies, reported in its news columns on the formal entry of the new Lord Lieutenant, Viceroy and Governor-General of Ireland, John Gordon, Earl of Aberdeen, into the city of Dublin on the previous day:

> As a military display it was an imposing sight. As a popular demonstration it was no more than what usually takes place in the Irish capital. All the idlers, paid and unpaid, looked on. As usual the rowdies of Trinity College were conspicuous by their rowdyism.[1]

Six months later, the Viceroy's departure was reported in the same newspaper, but in very different terms. Lord Aberdeen and his wife left Dublin on Tuesday, August 3rd and their farewell procession was described in the *United Ireland* of August 7th as having evoked 'the most memorable manifestation ever witnessed in Dublin'. It was an expression of affection for the 'friendly ex-Viceroy and his amiable wife', and was 'enormous, stately and never-to-be-forgotten'. The route from Winetavern Street to College Green was a solid mass of citizens, all wishing a 'national God speed' to the popular couple. The crowds were sad to lose the Aberdeens and the 'departing guests were visibly affected by the warmth of the leave-taking' as the loud cheers echoed through the streets. It was observed that Lady Aberdeen had 'very great difficulty in restraining her emotion', and her name was frequently heard on the lips of the crowd amid the cries of "Home Rule" or "Gladstone". She wore 'a pale-green toilette' in response, it was said, to the declared intention of the citizen-sharers in the departure ceremonial of wearing the badge of the Gordon clan – an ivy leaf. It was not only the members of the official party who paid the Earl and Countess the compliment of wearing the Gordon emblem – the city was stricken with 'ivy fever'. The car-men had wreaths of ivy on their horses' heads, and even the tramway drivers decorated their harness with it. Indeed the ivy was seen 'almost as frequently as shamrock on St Patrick's Day'.

The demonstration at Kingstown was equally enthusiastic and 'it was remarked that the Countess never looked more animated' as when she acknowledged the 'storm of cheers' for the ex-Viceroy and 'the distinguished lady who, with him, won the esteem of the people of Ireland.' The ceremonial was, as might be expected, a 'marvellous living panorama' but the *United Irelands'* writer emphasised that this was 'no flunkeyism' but a personal tribute. Then, the last farewells having been said, the ship pulled away to the strains of the 'Shamrock and Thistle', or 'Aberdeen March' (dedicated by special permission to the Earl and Countess by its composer, John O'Donnell) and it was seen that Lady Aberdeen was showing 'evident signs of grief'. 'Indeed,' added the writer, she appeared 'almost as full of emotion as if she were leaving her native country on her way to a foreign land.'

Who were these two people who called forth such an outpouring in a nationalist newspaper and what was the secret of the popularity they gained in such a short time? Of the two, Lord Aberdeen was the more distinguished in lineage, but his wife, Lady Aberdeen, was the more interesting, and certainly the more forceful personality. John Campbell Gordon, seventh Earl of Aberdeen, was a member of a family that could trace its ancestry back to 1315. The most famous member of the clan was the fourth Earl, who was Foreign Secretary of Britain and later (1852-1855) Prime Minister. William Gladstone greatly admired the fourth Earl and accounted him one of the few men he truly loved. The fourth Lord Aberdeen improved the estate (but not the house) by draining waterlogged lands, planting trees, building roads, and improving farming methods. Queen Victoria and Prince Albert visited Haddo House in 1857, and two giant sequoia trees were planted in commemoration of the visit. Coincidentally, that was also the year of the future Lady Aberdeen's birth.

The fifth Earl, George, succeeded to the title on his father's death in 1860, and reluctantly accepted the burden of running the family estate in Aberdeenshire. He was not popular with his tenants, in spite of building better cottages for some of them (for he increased the rents) and tried to ensure that a high moral tone was maintained at all times. With his six children he was both stern and strict, and the household was a gloomy one, theatricals being forbidden, jokes in short supply, and no toys for the children apart from those they made for themselves. This was the atmosphere in which John, the youngest son, grew up, and it was not lightened by the death of the fifth Earl at the age of 47. John's elder brother, now sixth Earl and named George after his father, remained in charge of the estate for only two years before running away from the family home to America. There he assumed the name George Osborne and worked as an ordinary seaman. An occasional letter to his mother indicated that he was still alive and well, but there seemed no prospect that he would ever return. Fortunately, his younger brother, James, seemed a more stable character, who would, if George never re-appeared and was presumed dead, make a worthy seventh Earl. Then, in what was described as a 'tragic accident,' James shot himself in his rooms at Cambridge. It was therefore essential to find George, and a frantic search was made for him in America, only to find that he had been drowned some time previously. Father N Walsh, SJ in an article in the *Irish Ecclesiastical Record*, November, 1897, entitled 'The Aberdeen Romance' put forward the theory that George's flight from family duty was, in fact, a spiritual quest, but it is spectacularly unconvincing).[2] This double blow to the family was followed by long legal proceedings before the title and estate were settled on the youngest brother, but eventually, John Campbell Gordon became the seventh Earl of Aberdeen and owner of the Haddo estate in the flat windswept lands of north-eastern Scotland.

Given the recent family history, and the gloom of his upbringing, it was not surprising that the seventh Earl was a shy and nervous young man. He was, however handsome, not very tall, but neatly put together, and with a fine-boned sensitive face. He did not care for the social round and avoided dances, soirées, receptions and so forth, whenever he could. Marriage was a state into which he must, for domestic and dynastic reasons, eventually enter, but he was in no hurry, and society matrons, ever-eager to make good marriages for their daughters found the young man extremely elusive. His manners, though, were impeccable and when, out riding in Rotten Row, the wonderful social centre for the élite of London, he met a young girl, sister of a friend's fiancée, he spoke seriously and courteously to her. Although he did not realize it at the time that meeting determined his future life and career.

The well-brought-up young girl whom he met that day was Ishbel Marjoribanks, and family tradition has it that, although only fourteen, she fell at once in love with John Gordon, Earl of Aberdeen, ten years her senior. Ishbel (a Gaelic version of her mother's name, Isabella) was one of five children of Dudley Coutts Marjoribanks, wealthy owner of a brewery, Liberal member of Parliament for Berwick-on-Tweed, later Lord Tweedmouth, and his wife, Isabella. Dudley Marjoribanks was connected to the famous Coutts banking family but had no position in the bank. His grandfather, Edward Marjoribanks, originally from Scotland, had been taken into partnership by Thomas Coutts, founder of the prestigious London establishment, and had been a very successful man, financial adviser to the royal family, and banker to Queen Victoria. Thomas Coutts had seen to it that the bank remained a family institution, and partnerships were both scarce and carefully selected. So, in spite of Edward Marjoribanks' position, only one of his sons could be taken into partnership, and his eldest son, another Edward, was chosen. He, in fact, was not a success, and in 1877 was found to be on the brink of bankruptcy and therefore likely to bring the bank into disrepute. The partnership was dissolved and Edward was ejected. Dudley, however, showed a talent for moneymaking, and soon became prosperous.

Ishbel was born in London in 1857 in the family home in Mayfair, taking her place behind a much older brother and sister. Two younger brothers arrived in due course, but Ishbel was nonetheless a solitary child. Her mother, who believed that she was in direct descent from the Plantagenet kings of England, was the eldest daughter of Sir James Hogg, originally from Lisburn, Co Down. He was a lawyer and a Tory member of parliament. The Hogg family were devout Evangelicals. Quintin Hogg, Isabella's brother, was one of the sponsors of the American evangelists Ira D Sankey and Dwight L Moody on their missions to Britain, and in 1882 founder of the Youth's Christian Institute in London, which later developed into the Regent Street Polytechnic. His grandson, the second Lord Hailsham, became Lord Chancellor of Britain in the nineteen seventies.

Isabella instilled her religious principles in her children, most notably in Ishbel. As was the case with John Gordon, her future husband, Ishbel's upbringing was extremely strict, possibly more so even than his. Admittedly she was surrounded by luxuries and had lavish toys, but she was lonely, and as Lady Marjoribanks disapproved of young girls as being too frivolous she was not allowed to make female friends. Instead there was a régime of study with governesses, piano lessons, dancing lessons and singing lessons. Games were forbidden – 'as a source of quarrelling' – and no holidays were allowed, not even Saturday half-days, nor summer holidays. The only exceptions, Ishbel recalled in her memoirs, *We Twa* were 'whole holidays on the birthdays of children when at home ...and expeditions to the shooting-lodge'.[3] Later Ishbel was allowed to attend French classes outside the home, accompanied, as were the other girl students, by a governess. Ishbel worked very hard in what was a highly competitive atmosphere, and gained first place in the class. This success gave her self-confidence, a quality she then lacked, possibly due to the unrelenting pressure of her parents' demands and expectations.

Lady Marjoribanks and her husband, Dudley, did not have a happy marriage and although appearances were, of course, preserved, Ishbel was aware of the tensions between them. It is not clear what Dudley's faults were, although by all accounts he had a savage temper and flew into fearsome rages, but what is clear is that after a short period in her childhood when Ishbel adored her father, she transferred her love to her mother. More than that, she saw herself as her mother's protector against her unpredictable and tyrannical husband. Lady Marjoribanks seems to have encouraged this attitude and to have bound Ishbel to her so closely that the girl gave her her total loyalty and support for the rest of her life while disliking her father up to the moment of his death in 1897.

There is no doubt that Dudley Marjoribanks was an extremely strict father, and that from his verdicts, capricious though they might be, there was no appeal. Ishbel was a lively little girl, but she was subjected to the usual rigorous upbringing of a well-to-do young lady. She was taught to sit up correctly in a chair with a straight back, a posture she would have to maintain for hours on end. Lessons were not meant to be enjoyable, but fortunately Ishbel had an inquiring mind and she did find pleasure in her studies. She would have liked to study mathematics, but was not allowed pursue such an 'unfeminine' path. After the successful course of French lessons she was later allowed to attend some lessons in literature (accompanied, as before, by a governess) given by Mr J M Meiklejohn. She found these inspiring, and was delighted when her teacher suggested she should enroll at Girton, the new college for women at Cambridge. Needless to say, Dudley Marjoribanks would not give his consent, and that was the end of that. Ishbel does not seem to have brooded over this decision – probably she expected it – but her later interest in women's education was almost certainly sharpened by her own girlhood experience.

If Ishbel's conventional education was deficient in many respects the same could not be said of her political and social upbringing. Dudley, as a Liberal member of parliament, although an almost mute one, was on familiar terms with the leading Liberals of the day and William Gladstone called occasionally to the house. Isabella Marjoribanks had cannily kept up her family's Conservative ties as much, one feels, from conviction as from expediency, although ambition for a new son-in-law was a powerful factor. Polly, Ishbel's elder sister, had married Matthew Ridley, son of a viscount who was also a Conservative, and it was only prudent to keep on friendly terms with the Tory party.

On one occasion the dreaded Benjamin Disraeli was entertained to dinner and Ishbel, already a fervent Liberal, had perforce to shake his hand. She had developed an interest in politics and by the time she was eighteen had read both Edmund Burke and Thomas Macaulay. She was given advice on speech-making by John Bright, the resolute radical, held to be the most eloquent speaker of the age, next to whom she sat one night at dinner, but it is not likely that she accepted the advice as anything more than of intellectual interest.

Ishbel was an intensely religious girl, encouraged in her fervour by her mother, and throughout her long and busy life she was consoled and strengthened by her faith. She found her fervently religious young uncle, Quintin Hogg, a great source of inspiration, and would dearly like to have accompanied him to the Moody and Sankey meetings, but predictably, Dudley disapproved. However, now that she was older she was allowed young feminine companionship and Quintin Hogg gave her tickets to pass on to her friends so she at least heard their songs and sermons at secondhand. Part of the admiration she felt, even as a young girl, for Gladstone, was the fact that he was a sincere believer, whose actions, even his political ones, were guided by his Christian principles.

It was inevitable that Ishbel should feel it her duty to do good in the world, and she started by teaching at a Sunday school for Cockney boys in London. Her father initially opposed this, but relented, and she was allowed walk there alone in the morning, but had to be accompanied by a footman in the afternoon. Although only seventeen, she organised a regular Sunday school for the children of the tenants at Guisachan, the family estate in Scotland, and concerned herself with the welfare of the cottagers. Dudley Marjoribanks had bought the vast estate near Inverness in 1856 and the family moved there late every summer – a huge undertaking involving coaches, horses, servants and numerous household goods all sent in advance of the family. Mother, children, governesses and ladies' maids and pets came next, first by train and then by horse-drawn omnibus. Finally, Dudley arrived, usually with guests for one of the regular shooting parties. The whole move was made in reverse some six months later when Parliament re-assembled and Dudley was required on the Liberal backbench.

Ishbel was extremely happy at Guisachan, where there was somewhat more freedom than in London. She learned some Gaelic, but her father disapproved, so she never acquired fluency but she did know enough to understand what some of the Gaelic-speaking cottagers were saying. She and her mother regularly visited the tenants and looked after their moral and material welfare. Mother and daughter became skilled in administering first aid for small accidents, – a necessary skill in the absence of a local doctor – and learned to value homely and traditional remedies for minor illnesses. Ishbel also became quite a competent water colourist, a necessary accomplishment of the day, and one which alleviated the occasional boredom of wet Highland evenings. Novel reading was totally forbidden, but there was no scarcity of religious books, pamphlets and tracts.

Ishbel grew to be a tall well-built young woman, rather solemn, and handsome rather than conventionally pretty. In those days marriage was the ambition every mother had for her daughter, and with elder daughter Polly satisfactorily wed, Lady Marjoribanks looked over the social scene for a husband for Ishbel. Fortunately, there was to be no conflict on this issue between mother and daughter, for when Lady Marjoribanks became aware that young Ishbel had taken a fancy to Johnnie Gordon, the Earl of Aberdeen, after their casual meeting in the Park, she was fully approving. It wasn't all that simple, however. The match would be a good one and eminently suitable, but the trouble was, that unlike Ishbel, John Gordon did not appear to have fallen in love. He was polite and normally attentive in the social sense, but that was all. Ishbel suffered agonies, made worse by the fact that all London (the part that mattered) seemed to expect an engagement.

In the midst of all this emotional upheaval Ishbel was presented at Court to Her Majesty, Queen Victoria. This was normally an ordeal for a young girl, who had to manage her wide skirts and a fan, while curtsying seven times to the Queen and various members of the royal family. Ishbel coped well enough in her white satin gown, embroidered with thistles and bearing a train three yards long, and was patted on the cheek by the Queen (a rare honour), no doubt in memory of the canny banker Thomas Marjoribanks. On the way out, formalities completed, Ishbel stumbled on the way down the staircase, broke her fan and bruised her face. That was nothing, however, as against the fact that Aberdeen, the longed-for-one, showed no signs of proposing.

Nor did he for the next two years, so that Ishbel reached the dangerously late age of twenty without the coveted marriage in sight. She tried to resign herself to the Divine Will, but her patience was indeed 'sorely tried': However, years later, in her memoirs she indicated that the two years she was 'out' in society were, in spite of her unrequited love, happy and enjoyable ones. She attended balls, country house parties, dinners and concerts, fully participating in the social round. Seemingly, there were proposals of marriage but nothing came of them – her heart had been captured by young Gordon. Then, when Ishbel had almost given up hope, there came a resurgence of the relationship. She met Aberdeen at a tea-party and told him frankly of the annoyance caused by the linking of their names together. He took the hint, but it was hardly in the way she would have expected. He called on Lady Marjoribanks and told her firmly that his feelings for Ishbel were those of friendship only, and took his leave. Back in Scotland, however, a letter reached him from Lady Marjoribanks, telling him of the discomfort his behaviour had caused to the entire family and going on to say, as Lady Aberdeen's daughter, Marjorie Pentland, recounts in her biography of her mother, *A Bonnie Fechter*:

> In conclusion, I venture to tell you that I am sure you are deceiving yourself. What is the evidence of love but the seeking of companionship? Continual introspection is a fatal error. For your own sake I would not have you throw away a priceless blessing.[4]

One can only speculate on what Aberdeen's feelings were when he received this inimical message. As an honest, God-fearing young man he must have worried in case he had trifled with Ishbel's affections. That most certainly would not do, and would never be forgotten in an unforgiving and rigid society. The easier, and indeed, more honourable, course, would be to marry the girl and be done with it. As the seventh Earl it was his duty to marry and to secure the succession, and perhaps the mother was right and she was indeed 'a priceless blessing.' Although

Aberdeen could not have known it at the time, and could probably not have discerned her potential, Ishbel was a rare find, and the most suitable wife he could have acquired if he was to make his mark in the world. Whether that is what he wanted, is, of course, another story, but the picture that reveals itself to us through the mists of the years is that of a man who was agreeable, eager to do the right thing and anxious to avoid trouble. As such, he answered Lady Marjoribanks, replying that, on consideration, he realised that his feelings for Ishbel were not, after all, those of mere friendship but of something much deeper. Shortly afterwards, having received her father's permission to do so, he proposed to Ishbel and was accepted. So began the next phase of Ishbel's life.

Now, aged twenty, she became the Countess of Aberdeen in a fashionable ceremony on the 7th November, 1877. She would have liked the wedding to have been held in Guisachan, but too many guests had to be accommodated, so it was held in St George's, Hanover Square. In December of that year, after a honeymoon spent in England, the young couple went on a trip to Egypt and travelled up the Nile, distributing medicines, tracts and cigarettes to those natives fortunate enough to meet them. Slavery was a fact of life in Egypt and the kind-hearted Aberdeens rescued and adopted four young boys, having them baptised and then sent to a Presbyterian mission school. They also smuggled back to England a young man, Ahmed Fahmy, who had been introduced to them in Cairo. He was a Christian convert from Islam, and his Muslim family were threatening him with death. Lord Aberdeen supported him for nine years at Edinburgh University, and was most gratified when Ahmed chose to go to China as a missionary.

During their trip the Aberdeens met General 'Chinese' Gordon, Governor of the Sudan and a relative of John's, who was later to achieve fame by his ill-fated defence of Khartoum and death at the hands of a fanatical mob. He greatly impressed Ishbel by his rampant Christianity and his determination to wipe out slavery, but he was not enamoured of her, describing her in a letter to his sister as 'a great fat girl'.[5] Rather unkind, and judging by her wedding photograph, most unfair, because although large in build, Ishbel could not at that stage of her life, be described as 'fat'.

When the protracted honeymoon finally came to an end, the Earl brought his young Countess north across the border to the family home in Aberdeenshire. Ishbel's first sight of Haddo House was on a cold June day, and a wind from the grey North Sea chilled the Earl and Countess as they drove in their open carriage across the flat treeless fields marked by stunted hedges. It was all so different from Guisachan, the Marjoribanks' Highland estate, with its mountains, glens, lakes and forests, but the Haddo tenants' welcome was a very warm one, expressed in loud cheers and fervent blessings. Haddo House, though sturdily built, was neither beautiful nor comfortable, and Ishbel realized immediately that major improvements were needed. Significantly, one of the first improvements was the completion of a small chapel which Lord Aberdeen had begun and where family, servants and guests could attend Divine Service. Then more material concerns took over. A major change was made to the entrance, which when Ishbel first saw it was on the second floor approached by a narrow stone staircase and led through what appeared to be a large window into a space no larger than an ordinary room. As she recalled in her memoirs 'it was distinctly unsuitable,' and a new entrance was made on the ground floor, leading into a foyer out of which rose a grand open staircase. Other large-scale works were put in hand, including a new wing and a library, and all the modern Victorian conveniences were added for practicability and for comfort.

Marriage to Aberdeen must have been bliss after Ishbel's life in her father's household. In place of Dudley's disapproval of almost everything she wished to do she had John's full-hearted support, and as he was a mild-natured man, there were no more of those terrifying rages that had made Ishbel's childhood a time of worry and dread. The alterations cost a great deal of money, but Aberdeen was agreeable, in spite of the fact that his income from the estate dropped during the year 1878-79. It had been a very hard winter and there was much distress on the estate. The young bride, who became mother of her first son, George Haddo, in January 1879, was sympathetic and as helpful as she could be to tenants in difficulties, but her husband went further and took the generous step of cancelling all rents for that half year. The Aberdeens were conscientious landlords, Ishbel taking as much interest in the lives of the tenants as did her husband. The couple set up a cottage hospital in the estate village of Tarves, complete with district nurse, and a doctor whose salary was paid in a lump sum by Lord Aberdeen every year. Medical and nursing attention was, therefore, free to tenants. There was also evening school for young men in the village of Methlick, and hot penny dinners were supplied for poor school-children.

A large house such as Haddo House required a large staff for smooth running. A good butler and a good housekeeper were essential, and once they had been engaged, they, in many instances, engaged new servants. These included cooks, parlourmaids, footmen, housemaids, page boys, boot boys and scullery maids. There was a very strict hierarchy among the staff and distinctions were as carefully drawn below stairs as they were above. The mistress of a large staff, if she was to be successful in obtaining good service had to have several qualities, including an observant eye, firmness of character, a strong sense of duty and responsibility, and, almost as important as all the others put together, a tactful and kindly manner. Ishbel possessed all these qualities, and although in later life she acted sometimes in a curiously tactless way it was not those who worked for her, or who were employed by her, who caused her to be abrupt, abrasive and domineering but bureaucrats, politicians, medical men and various obstructive officials. No doubt she was often reminded of her father's obduracy and automatic disapproval of anything she wished to do, and perhaps she felt a particular and personal pleasure whenever she overcame difficulties put in her way by male opponents – some consolation for the disappointments of the past. Indeed the Aberdeens, and especially Ishbel, soon got the reputation of being too familiar with their servants and failing to observe the proper distance between employers and employees. There was, it is true, an attempt by the Aberdeens to relax a little of the formality customary in grand households, but it was never on the scale alleged by their detractors.

They founded what they called the 'Household Club', and invited the servants to join. One wonders what would have happened if they had refused. Lord Aberdeen was elected President, and Lady Aberdeen Vice-President and one or other of them usually attended the meetings. The formation of the Club was due, as Ishbel recalled:

> ...to an uneasy feeling on our part that we were doing nothing for the members of our own household ... beyond our daily gathering in the Haddo House Chapel for family worship day by day, and on Sunday evenings.[6]

The main concerns of the Club were education and recreation and so there were carpentry and drawing classes, readings, lectures, piano and violin recitals, as well as those on the more humble melodeon and concertina. It was the personal involvement of the Earl and Countess in those activities that aroused the criticism of their peers, and Lord Aberdeen gained the reputation of being something of a radical in social matters. Stories about the Aberdeens' domestic arrangements grew wilder with the years, and in 1902 J M Barrie's play *The Admirable Crichton* in which the roles of master and man were reversed, was popularly supposed to have been based on Lord Aberdeen's behaviour towards his butler. Normally a mild man, Aberdeen was so incensed by this that he demanded an apology from Barrie and was immediately granted it.

Servants were encouraged by the Aberdeens to make suggestions about the running of the Club, and one made by an odd-job man, had what proved to be a lasting effect on social life in Britain. In his account of the Haddo House Club in his book *Onward and Upward* James Drummond quotes from the minute book kept by the under-butler:

> Fred Hurst (odd job) strongly objects to the stiff way in which the Social met on Thursday. If possible to get small tables and to mix freely.[7]

The proposal was seconded by Maggie Gall (housemaid), was carried and was put into effect. Ishbel saw the advantages of this seating arrangement, and introduced it at her dinner parties. Smaller tables for eight or ten guests took the place of the traditional long table with its strict placement and almost inevitable boredom. The innovation caught on and became standard in society. In their memoirs the Aberdeens refer to the criticisms, which continued throughout their public life, particularly in Canada. It was not true, Ishbel insisted, that they played 'hide and seek with the servants' nor that she told parlourmaids to remove their caps, those 'badges of servitude'. Queen Victoria, Lady Aberdeen recalled, had asked Lord Rosebery, the Prime Minister, to find out 'if we dined with staff in the servants' hall once a week', but was assured of 'the orthodox character of our household arrangements'. King Edward VII was also perturbed by rumours and had to be reassured that:

> ...all dinner parties [were] carried on in the most correct manner, according to precedence and under the Chamberlain's rigid directions.[8]

Actually, it is difficult to conceive of the Countess of Aberdeen being other than strictly correct and conventional in her domestic arrangements

– she was sensible enough to realise that the discipline of a large household had to be maintained, as otherwise chaos would follow.

Ishbel's zeal for doing good and improving the lives of those around her did not evaporate outside the doors of Haddo House. Although she was satisfied that, as far as was humanly possible, her own female servants were properly cared for, both materially and spiritually, she knew that other young girls in service, particularly those in farmhouses, were lacking both the protection of a Servants' Hall with its strict insistence on good behaviour and the opportunities for education and recreation which a large household could afford. To help these girls, therefore, Ishbel set up evening classes in Haddo House for maidservants from local farms. The farm wives, however, refused to allow their servants to attend the classes, fearing for their morality if they were let out at night. Ishbel solved the problem by setting up correspondence classes in 'Bible topics, history, geography, literature, domestic science, needlework, etc'. The Education Act of 1870 had spread literacy among the population and most servants could now read. Female farm workers were invited to join the 'Haddo House Association' and supervised by their mistresses, the servants studied in the farm kitchens, and prizes and certificates were awarded annually. Ishbel hoped that this shared activity would give mistresses and maids a common interest and a common purpose, which would be to the benefit of both parties.

She liked the idea of having different groups and classes of people mixing together, and in the various working parties which she set up in farm houses on the estate where farmers' wives and daughters made garments for the destitute, had tea, and listened to an uplifting book, she tried to have a mixture of 'different and hostile cliques – religious, political and social'. When she opened Haddo House in August 1878 for the annual holiday festivities for the servants of the area, in an attempt to curb the rowdy excesses that usually marked the day when it was celebrated elsewhere, all the ladies of the locality, middle-class and gentry, served refreshments (tea and lemonade, no strong liquor) to the estimated 8,000 who attended

Out of all this charitable and uplifting activity there grew the 'Onward and Upward Association', an organisation dedicated to the betterment of the lives of young working girls. It spread throughout Scotland, and its President, Lady Aberdeen, when asked why she had chosen that particular name for the organisation retorted that it was the 'opposite of

Backward and Downward'. The Association later published a monthly magazine under the editorship of Lady Aberdeen and her children contributed to its junior supplement, *Wee Willie Winkie*. The Association was eventually absorbed into the Scottish Mothers' Union, an amalgamation with the Girls' Friendly Society having failed because Lady Aberdeen could not accept the Society's 'Central Rule' which required that a girl who had succumbed to temptation outside marriage must surrender her membership.

An insight into Ishbel's character in those years is provided by notes she made for a speech at the opening of male farmworkers' classes at Tarves in 1879, to be held every Saturday evening at 8 pm. There would be lessons in reading, writing, arithmetic, history, chemistry and astronomy, but there would also be classes in carpentry, cooking and tailoring. 'Don't laugh,' she wrote, 'missionaries and emigrants have to learn a little of everything'. Religious instruction would, of course, be pre-eminent, and a religious belief would infuse every subject. She insisted:

> We must improve ourselves, it is our duty to ourselves, our country
> and to God. Our talents must be improved, and we must recollect
> that they are not our own bodies, minds and souls. Above all, we
> must know why we believe.[10]

It was not only in the Haddo House estate that Ishbel practised her Christianity in the form not alone of prayer but also through good works. From their Grosvenor Square home in London, where the Aberdeens lived while the Earl attended to his parliamentary duties in the Conservative interest, she engaged in various good works, including visits to the Strand Rescue Mission every Friday evening, where she tried to save 'women of the streets'. In this, as in so much else, she was inspired by Gladstone, and like him, she ventured into dark alleys in search of souls she could save. She was still very young and had led a conventionally sheltered life, but, buoyed up by her faith, she braved the dangers of the streets.

London streets were truly dangerous. There were indeed great houses inhabited by wealthy members of society, and spreading areas of middle-class respectability, but there were the dark, dirty and stinking regions that Charles Dickens had written about, where a whole underclass festered in rags and filth. It was dangerous for a woman to walk unescorted even in Bond Street, and in Lower Regent Street alone it was estimated by the police that there were 500 prostitutes. Burlington Arcade, Picadilly, Coventry St, Haymarket and the Strand were also favourite beats for prostitutes, so there was no shortage of women and girls to be rescued. It is doubtful if many wished to *be* rescued, for bad and all as was life for a prostitute, the alternative was not much better. Girls had generally taken to prostitution not from choice but from economic necessity, and a future in a home for fallen women, or a refuge, with little chance of employment apart from the most menial work, hardly looked like a glittering one. An occasional soul was saved, however, and forty years later Ishbel received a letter which her daughter quoted in her biography of her on the occasion of her Golden Wedding:

> When I look at your picture I see again your sweet face as on that first night we met. How lovely you were to me then – when so few can understand the torture of the struggle that has to be borne – and have been ever since.[11]

At least one girl appreciated Ishbel's efforts.

Dudley Marjoribanks owned a house in the country outside London – Dollis Hill – and he made it over to the younger couple (or perhaps they bought it, the transaction is unclear). Here, in the summer time, they entertained their friends, among whom they counted Gladstone. He became very fond of the place, and used it extensively almost up to the end of his long life. Less exalted visitors were welcome also, and on the August Bank Holiday the inmates of the Working Girls' Homes were invited for refreshments. Most Sundays, too, when the Aberdeens were in residence, the barns were filled with workmen singing hymns and listening to lectures. Every week there were excursions to Dollis Hill by mothers and children from poor London districts, and the Aberdeens became recognised as assistants to the famously philanthropic Lord Shaftesbury.

Social life and its demands were looked on as a burden, lightened only by the fact that they might be useful in 'influencing for good' the top stratum of society. Furthermore, Ishbel consoled herself, 'the disciplines of society and ... the necessities of suppressing personal likes and dislikes' were useful experiences. She really was a most solemn young woman, earnest and much given to introspection, especially on religious matters. Although she never really wavered in her religious beliefs she was affected by the contemporary tensions between religion and science that followed the publication of Charles Darwin's *The Origin of the*

Species in 1859. Then into her life came the man who was to be her greatest friend and inspiration – Henry Drummond, one of the most appealing of Victorian preachers.

Henry Drummond was born in Stirling in 1851. His father was William Drummond, a seedsman and head of William Drummond and Sons, Stirling and Dublin. Henry was handsome, charming and intelligent, and coming from a family of Free Church believers, he quite naturally gravitated towards the religious life. Having completed a divinity course at New College, Edinburgh, he then went to Tübingen in Germany for further study. In the autumn of 1873 he was drawn into the evangelical revival inspired by the American gospellers Moody and Sankey whose combination of music and sermons evoked a popular response to religion. Henry followed up the evangelical work of Moody and Sankey in the cities of England and Ireland and worked with them in London. His personality and his gift of oratory made him an expert at running meetings, and he came into contact with all manner of persons. In 1875 he returned to New College, and in 1877 was appointed lecturer in Natural Science at Free Church College, Glasgow, not an incongruous post for a clergyman, as the dearest hope of religious believers and thinkers of the time was the reconciliation of Darwin's startling and disturbing theory of evolution with the truths of the Bible. Henry lectured brilliantly and captivated students, but he considered that the most valuable work he could do was to influence young men for good, not only in the academic world but in the harsher world outside. He therefore combined his college lecturing with mission work in Glasgow's poorest and roughest areas.

In 1879 he went on a geological trip to the Rocky Mountains and in 1883 he travelled to Africa for the African Lakes Corporation on a surveying expedition to Lake Nyasa and Lake Tanganyika, travelling home via Zanzibar and Mozambique. The natural wonders he saw on his trips confirmed his view of the world as a place where the natural and the spiritual laws were one and the same. Henry Drummond was ordained in November 1884 in College Free Church and the title of his inaugural address was, fittingly 'The Contribution of Science to Christianity'. He had, already in that year published a work which was an immediate success, and by which he is remembered (if at all) today. Entitled *Natural Law in the Spiritual World* it contended that the scientific principle of continuity operated in the spiritual world as well as in the physical one.

An enthusiastic review in the *Spectator* helped sales, which reached 70,000 within five years, but critics of his tenets had no difficulty in demolishing his arguments. That, however, was irrelevant, for the book beguiled by the beauty of its writing and the joyous simplicity with which Drummond reconciled science and Christian belief. He understood the fears of those who worried lest the new discoveries would destroy men's faith and he strengthened the belief of those who might otherwise have been tempted to waver, 'haunted', as he said, 'by a sense of instability in the foundations of their faith'. That there was, indeed widespread disquiet, he fully accepted:

> It is recognised by all that the younger and abler minds of this age find the most serious difficulty in accepting or rejecting the ordinary forms of belief...Science cannot overthrow Faith but it shakes it.

The Christian need not be afraid, because science and nature could be drawn together again by 'the disclosure of the naturalness of the supernatural'.[12]

The Aberdeens met Drummond some time in 1883, possibly through an introduction by Ishbel's uncle, Quintin Hogg, one of the sponsors of the second Moody and Sankey Tour in 1882, which Drummond had joined. Henry, now Professor of Natural Science at Glasgow, was invited by the Earl and Countess to preach in the chapel at Haddo House, and it was there in August 1884, that he gave what became one of his most famous sermons 'The Greatest Thing on Earth' (often reprinted by the Church of Scotland). The greatest thing, was, of course, 'Love.' If a man had that, all else fell into place. Henry's version of Christianity was a very attractive one, and his message was one of hope. His teachings made people feel better, more tolerant of their own and others' failings. A good Christian life was not a joyless one, but was full of sparkle and gaiety. There must be fair deals for all, study of the Bible and the great truths of Christianity, but there must also be fresh air and exercise, games and laughter. To him religion was not negative but consisted of spiritual evolvement.

Ishbel was captivated by him, both by the man and the message he preached. It appealed to her with its mixture of practicality and spirituality, and evoked a strong response. Now, more than ever, she wanted to get on with doing good for others, extending the work she had already started at Haddo House. Henry also proved to be a delightful and understanding companion and he became a close friend. It was a friendship which lasted to the end of Henry's life, and his death from bone cancer in 1897 affected her deeply. Letters between Ishbel and Henry, quoted in his biography by George Adam Smith are sometimes light and inconsequential, sometimes more serious, but always indicators of a happy relationship.

Henry's personal creed took no account of doubts or of sectarian squabbling, though it always remained firmly Christian. He wrote:

> No distinct or new thing [is] added to souls of those who profess
> Buddhism. These religions may be developments of the natural,
> mental or moral man. But Christianity professes to be more. It is
> the mental or moral man, *plus* something else.[13]

His beliefs were a great comfort to Ishbel, especially at dark periods in her life, and this helped her to lose some, if not all, of her solemnity. Later on, looking back, she marvelled at 'what prigs' she and her husband must have been in their early life. Aberdeen, the conscientious landlord, fine Christian gentleman, and ever-supportive husband, comes across, even in the joint memoirs, as a rather shadowy figure, lacking both his wife's dash and her energy. At all events he seems to have welcomed Ishbel's new friend and Henry soon became accepted into the family circle.

The Aberdeen's daughter, Marjorie Pentland, delicately described Ishbel's friendship with Drummond in *A Bonnie Fechter*, pointing out that Ishbel:

> ... had always been most at ease with men friends; objectively,
> constructively, discussing things and plans rather than emotions and
> acquaintances.[14]

That may have been so at that stage of Ishbel's life, but later she had no trouble whatsoever in being at ease among women, as her career in various organisations was to prove. In her journal, quoted by Marjorie Pentland, Ishbel speaks in general terms of her friendships with men, and that with Drummond in particular:

> Our first great friendship with a contemporary was with Henry
> Drummond and more recent years, too, some of our men friends
> have become real comrades and have taught me more about 'the
> joy of living' than ever I knew in my youth. I do not suppose that
> any woman can have enjoyed the satisfaction of such friendships
> more fully than I have; I am sorry for those who have no such

opportunities. A. [Aberdeen] has rejoiced so much in this that for me all has been plain sailing. Of course, I owe it to the blessed lack of jealousy in his composition, and I believe that he too has reaped benefit from his generosity.[15]

The 'benefit' may well have been the diversion of Ishbel's formidable energies. Enlivened, exhilarated and stimulated by Henry Drummond she set forth on a new campaign. Henry must bring his joyous message to politicians and to high society. She personally supplied Liberal MPs with his writings, and then set up four Sunday afternoon talks in May in the ballroom at Grosvenor House. These were a huge success and were attended by members of the fashionable set all of whom went away, not only impressed by the young man, but cheered by his kindly version of religion.

Following on this success, in July 1885 Ishbel and a friend, Lady Tavistock, set up an organisation, the Associated Workers' League, to co-ordinate the charitable work of London ladies of fashion. The social historian, Geoffrey Best, in his study *Mid-Victorian Britain*, opines that the poor of central and western London 'were corrupted by the amount of indiscriminate charity poured on them'.[16] Some evidence to support this statement comes from Henry Drummond's rather mischievous comment, while he was advising and assisting the organisation, that it was 'an agency for the unemployed of the West End'.[17] A workers' exchange was set up where volunteers could learn about the most suitable field for their gifts. Ladies could help at evening classes run by the London School Board at clubs, and also as hospital almoners, school managers, parish visitors, and so on.

There was great enthusiasm among women for such work, and it is estimated that in 1893 there were half a million voluntary women workers in charitable organisations and a further 20,000 women as paid officials. Women had been granted the municipal vote in 1869 and were later allowed to stand for school and poor law boards. The Liberal party brought many women into public service, although Gladstone was against votes for women, fearing perhaps that it would tend to be a Tory vote. Ishbel was by now keenly and actively interested in politics, and a firm supporter of Mr Gladstone, the Grand Old Man of the British political world.

Gladstone, who according to his recent biographer, Roy Jenkins, believed that his 'primary task in politics was to uphold religion',[18] and was like Ishbel, an Evangelical, had been Chancellor of the Exchequer in 1853 while John Gordon's grandfather had been Prime Minister of a Coalition Government. Gladstone had himself been Prime Minister from 1868 to 1874 when his Liberal government fell, and his old opponent, Disraeli came back in again as Prime Minister. In 1875 Disraeli, the imperialist, eager to extend the bounds of British Empire, mounted a 'dawn raid' on Suez Canal shares which led to British half-ownership of the vital east/west link, and in 1876 he conferred the title of Empress of India on Queen Victoria, which pleased her mightily. Disraeli's relationship with the Queen was a warm one, oiled and eased by his instinct for flattery – exemplified in his bracketing their two names together in the phrase "we authors, Ma'am", a reference to the publication of the Queen's *Highland Journal* in 1868.[19]

In 1878, ever-expansionist, Disraeli authorised a punitive expedition against Afghanistan, the buffer state between Russia and India. Aberdeen, like other members of the Tory party, was not in favour and was possibly influenced by his own, and his wife's, admiration of Gladstone. Gladstone was very much against the Afghan War, as he was against the Zulu War, also entered into by Disraeli, for he was an anti-imperialist, correctly foreseeing the rise of the United States as a world power and the consequent decline of a British Empire, over-extended and difficult to govern.

Aberdeen spoke in the House of Lords against the Afghan War and this was the beginning of his conversion from the Tory Party to the Liberals, a process accelerated in early 1880 when he spoke at a Liberal rally in Aberdeen in support of Gladstone and completed in March when he took his seat on the Liberal benches in the House of Lords. Gladstone swept back into power and his popularity had been recognised and enhanced by the campaign in Midlothian where he was heard and applauded by huge crowds.

When Disraeli dissolved Parliament Gladstone once again became Prime Minister, and Lord Aberdeen received his first public appointment – Lord Lieutenant of Aberdeenshire. In the following year, 1882, through the good offices of Lord Rosebery, the planner of the Midlothian campaign, Aberdeen was appointed Lord High Commissioner to the Church of Scotland. In a letter to Ishbel proposing the appointment, Rosebery opined that 'not the least of his [John's] qualifications being the Lady High Commissioner.'[20] Ishbel's talents were now being recognised outside the family circles and she entered into public life with great enthusiasm.

The Lord High Commissioner's function was to represent the Queen in Edinburgh at the General Assembly of the Church of Scotland, an independent, nationalistically-minded body. Most of the duties were ceremonial, but much official entertaining had to be done. Ishbel enjoyed this, and broadened the guest lists to include people from outside Church circles. She also made overtures to the Free Church of Scotland, going so far as to attend one of their Assemblies, but nothing came of her efforts, and in any case, they were not officially appreciated. More worrying was the fact that all this entertaining cost money, considerably more than the official allowance of £2,000 per annum (plus free apartments in Holyrood Palace) and the Aberdeens found the expense so much a drain that when Gladstone offered a second term in 1885 they were most reluctant to accept, pointing out how costly the position had proved to be. Gladstone was unsympathetic, suggesting that they economise – 'restrain the free and large current of your hospitable entertainments,' was how he put it, although he added approvingly that the position had become a 'different office,'[21] and 'a channel of much influence, most munificently conceived by yourself and Lady Aberdeen,' and he asked them to stay on. It was hard to say 'no' to a Prime Minister, especially when he was a family friend and godson to their second son Dudley, so the Aberdeens stayed on.

The expressed anxiety about money was a theme that recurred throughout the Aberdeens' life, and was often, especially during their time in Ireland, converted by malice into rumours of parsimoniousness. At this remove facts and figures are hard to come by, and there are conflicting stories about their largesse, or lack of it. Yet, it is well known that persons in public positions quite often have to pay heavily from their own pockets for expenses that should properly be the concern of the State, so it is not surprising that the Aberdeens should have had to use their own money while in office. Nor is it surprising that they should complain, however mildly, about the drain on their income at this time. The estate was affected by the general agricultural depression of those years and there were demands on what was now a limited income. In earlier days, John, or Johnnie, as he was affectionately known, had had great plans to run a railway through the Haddo House estate but it proved too expensive a project and he had had to abandon it, much to his sorrow, as he was a real railway enthusiast. Gladstone and Lord Rosebery among others were said to have greatly admired and enjoyed his party-piece – the imitation of various locomotive noises.

By 1885 there were four children to care for (another, Dorothy, had died, only eight months' old, in 1882) and the eldest, George Haddo, was sickly and needed constant attention. Furthermore, Ishbel's young brother, Coutts, as the result of a family quarrel, had been cut off by his father, Sir Dudley, and was receiving an allowance from the generous Lord Aberdeen, an allowance that was to continue for years. Coutts involved the Aberdeens in considerable expense when they set him up as a rancher in British Columbia. The venture failed, due to Coutts's indolence and extravagance and Lord Aberdeen's investment provided no returns. The Earl and Countess, however, loved the landscape of the Okanagan Valley in British Columbia and made further land purchases there against the advice of their Edinburgh lawyer. As a business venture it was a failure (plans for fruit growing on a commercial scale were particularly ill-advised) and the Scottish estate had to pay for the losses. Ishbel admitted in her memoirs that the results of the investment in British Columbia had been very sad and 'that neither the purchase money nor all that was spent on development ever came back.'[22] However, although the Aberdeens lost money in the Okanagan Valley they gained personal happiness there, especially during Lord Aberdeen's stint as Governor-General of Canada from 1893 to 1898 when the Viceregal couple and their family retired there on vacation.

On balance it would seem that the Aberdeens were not the tight-fisted Scots of caricature, but were people on whose purse – not a bottomless one – many demands were made. Their house in London had to be maintained for use during sessions of Parliament, and then there was the upkeep of Dollis Hill, the country house outside London. An estimated £500 a year was set aside for charitable purposes, and quite possibly more than that was spent at times. An interest, therefore, in reducing expenses, was not only natural, but in the circumstances, prudent and desirable.

Lord Aberdeen's second term as Lord High Commissioner, with its attendant expenses, did not last very long, however. An unexpected honour came his way in 1886, when Gladstone, once more Prime Minister, after a short-lived Conservative administration, offered him the post of Viceroy in Ireland. He accepted, without consulting Ishbel, later explaining to her that he had had to make up his mind at once, and that there had been no time to consult her. She was not happy about the new post, but had no choice in the matter. With her husband and family she set off in February for a land of which she knew very little and what little she did know did not greatly appeal to her. In a letter to the ever-understanding Henry Drummond, quoted in her daughter's biography, apprehension is mingled with resentment:

> Don't you think that I ought to be very much offended at not being consulted, I who have registered a solemn vow never to set foot in Ireland? ... Certainly the idea of going there had never occurred to us and it was the very last post one would have chosen. So that one feels it all the more a direct call which one can only obey blindly, plunging into the unknown.[23]

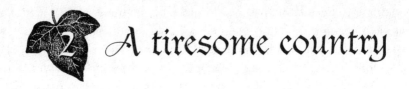# A tiresome country

SHBEL HAD GOOD REASON to be apprehensive about the posting to Ireland. Violence was never far below the surface there, and indeed, had come close to the Aberdeens, with the murder in the Phoenix Park in 1882 of their friend, Lord Frederick Cavendish, (husband of Gladstone's niece, Lucy) Chief Secretary to Ireland, and his Under-Secretary, T H Burke. Ishbel, in her letter to Henry Drummond, expressing her distaste for the new appointment, had made little of 'the DANGER', saying, 'we do not think of it,'[1] but nevertheless it was there as a possibility. There had been widespread and active land agitation from 1879 following the foundation by Michael Davitt of the Land League, with its twin objectives of tenant protection and ultimate ownership of their holdings to 1882, and the fires of Fenianism, although damped down, continued to smoulder. Successive administrations were faced with the problem of violence and harsh punitive measures were applied wherever considered necessary. Two Coercion Bills were passed in 1881 in an attempt to impose order, but agrarian crime continued to rise.

The potential for violence sprang from a well-founded sense of injustice. Irish tenant farmers suffered not only from poverty but from insecurity of tenure. For centuries they had been at the mercy of their landlords, who could raise rents at will and then evict them for failure to pay. The Land Act of 1870, which was driven through by Gladstone during his Premiership of 1868-1874 had made an attempt to deal with the problem, but its results had been disappointing. In 1881, again inspired by Gladstone, during the Liberals' short spell in power, a second Land Act was passed which gave tenants what were popularly known as the three 'Fs' – fair rents, fixity of tenure and free sale. There were deficiencies in the Act, and it fell short in some respects, but it did go a fair distance in removing grievances. In spite of this a sense of historic injustice remained, and in certain instances there were real and present injustices. Evictions continued in some estates, especially in the west and south of Ireland, for landlords themselves were in difficulties as tenants failed to pay rent, and it was usually only as a last resort that they carried out land clearances. Nonetheless the emotional impact of evictions obscured the very real difficulties of the landlord class. Britain was in the grip of an agricultural depression (due mainly to the American imports of beef and grain) and not only were prices low and still falling, but the earnings from migrant labour on which so many poor families depended were either not available or were so negligible as to be almost useless.

The two main demands of the Irish people were for land reform, and for Home Rule, rather than rule from Westminster. Of the two, it looked in 1886 as if the second of these had a chance of succeeding. Gladstone, even before the election of 1885, had decided that Home Rule for Ireland was inevitable. In 1867 he had seen that the outbreak of Fenian violence was a symptom of a deeper malaise. 'Irish violence,' he said, 'was a product of Irish grievance.'[2] The symptoms could be dealt with by a rigorous régime, but they were merely suppressed, and the underlying disease continued to fester. He had come to this conclusion, partly from a moral conviction that Ireland had suffered British injustice for too long, and partly from a well-founded belief that the granting of Home Rule was the only hope of keeping Ireland permanently linked to Britain. The 1885 election saw a complete collapse of the Liberal party in Ireland – they won no seats, while the Home Rule party led by Charles Stewart Parnell won 85 of the Irish seats. The fear then was that almost all the Irish MPs might withdraw from Westminster and set up their own legislative assembly in Dublin. The choice then facing whichever British party went into government would be one of military reconquest, with all its dreadful connotations, or recognition of the illegal assembly, which would be, in fact, an acceptance of the break-up of the United Kingdom. Gladstone, therefore, was in favour of granting Home Rule to Ireland and with the support of 74 Irish nationalist MPs he took up office again.

The Aberdeens, as friends of Gladstone, and believers, as he was, in the moral duty of eradicating injustice, would have broadly shared his views as to the desirability of granting Home Rule to Ireland. Ishbel, in the letter to Drummond already mentioned, noted that her husband had 'always felt inclined for some measure of Home Rule'. However, in a very personal way they would have had great qualms about the country to which they were being sent. The Irish were poorly regarded in England. As a people they seemed to be ungovernable, forever giving trouble. When they were not killing Englishmen they were killing one another, maiming cattle or burning homes and out-buildings. They lived in filth and squalor in dire poverty, and there was a widespread suspicion that many of their troubles were of their own making, for it was well known that they were lazy and improvident. The language they spoke could technically be called English, but it was often so mangled as to be almost incomprehensible. Their religion was a mass of unpleasant superstitions, and its dogmas were dictated by a foreigner, the Pope of Rome, who was anathema to all those Englishmen who had cast off his yoke centuries before. This view of the Irish was exemplified by the cartoons in *Punch* magazine which portrayed the Irishman as an uncouth simian being, little better than a savage, who shared his hovel with his pig and lived like him, on potatoes.

Irish fiction too, of the earlier half-century had helped plant in English minds this picture of a people who were below them in evolutionary terms and whose only hope of advancement lay in grasping the helping hand of their superior neighbours. Unfortunately, there were living specimens of Irish people in England, whose appearance and behaviour conformed to the stereotype. These were the hordes of emigrants who had come to the big cities in search of work, and who only too often sank almost to the bottom of the muck heaps there. They were no worse than their English equivalents, but they were identifiable by their accents, by their tribalism and by their Roman Catholicism. There were, it was true, some Irish ladies and gentlemen, even aristocrats, but these tended to be Protestant. A middle class was arising, but it was not as numerous or as prosperous as its counterpart in England. Not all English men and women felt this way, of course, or held all these views of the Irish, but there was, nonetheless, a residuum of belief that made the prospect of a term of office in Ireland not a particularly pleasant one.

Lord Aberdeen's position in Ireland would be most exalted. He would be Governor-General, Lord Lieutenant, and above all, Viceroy, the Queen's personal representative in Ireland. He would have wide statutory powers and the prerogative of mercy, but also be responsible for the 'peace and security of the kingdom'. In this awesome task he would be assisted by the Chief Secretary. In Aberdeen's case this was the clever and cultivated John Morley, one-time Secretary to Gladstone. By the end of the eighteenth century the Chief Secretary had become the Viceroy's partner, and it was through his department that the Viceroy's will was expressed. A position of power indeed, but not one regarded in some circles in England as being important, worthwhile or satisfying. As R

Barry O'Brien said in his study *Dublin Castle and the Irish People* the Chief Secretary 'is congratulated as a man who is promoted to an office on the Gold Coast is congratulated'.[3] There were rumours in Dublin every now and then that the position of Viceroy was to be abolished. These were particularly strong towards the end of 1885, and a loyal subject, John P Prendergast, was so dismayed at the prospect of losing the Queen's representative that he wrote a series of letters (later published as a pamphlet) to the *Irish Times* vindicating the office of the Viceroyalty. He wrote:

> If it were abolished it would be another step towards reducing this
> kingdom to a poor wretched province, and this capital to a
> provincial town.

The Viceregal Court, he said, was a splendid one, outshining in brilliance that of St James's, where, unlike the hospitable Dublin Castle, not even a cup of tea was to be had. In Edinburgh, where lately, as Lord High Commissioner, Lord Aberdeen had hosted receptions, society was composed of 'solemn sour-faced ministers and their wives, without the graces or the airs of good society'. Such would be the case in Dublin, he concluded gloomily, 'when Ireland is reduced to a country of small landowners ... and the Republican crowd wait upon President Davitt'.[4] The rumours were false, as usual, and the normal pattern of the Viceroyalty was not broken. The Viceroy would be expected to live in great state, as befitted the representative of the Queen and the embodiment of the 'dignified' aspects of the monarchy. He would, in short, be the official leader of Irish social life.

Ishbel, Countess of Aberdeen, did not look forward to this feature of her new life. As Vicereine she would be hedged about with protocol and she would have 'to observe' in her daughter, Marjorie Pentland's, words 'just the sort of "flummery" and social convention against which she had rebelled from her youth'.[5] It was bad enough 'being sent off to a tiresome country for which she felt a strong dislike' without also being confined and constrained by court etiquette, and the decorum demanded by her official position. Lady Spencer, wife of one of Lord Aberdeen's predecessors, was both amused and horrified by Ishbel's naïve assumption that she could go walking in the Phoenix Park and exclaimed:

> My dear Lady Aberdeen, you don't know what you are talking
> about. You must never take a walk in Dublin except in the Pound –
> the enclosure behind the Castle – you must not take a drive in the

Park without an A.D.C.; you must not go to a shop without telling them, so that they can put down the red cloth.[6]

Not a pleasant prospect, particularly as the Vicereine had no official duties. Marjorie Pentland quotes a letter written some years earlier about Lady Cowper who was to take up that position in Ireland. Her brother-in-law, Henry Cowper, wrote:

I am afraid she will be bored, as a lady lieutenant has no duties; her household duties are interdicted and she can hardly order a carriage except through a controller or master of the horse. The Dean of the Chapel Royal does all her charities and school work.[7]

All, therefore, that seemed to be left to Ishbel was the opportunity to shine as a social star, and satellite to her husband. For a woman who had been active in philanthropy, had engaged in religious debate, and had had an addictive taste of political life this could hardly be enough. The ban on political activity was absolute – Lord Aberdeen, although the representative of the Queen, was also a member of the Government, so had to keep away from anything that was tinged with party politics. Not only would his every word and action be scrutinised, those of his wife would also be noted. 'Politics' in Ireland, as it turned out, seemed to come into everything. Not only was there the familiar Tory/Liberal conflict to be avoided, there was also the problem of nationalist susceptibilities. Before Ishbel even arrived in Ireland she was made aware of problems that would never have occurred to her at home. Although she was far from happy about the move to Ireland she pragmatically decided to make the best of it, and resolved on making a gracious personal gesture towards the Irish people. Her four children were to make their State entry with their parents in an open carriage and they would all wear green in honour of the Emerald Isle. Unfortunately, an adviser pointed out to her, this could be interpreted as an overtly political act, as 'green' was in opposition to 'orange', and one was immediately stating a preference. And then, of course, there was the resolutely nationalist song 'The Wearing of the Green'; it simply would not do, so the children had to be arrayed in neutral white. The material was Irish poplin, however, so Ishbel got that one right.

The Viceroy and his wife, accompanied by their children, who ranged in age from sixteen months to seven years, made the State entry on the 20th February 1886, a bright, sunny, spring-like day. The Earl of

Aberdeen rode ahead on his bay horse, Splash, accompanied by his staff and a military escort, and then came the open carriage with the Countess and her children. The *Dublin Evening Mail* of that date reported that 'the Countess wore a plain black dress, and a grey wrap and veil with a small bonnet of the same colour'.[8] She had arrived at Kingstown at 8 am having left Holyhead, at 4 am and had experienced a calm crossing. The crowd's general attitude was one of reserve, mingled with some optimism about Home Rule. The *Irish Times* described the State entry as not being 'remarkable for any degree of enthusiasm' but added that 'nothing could exceed the heartiness with which the Countess and her children were cheered by the crowds'.[9] The Viceregal party then disappeared into Dublin Castle, the seat of British power in Ireland. It was also the venue for glittering state occasions and the building contained a Throne Room, a large Reception Room known as St Patrick's Hall, a large Drawing room, a small Drawing Room, a Picture Gallery, a Supper Room, a Boudoir, and a Banqueting hall. There were also more than thirty bedrooms for the Viceroy, his family and their guests. There was, of course, a large staff, the most important of whom was the housekeeper, who was responsible for the general caretaking of the State Apartments. She lived in the Castle for ten months of the year, while the Viceroy was living in the Viceregal Lodge in the Phoenix Park. During the other two months she moved to the Viceregal Lodge, and he moved into the Castle for the Season, which normally came to an end on St Patrick's Day. As the Aberdeens did not arrive in Ireland until almost the end of February they had to plunge immediately into the round of Receptions, Soirées, Drawing Rooms, Balls and other social functions.

In her memoirs Ishbel recalled that she found the routine very irksome at first. The family was never allowed to be alone, but had two detectives in constant attendance. When they went to Sunday afternoon service in Christ Church, a very short distance from the Castle (admittedly through 'rough streets') they had to go in a procession, consisting of two policemen, followed by two plainclothes detectives, who in turn were followed by two ADCs; then came Their Excellencies, two more ADCs, two detectives and two policemen.

Ishbel may have affected to scorn the 'flummery'of social life, but she never failed to dress up for the occasion. For the Drawing Room on Wednesday, 24th February she wore, according to newspaper reports:

… a court train of richest sapphire Lyons velvet, lined with richest pale blue satin surah and trimmed with plumes of pale blue ostrich feathers and bouquets of silver coral.

Her corsage was 'trimmed to correspond', and her head dress was a 'court plume of ostrich feathers'. A tiara, necklet and stomacher of diamonds completed the glittering picture. For the St Patrick's Ball ('Full Dress, feathers and lappets to be worn' and no person admitted 'in mourning, by Order of the Chamberlain') she again wore pale blue, but this time it was trimmed with silver and green shamrocks. The Castle entertainments were taken seriously by a section of well-to-do Irish. Débutantes were presented to the Viceroy, at a Drawing Room, and this marked their entry into society; in reality it placed them in the marriage market. There have been various accounts of the procedure followed in the Castle, but the most striking is that given by George Moore in his novel, *Drama in Muslin*, which follows the fortunes of a group of girls who were presented at the Irish Court. The action takes place in 1882, only four years before the Aberdeens were in Viceregal state, so the book is pertinent. Interestingly, Moore's description of Her Excellency's gown in *Drama in Muslin* prefigures that of one of the newspaper reports already quoted:

> ... many yards of azure blue richest Duchesse satin, ... trimmed with plumes of azure blue ostrich feathers and bunches of silver coral.[10]

It is doubtful however, if gentle Johnnie Gordon would have sensed, as Moore the novelist did, that his Viceregal kiss on each débutante's cheek was 'a lingering survival of the terrible *Droit de Seigneur* of olden times'. This was the crowning moment of the ceremony, but it took patience and stamina to get there, and money, of course, and much planning. Rooms had to be taken in Dublin for the Season, either in a rented house in Fitzwilliam Square, Merrion Square, Stephen's Green, or next best thing, in the Shelbourne Hotel. Then there was the vitally important matter of dress. Costumes would be needed for every outing, especially for the many fashionable tea parties, and above all, for the Presentation. Every seamstress in Dublin was kept busy preparing for those two months of social activity, and good dressmakers became haughty creatures, much sought-after. In Moore's novel, Mrs Symond, the dressmaker who made the gowns for the Barton girls, central figures in the book, was the confidante of 'the giggling Countess' and the 'sighing Marchioness' and was known for her 'genial sympathy'. However, to her less exalted clients she was known always as Mrs Symond, for 'to the Christian name of Helen none less than a Countess dare aspire'.

On the actual night of the Drawing Room, the young girls in their white silks and satins travelled with their mothers in horse-drawn carriages across the slippery, grimy cobbles to the menacing bulk of Dublin Castle. The Drawing Room did not begin until eleven but the more wily mothers, such as Mrs Barton, aimed to be there about half-past nine, because if you got into the first lot you could 'stand at the entrance to St Patrick's Hall and have the pick of the men as they came in'. As the carriages approached the Castle groups of onlookers peered in to have a good look at the occupants in all their finery. In Moore's words, 'never were poverty and wealth brought into plainer proximity'. The exquisitely-gowned girls looked upon young women:

> ...in battered bonnets and draggled skirts who would dream upon ten shillings a week; a drunken mother striving to hush a child that lies beneath a dripping shawl; a harlot embittered by commercial resentment; [and] troops of labourers battered and bruised with toil.

These miserable creatures looked in and by the flickering light of the street gas lamps saw 'the bloom on every aristocratic cheek, the glitter of every diamond [and] the richness of every plume'.[11] Inside, there was a long wait, usually in the Blue Drawing Room, where the sofas and chairs had been pushed back against the wall, but where the crush and the heat became almost unbearable. Eventually, through an anteroom, and into the Throne Room, where the girl's card was given to an aide-de-camp who passed it on, spread out the débutante's train, and then came the big moment, the double kiss from His Excellency, and a grateful, graceful curtsey from the recipient of the kiss. The girls who had gone through this ritual were then eligible, in keeping with Court etiquette, to appear at the St Patrick's Night Ball in 'the full glory of Court plumes and veils, many of which' said an article in *Every Woman's Encyclopaedia*, published in 1913:

> ...get rather damaged in the hours after supper when the Viceregal party retire and dancing grows fast and furious ... In days gone by the regulations for St Patrick's Ball were rather less formal than today, and there are accounts of lively scenes when the guests picnicked on the floor of the supper-rooms.[12]

Sad to say, I haven't been able to trace any of these accounts, but an item in *Modern Society* in March, 1907 suggests that there were indeed high jinks on these glittering occasions:

> It is whispered that their Excellencies have not been quite pleased with the conduct of some of their guests. At the last State Ball a section of the young people quite lost their heads, and a set of the Lancers degenerated into a romp ... Perhaps His Excellency will cause a guide to Castle manners to be written.[13]

The Dublin in which these festivities took place was a sad and gloomy city. In common with other towns and cities of the 1880s it was grimy with coal dust, poorly lit, and smelling of horse dung and worse. Unlike many other cities, however, Dublin was declining, not prospering. It had no industrial base, and its dependence on Irish agriculture left the city in a vulnerable position. As Mary E Daly points out in her social and economic history *Dublin, the Deposed Capital*:

> ...agricultural depression could act as a key factor of the city's economy. Changes in the volume of agricultural exports travelling through Dublin port was the most direct link. Bad harvests leading to higher food prices impinged on the living standards of the city's workers and might generate distress. Agricultural depression also brought an influx of rural migrants to the city in search of work or relief, a phenomenon of particular importance during the famine of the 1840s and also during the agricultural recession of 1879-82.

Other factors contributing to the lack of economic growth in Dublin were:

> ...the failure of Dublin businesses to manufacture, and, in some cases, even to distribute the manufactured goods which rural Ireland needed, plus the apparent stagnation of the port in the third quarter of the nineteenth century all meant that Dublin failed to provide adequate employment either for the indigenous Dublin population or for even a small proportion of the surplus population of rural Ireland.[14]

What employment there was available was, in many cases, casual work. It would seem that 'a substantial proportion of the city's working class lacked steady employment' – a hand-to-mouth existence, in other words, and a very precarious one. Illness or an accident, would, even for those in steady employment, be almost disastrous, for casual labourers absolutely so. One consequence of the under-employment of men was that there was a high proportion of women and children working as dealers and hawkers – a notable feature of Dublin street life at the time. Another notable feature was the number of beggars visible on all the major streets of the capital – an Irish phenomenon that had been commented on by many foreign travellers since the last days of the eighteenth century. Given this economic uncertainty in many Dublin households it is clear that a family that could supplement the main income by means of female labour – as seamstress, washerwoman, milliner, charwoman – would look with intense interest on the doings of the Viceroy and his wife. If they were to continue the customary Castle season then there would be employment for a time, but if anything happened to disrupt it, such as a period of Court mourning, or a cancellation due to agrarian outrages or extreme rural violence, then the future would be very bleak indeed. In that way, so, the lives of the most important personages in Dublin and those of the most insignificant were linked in a very real sense.

There were still elegant and beautiful houses in Dublin where gracious living was practised, and there were also, in the new suburban areas, the respectable dwellings of the new professional and upper middle class. There was also sound lower-class housing, especially that built by good employers such as Guinnesses, Pims and Watkins. Below this surface, however, there were the tenements, the once-grand houses that had originally housed one wealthy family apiece, but that were now home to two or more large families. The tenement system was described by the members of the Royal Commission on Sewerage and Drainage in 1880 as 'the great sanitary sore of the city', and Joseph V O'Brien, in his account *Dear Dirty Dublin*, of 'a city in distress', quotes from official reports on the state of these dwelling places. Inspectors spoke of:

> the narrow courts of over-crowded tenements with their cellar dwellings devoid of light except through the door; the privies ("never cleaned until impossible to use") in lobbies and under staircases; back yards ankle-deep in human filth; adjoining ruined sites serving as dung yards; nearby slaughterhouses and dairy yards with their "noxious effluvia," refuse-laden streets lacking any regular system of scavenging … and pervading all, the noisome smell.[15]

Most tenement dwellers had only a single back yard tap as a water supply, while those without such a basic amenity had to go to the public fountains. There was no way of bathing or washing clothes until a Public

Baths and Wash House was erected in Tara Street for the entire city.

The Viceroy and his wife did not, of course, visit these teeming dwellings, but the decaying houses and their miserable occupants would have been visible as the Viceregal pair rode in their carriages through the city on their various official and charitable outings. Even if they had closed their eyes and covered their ears they would still have found it difficult to avoid the fact that they were in Dublin, for it had its own distinctive smell – not only that of the streets that were never cleansed, but the vile odour that emanated from the Liffey, which was no more than a great open sewer, into which the city sewers emptied unchecked. From Dublin Castle out to the Phoenix Park, part of the Viceregal route lay along the Irish Styx, considered by many to be the cause of the very high death rate in the city. Every town and city in the late nineteenth century was, of course, an unhealthy place, its inhabitants at risk from infectious diseases – cholera, typhus, scarlet fever, typhoid, tuberculosis, measles, diphtheria, etc – but Dublin was worse than most.

Lady Aberdeen, although she had not wanted to come to Ireland at first, soon identified herself with the cause of the poor, and even before she arrived in Dublin, had made enquiries about the extent of the distress in the city. What she learned inspired immediate action. A letter to her from a prominent English philanthropist, Arnold White, dated February 22nd 1886, is obviously in response to an appeal of hers for assistance in providing dinners for poor Dublin men. It contains not only a promise of help but guidelines as to how that help is to be given. He writes, 'I could not decline to help, however feebly, in the true message of peace your Excellency is to carry to old Ireland', and then lists his suggestions as to how the dinners are to be organised – the helpers are to be voluntary workers, each diner's name is to be registered for future employment, and at least twelve to fifteen men are to be found work as a practical result of the dinners. This, he points out, 'will redeem the movement from the taint of "dole."' And of course it is extremely important to have the co-operation of the clergy, especially the Roman Catholics. Admission to the dinners is to be by ticket and tickets will be issued only to the 'bona-fide unemployed'. The menu will consist of thick soup, followed by plum pudding, and a half ounce of tobacco is to be distributed to each man. There will be one male or one female helper to each ten men, and the ladies are advised to dress very simply. Any speeches are to be practical and straightforward, and he recommends that 'plain analytical questions' be sympathetically put to the audience in order to classify the causes of distress. 'We are all missionaries for good or evil, high or low,' he concludes, and while politicians may do their bit, he believes that 'the only solution to trouble in India, South Africa or Ireland is a knowledge and faithful following of Christ'.[16]

His letter in places betrays the usual mid-Victorian fear that charity may be going to the 'undeserving poor,' those who bring their troubles on themselves by improvidence and drunkenness, and another letter, written on the 9th March expresses his doubts more openly.

> Is the distress in Dublin abnormal? Inquiries should be made among pawnbrokers, for if pledges redeemed are fewer than those pawned, and the articles are clothing and blankets, then distress must indeed be great. Fuel merchants could also be questioned about sales – are they much lower than at this time last year? Finally, what about whiskey? Are the poor forced to abstain?[17]

Dublin was renowned for the number of charities active at this time, and those who did not have recourse to Poor Law Relief or the workhouse, might have their distress relieved by, among others, the Sick and Indigent Roomkeepers' Society, the St Vincent de Paul Society, the Strangers' Friend Society, and the Association for the Relief of Distressed Protestants. Nevertheless, further voluntary help was needed, not only for the relief of distress in Dublin but in other parts of the country, and the Lord Mayor of Dublin, T D Sullivan, author of the popular ballad 'The Wearin' of the Green' proposed to hold a meeting in the Mansion House to set up a Committee to deal with the problem.

In terms of distance Dublin Castle and the Mansion House are not far apart, but in 1886 they were separated as effectively as if there was a wide ocean between them. The Nationalist Corporation of the city and the Viceroyalty had been on bad terms for years and there had been no communication between them. When, however, the Viceregal couple heard about the proposed meeting Lord Aberdeen, rather bravely, decided to attend and was fully supported in his decision by Ishbel. As she recalled in her memoirs, Lord Aberdeen sent an informal message to the Lord Mayor asking if he would be welcome in the Mansion House. The answer was "Yes", and the Viceroy joined the official platform where, as *United Ireland* reported, he sat 'beside a Protestant Archbishop and a Catholic Nationalist Lord Mayor'. Even more astounding, when Lord Aberdeen spotted Michael Davitt in the room he asked to be introduced to him and the 'ex-Fenian prisoner shook hands with the Lord-Lieutenant'. *United Ireland* was generous, even fulsome, in its praise for Lord Aberdeen, who, it said:

> ...gave proof not only of the genuineness of his sympathy with distress, but he, without doubt intimated on an occasion peculiarly well-chosen, that a state of perpetual estrangement between the Irish people and their rulers is becoming, or has become, unendurable for their rulers.

The paper took:

> ...his unassuming and straightforward conduct at the Mansion House to portend that the Lord Lieutenancy in its old unreal and mock-royal state is about to disappear.[18]

This incident established Aberdeen's popularity – no longer just a royal deputy, or even a 'Gladstone man,' but a kindly and caring person. His gift of £1,500 from his own pocket for the immediate purchase of seed potatoes to be distributed in the distressed areas was recognised and appreciated, as was his later contribution of £500 to Dublin charities. This latter sum was an offering to make up for the non-appearance of the Viceregal party at Punchestown – a break with tradition which was most unpopular. The Aberdeens allowed their staff to go, and gave the usual Punchestown Ball that evening, but their popularity, in a society where an interest in horse-racing was shared by high and low, was for a time somewhat diminished.

Lady Aberdeen soon began to appear in the public eye as a vigorous and hard-working woman, not simply an ornamental figure at official functions. She became patron of the Mansion House Ladies' Committee for the Relief of Distress. The Secretary of the Committee was a Miss Alice Crosby, who later, as Mrs Rushton, was Secretary to Lady Aberdeen's Women's National Health Association. Ishbel evidently entranced the Lord Mayor, for relations remained cordial between the Aberdeens and the Sullivans, throughout the Viceroyalty and on the morning the Viceroy and his wife were leaving Ireland for good (as they thought) Lady Aberdeen received a letter from T D dated August 3rd, 1886, and headed from the Mansion House. The letter asked if he might have a portrait of her – but it must be a large one. He added that both he and Mrs Sullivan would be pleased to accede to Lady Aberdeen's request that their names be added to the list of those on the Central Council of

Irish Home Industries.[19]

The promotion of Irish industries became Ishbel's main interest very soon after she arrived in Ireland. She had inherited from her predecessor, Lady Carnarvon, the presidency of the committee organising the Irish Stall at the Edinburgh International Exhibition in May of 1886 and she threw herself into this new task with all her youthful energy and enthusiasm. It was an outlet for all those organising talents which she had discovered over the past few years and it was also an enterprise which combined her new-found romantic love of all things Irish with practical good works. Irish craftsmen and women could be helped to improve their lot, and she could show the world what a wonderful country Ireland was. She had fallen completely in love with Ireland and it was a genuine passion, one that lasted for many years, and one that was given practical expression.

The first public announcement of Lady Aberdeen's vital interest in Irish Arts and Crafts appeared in the newspapers of March 29th, 1886. Notice was given of a garden party to be held in the Viceregal Lodge in May. The precise date would depend on the weather, but otherwise the instructions were clear. All those who had been invited to social functions by the four Viceroys preceding Lord Aberdeen were bidden to the party, along with their children, and were commanded to wear clothing of Irish manufacture, the children to appear as peasants from many lands. Men should wear suits of Irish tweed, Irish felt hats, and poplin ties of St Patrick's blue. Both ladies and gentlemen should wear 'Irish gloves exclusively'.[20] The advertisements began very soon from the big Dublin shops as the owners noticed commercial possibilities. Arnotts, McBirneys and Clerys all advised customers that they had materials of Irish manufacture in stock, including boots, shoes, hosiery, umbrellas, handkerchiefs, parasols, and so forth.

On May 22nd, after a week of rainy, windy weather, with the garden party still in doubt, the skies cleared, the sun shone, and a pre-arranged signal – a flag flying from the Castle – announced that the festivities would take place that afternoon. The *Irish Times*, in its report on the following Monday, told readers that 2,000 guests arrived at the Viceregal Lodge, watched by a large crowd who 'stood on the outer side of the steep ditch that forms the boundary of the property'. As instructed, the guests wore Irish-made garments, and the reporter commented that 'not a tie of blue poplin remained unsold in Dublin'. It was indeed, 'a picturesque and patriotic' spectacle, and the Viceroy and his wife followed their own instructions faithfully. Lord Aberdeen wore a suit of grey poplin, his boots, gloves and tie had all been made in Dublin, and he carried 'a blackberry stick'. Lady Aberdeen was dressed in what was said to be the costume of an Irish lady of the thirteenth century, designed for her by Major MacHenry, Curator of the Royal Irish Academy. It was of 'cream imperial poplin' and was embroidered in gold by students at the Dublin School of Needlework, from designs in *Book of Kells*. The head-dress was of gold, and her jewellery included a Tara brooch. Her stockings, embroidered with shamrocks, were Balbriggan-made, and her white poplin parasol was trimmed with Limerick lace. The shoes were of untanned Irish leather, fastened with Irish harp buckles.[21]

The guests were entertained by five bands, an Irish harper and an Irish piper. A portion of the lawn was boarded over so that 'guests could dance Irish jigs and reels'. These Irish capers had already been seen in Dublin Castle on the night of the St Patrick's Ball, and had been commented upon by Ishbel's mother, Lady Tweedmouth, who wrote to her:

> Fanny [Ishbel's sister-in-law, Lady Edward Marjoribanks] has
> returned with a glowing account of your success … at the ball; also
> how well you mastered the intricacies of the jig. The Duchess of
> Marlborough says she never saw a jig danced in Ireland – much less
> at the Castle – very infra dig! She is quite awfully jealous of your
> success! It is too amusing![22]

There is no record of Ishbel's having danced a jig or a reel at the garden party but perhaps she did, pleased by the success of her plans. The children, including the Aberdeens' own, were amused by various 'sports and pastimes' and were all presented with toys as prizes and keepsakes. The Viceroy was himself seen carrying various young folk around in his arms, enjoying himself almost as much as they did. 'The Earl and Countess,' said the *Irish Times*, 'have proved that they entertain the kindliest feelings towards all classes in the country', and the reporter wished that others would follow their example. He, or possibly she, believed that the Earl and Countess having shown how elegant Irish materials could be, lace, linen, poplin and tweed would now become fashionable. Ishbel, however, while all the fun and frivolity was going on, was doing more than just show off Irish goods; she was setting up an organisation for their design and marketing on a national scale. This was the Irish Home Industries Association, which came into being at a meeting on the tennis court of the Viceregal Lodge that day and arose from Ishbel's realization that much needed to be done to put Irish arts and crafts on a more rational basis.

While she was gathering material for the Edinburgh Exhibition it became obvious to her what was wrong, and in her preface to the *Guide to the Irish Exhibits, Women's Industries Section of the Edinburgh Exhibition,* Lady Aberdeen identified three things that were needed for the development of Irish craft work and industry –

(1) The overall organisation and bringing together of different centres;

(2) Good designs, and arrangements for their dispatch to isolated districts;

(3) Adequate provision for the sale of the work done.

She noted that Irish workers showed 'great ingenuity, power of adaptation, natural skill on working out designs and the patience shown in the work itself'. The committee in charge of the Irish entries had concentrated on the work done by groups, not on that done by individuals, which, however skillful, as the Preface noted, 'cannot affect the welfare of the country'.[23]

There was much plain needlework, but in the words of Paul Larmour, in his book *The Arts and Crafts Movement in Ireland* there were:

> ...exhibits ... that would undoubtedly have shown the artistic side of Irish women's industries, such as lace from Kenmare Convent, embroideries from the Royal Irish School of Art Needlework, and examples of illumination and woodcarving.[24]

On display at Edinburgh also were feather flowers, fishing lines made of silk, or silk and hair, and trout flies tied by Dublin girls. Perhaps the best-known exhibit was Irish lace which had, up to a few years previously been of limited artistic quality. A report by Dr William Sullivan, President of Queen's College, Cork, on the Cork Exhibition in 1883, had identified this as a problem and steps had been taken to solve it. With the help of Alan Cole of the South Kensington Museum, and James Brenan of the Cork School of Art, both of whom were working on improved designs, the quality of lace was improving all the time. New patterns were being produced and in convents in Ireland, especially in the south of the country (and in Carrickmacross, County Monaghan) nuns were both giving classes and themselves doing lace-making. Nuns also engaged in hand embroidery, not only for ecclesiastical use in vestments, but in gowns and trains for fashionable London and Dublin society.

Ishbel met many nuns as she carried out her duties as the Viceroy's wife. Since the beginning of the century the numbers of women in the religious life had increased dramatically. New orders had appeared and from eleven convents at the start of the 1800s the total rose by the end of the century to 368. This rise in the number of convents and that of women in the religious life was part of the nineteenth century religious revival which was experienced all over Europe. Two main features characterised this resurgence – an increase in the authority of the Pope within the Church, and an intensifying of emotionally-charged religious devotion among individuals. The devotion was notably focussed on the Virgin Mary, and gained a public recognition by the many apparitions of the Virgin reported throughout Europe at the time. Not all these apparitions were officially approved by the Church, but two of the most notable, at Lourdes in 1858 and at Knock, in County Mayo in 1879, were given official approval. The Virgin became almost a familiar figure; familiar, that is, in the sense of being approachable, understanding and sympathetic. For many girls and women the idea of emulating her and living a life of chastity was a beguiling one, especially when that life could be spent in the company of other women who had similar beliefs and aspirations.

Genuine piety was what motivated these women, and a willingness to work and pray for Mary's sake and that of her son, but there were other, lesser considerations that made conventual life an attractive prospect especially in nineteenth-century Ireland. For the majority of girls life offered few prospects apart from marriage and one could not be certain of that. Changes in the pattern of land inheritance, which meant that subdivision was gradually abandoned and property was passed on to one heir only, meant that marriage rates fell and rates of emigration rose. In any event, embarking on marriage in those days could be a perilous enterprise, leading as it almost inevitably did to pregnancy and to childbirth with its attendant risks to health, even life itself. The drudgery of farm labour could be exchanged for that of domestic service (and had to be if the farm was not prosperous enough to support a large family), but that too was a lonely life. Factory work was confined to the north-east of the country and to large cities, and the newer occupations in shops and offices were not as yet capable of absorbing female labour. Even well-to-do girls, daughters of prosperous farmers and businessmen, could be frustrated if they wished to have careers or lead independent lives. A convent, therefore, offered secular opportunities to women whether they were rich or poor, educated or uneducated.

Some communities led a purely contemplative life, but others were engaged in service to the community. Nuns ran hospitals, schools, orphanages, reformatories, industrial schools, asylums for mentally and physically disabled people, and homes for 'fallen women'. Many of the women in charge of these institutions were not only truly pious and animated by a strong belief that they were doing God's work, but were talented and able administrators, allowed to shine in a world somewhat removed from the power of dominant males. Nuns were, of course, bound by the authority of bishops, but they were adept at dealing with every kind of bureaucrat and civil servant and Caitriona Clear, in her essay on nuns in nineteenth century Ireland in the collection *Women, Power and Consciousness* writes that 'stories of strong-willed superiors outwitting bishops abound in convent lore'.[25] They were useful to the state by reason of their institutional work, and were, in every practical sense identified with the state. Individuals may have had rebellious stirrings of nationalism, (as imaginatively described by Kate O'Brien in her novel *Land of Spices*) but the communities and congregations dutifully and efficiently administered the rules, laws and regulations of the Imperial government.

When Lady Aberdeen met these nuns in their polished parlours or surveyed their work in their institutions she was meeting women with whom she had much in common. They all shared a belief in a Christian God, and they all worked to help those less fortunate than themselves. Also, though unlikely to have been acknowledged, there was the shared triumph of wielding a measure of power. Admittedly, Ishbel's power and status derived from that of her husband, while the power of the nuns was a different, and perhaps more hardly-won weapon, but power it was, and Ishbel was rapidly discovering its pleasures. She might only be the wife of the Lord Lieutenant but she was very much emerging as a person in her own right – and a popular one in Irish eyes, 'foremost,' as she was, 'in every good and kindly duty'.

These duties were from the end of March onwards, carried out from the comfort of the Viceregal Lodge in the green and pleasant surroundings of the Phoenix Park to the west of the city. The Viceregal Lodge stood in its own demesne, and had originally been a private residence before being bought by the government in 1782 as an 'occasional residence' for the Lord Lieutenant. Alterations and extensions to the building were made in later years, and artists involved included Francis Johnston who, in 1815 was responsible for the eastern and western additions to the house, the Ionic portico, new gates and lodges, and Decimus Burton who laid out the formal garden in 1840, and designed several of the park lodges at the same time. The house was further extended for Queen Victoria's visit in 1849. Typically, one of the first of Lord and Lady Aberdeen's acts was to add a chapel for Divine Service and Worship, a wooden building which was not too expensive. The Lodge was comfortable, and not too grand or too ornate, and one might as well be in the countryside, but to quote R Barry O'Brien, in *Dublin Castle and the Irish People*, the 'Viceregal Lodge is no more Ireland than Park Lane is England'[26] and the life of the Aberdeens was far removed from the stark realities of rural Irish living. Ishbel was an energetic chairwoman of the Ladies' Distress Fund, and she organised her committee in sewing bolts of flannel for clothing the women and children of the west, gathered blankets for them, and supported every fund-raising activity, but she never saw for herself the scenes of misery and want in remote country areas. However, even a casual reading of the *Irish Times*, the 'Castle' newspaper, would have brought the distress starkly to their Excellencies' attention.

Letters asking for donations to relief funds, and acknowledgements of monies sent appeared regularly in the *Irish Times*, and in April 1886 alone there were reports from special correspondents in the affected areas. A particularly vivid description of conditions in Ballycroy in County Mayo told how, in a 'cheerless and sodden landscape' the population was living on seed potatoes and meal bought on credit. The wretched cabins with their dripping thatch and discoloured walls were filled with stifling smoke, through which one could dimly discern emaciated children 'whose limbs and bodies [were] showing through the ragged remnants that they wore'.[27] Lack of clothing was commented on by the special correspondent who visited Gweedore, Donegal, and reported on the conditions there on April 24th.[28] 'It is a common necessity,' he wrote,' that many have to stay at home on Sundays for want of sufficient clothing.' In Aran too, it was noted that lack of clothing prevented many from leaving the shelter of their homes. Gweedore was never a prosperous district, said the *Irish Times* writer, adding, with considerable understatement, 'the relation of landlord and tenant [there] is far from desirable'. One hundred families were about to be evicted for non-payment of rent because there was no longer any money coming in from migrant labour. The potato crop 'the miserable produce of spongy bogs' had never been good, but this year it had failed altogether. Families had lived on food bought with credit, which they could not now repay. No more credit was available, and the merchants themselves were now in trouble. The writer concluded:

> The condition of the people is thus rendered hopeless. There is no food, no means, no credit and no marketable commodities. All is misery and utter destitution.

In Clifden, at the same time, where there was also much distress, the Parish Priest was engaged in the distribution of seed potatoes, and was accompanied by an English gentleman named Mr Arnold White (the same man who had been in correspondence with Lady Aberdeen about dinners for unemployed men in Dublin). The distribution was done on orderly lines, and recipients had to present their ticket of entitlement. The plight of one poor man who had no ticket so moved Mr White that he gave him two pieces of silver. Mr White then addressed the crowd from a spot outside the seed store and told them that while thousands of unfortunates were starving in London, at least they were not totally forgotten by the rich, who set up schemes to help them. Here, in the West of Ireland it was different – the hungry people seemed to have been forgotten by everyone. He himself did not have the power to do much for them, but he would 'make public the conduct of those who neglected them'. As he drove away he was showered with expressions of thanks and 'many of the poor cheered, "God bless the stranger"'.[29]

Terrible though these scenes of destitution were, they were surpassed in horror by what happened when families – sometimes whole villages – were evicted from their homes. William Carleton, the peasant who knew his rural world intimately, had written movingly about evictions almost fifty years previously, and what he had described in his novel *Valentine McClutchy* could still be seen in areas owned by unfeeling landlords. Cabins were tumbled down by wreckers acting, as they had been in Carleton's words 'with wanton cruelty and inhumanity'. The inhabitants:

> … poor shivering wretches, with all the marks of poverty and struggle, and, in many cases, of famine and extreme destitution, about them were thrown out to seek shelter wherever they could find it, in a ditch or a cave, or an overhanging rock. Even the grievously ill were taken from their beds to die under the fury of the wind and the rain.[30]

The Freeman's Journal had pointed out in an article in February 20th of 1886, that in England, during a period of agricultural depression, landlords reduced their tenants' rent, but that no such mercy (or sound sense) could be found in Ireland.[31] A letter in the same newspaper from Wilfred Scawen Blunt the English poet and pamphleteer, in the following June also adverted to the folly of Irish landlords in insisting on the full rental during times of recession. Speaking of the evictions in Kerry, which were being carried out on the Listowel estates of Lord Ormothwaite, and Miss Fitzmaurice, he pointed out that 'a little leniency and human feeling' (such as that shown elsewhere in Kerry where Lord Kenmare had reduced rents) would have saved tenants from ruin. These people were all dairy farmers on 'leases or yearly holdings judicially rented at figures far above present value'. Prices for produce had fallen, but no rent reductions had been granted and 'tenants who had sunk hundreds of pounds in building and reclaiming their farms [were] turned remorselessly out, beggars without a penny'. Blunt emphasised that he was bringing these cases to the public's attention because of the reputation North Kerry had gained for lawlessness. The trouble there, he said 'arises from cruel evictions, precisely similar to those now going on at Listowel.' If there are new outbreaks of violence in Kerry, it will be the fault of Lord Ormothwaite and Miss Fitzmaurice, but the English people will not see it in that light. 'They will cry out once more,' he said, 'that Irish people are lawless and unfit for self government.' But, if only one tenth of this injustice took place in England, he believed there would be 'before Christmas, a general Jacquerie'.[32]

There was no question of Lord or Lady Aberdeen witnessing these scenes, where in the words of the Bishop of Meath, quoted by Blunt:

the wailing of women, the screams, the terror, the consternation of children, the speechless agony of men [so affected] the officers and men of a large police force who were obliged to attend on the occasion [that they] cried like children.

Even if the Viceregal pair had, by some mischance, happened on such an incident, there was nothing that they, prisoners of their position, could have done. They were of course, aware of the unrest in Kerry when they set out on their tour of the south west of Ireland late in the month of May, but in *We Twa*, their book of memoirs, Ishbel recalled how they had dispensed with the usual military escorts, having instead 'guards of honour and ceremonial escorts'.[33]

They travelled by train, in their customary state, but the *Irish Times* noted in its account of the tour, that there were no popular demonstrations until they reached Millstreet, County Cork. There they were enthusiastically received, and the band of the local National League played 'St Patrick's Day' to loud applause. The reporter from *United Ireland* commented on the difference between this reception and that accorded to a previous Lord Lieutenant – Lord Spencer – some years before, 'then the populace stood silent and scowling at their doors, or kept inside while the Earl and his heavy military escort were riding through'.

The 'most enthusiastic' greeting to the Earl and Countess of Aberdeen was not alone for 'their amicable personal qualities' but was an indication of how the political situation had changed. The warmth and cordiality continued and from then on there were cheers 'for Gladstone and for the Countess of Aberdeen'. In Killarney (where the rain poured down) the party visited the Presentation Convent, and were greeted by children 'waving green boughs' and singing verses of welcome. Lady Aberdeen complimented the nuns on the excellent quality of the lace they produced, and Lord Aberdeen in a speech to the assembled dignitaries and townsfolk emphasised the importance of supporting Irish industries, pointing out that he and the entire Viceregal party were all wearing 'garments of Irish manufacture'. The official party included Henry Drummond, who was a frequent visitor to the Viceregal Household, and whose ties of friendship with the Aberdeens, especially Ishbel, were as close as ever. Ishbel had persuaded her husband to offer Drummond an official position on his staff, in Dublin, but Drummond had declined, pointing out, as he had done to Gladstone when the statesman invited him to enter policies, that he could do more good privately with his mission work, his lecturing and his writing, than he could in public life. In Kenmare a triumphal arch had been erected at the entrance to the town, and the local band played 'God Save the Queen'. Ishbel did not recognise the tune at first, commenting that it was obviously unfamiliar to the band, having always been regarded as a 'party tune'.

The Aberdeens were at the mercy of politics, and their friend, Gladstone who had sent them to Ireland, was by then in political trouble. His Liberal party had never been entirely happy with the Home Rule policy, and he had failed to convert those within it who, in common with the Conservatives and a large body of British opinion, associated the Irish party with Fenianism and agrarian crime. The old right-wingers among the Liberals, under the leadership of Lord Hartington, and the newer radicals, led by Joseph Chamberlain, grew more and more dissatisfied with Gladstone's plans for Ireland, and scarcely two months after his appointment to the Cabinet, Chamberlain not only resigned but set about gathering the dissidents in the party around him. Gladstone's Home Rule Bill, while providing for the government of Ireland by an executive in Dublin, responsible to an Irish parliament, retained the Union of the two countries, with the parliament at Westminster still exerting ultimate authority. When he presented this Bill to the House of Commons in April, its fate depended on the dissident Liberals, led by Chamberlain. In the event, they voted with the Conservatives against it, and the bill was defeated on its second reading on the 8th of June by 343 to 313.

Ishbel and Aberdeen had gone over to London for the weekend and Gladstone had spent the Saturday and Sunday with them at Dollis Hill. They had watched from the galleries of the House of Commons and had heard Gladstone make a 'magnificent' closing speech, but to no avail, and they shared in the disappointment of his defeat. In spite of the defection of so many of his party, Gladstone would not give up and he gained the Queen's reluctant assent to a dissolution of Parliament. A general election followed and Gladstone's Liberal party was soundly defeated. Seventy-eight Anti-Home Rule Liberals (later known as Liberal Unionists) joined 316 Conservatives in the House of Commons, easily outnumbering the 191 Liberals faithful to Gladstone and the 85 Irish Home Rulers. Gladstone resigned, and the Conservatives, under Lord Salisbury, took office, and the prospect of Home Rule seemed to have vanished for ever.

The incoming government made new appointments, including that of a new Viceroy in Ireland (the Marquis of Londonderry) and the Aberdeens left Dublin on August 3rd. The atmosphere was one of intense good will, tinged with sorrow and with thoughts of 'what might have been', while according to Ishbel, the Lord Mayor, T D Sullivan, asked Lord Aberdeen to tell the Queen that there would be an 'outburst of joy on the day when she comes to open the Irish Parliament on College Green'.[34]

As was customary when a Viceroy departed, Lord Aberdeen, was presented with 'loyal addresses', minor works of art, beautifully illuminated on expensive vellum. Sincerity resonates through some of these addresses, and unexpectedly vigorous language. That from the United Trades Council and Labour League reads:

> Your Excellencies have discorded the "Praetorian Guards" of Spies,
> Police and Soldiery which formed the entourage of many of your

predecessors; and by going about amongst our people trying to soften their misfortunes, you have won from them esteem and love where tyrants failed even to make themselves feared.

The Corporation of Limerick, which had never, in former years, given an address did so this time because they were so impressed by Lord Aberdeen's concern to 'ameliorate the condition of the people, develop industrial resources and in harmony with Irish aspirations'.

Lady Aberdeen came in for special mention – the Corporation of Dublin recalled the:

> ...noble part borne by the Countess of Aberdeen ... By her good example, her wise counsel and her liberal assistance, she rendered to the public a priceless service.

Her initiative in promoting the cause of Irish industries was particularly applauded and the addresses refer to her 'practical interest' in the project, the 'admirable results' which are sure to follow, and the 'time and energy' she expended on the development of native resources. An 'admirable convert' indeed, and a woman who had not only received public recognition as a person in her own right, rather than an adjunct to a government official, but a woman who had now discovered a cause which was to occupy much of her thoughts and energies for the rest of her life. Ishbel wrote in her journal 'Ireland is laid upon us to do all in our power for her for ever', and what was in her power to do, she did.[35]

The scars of battle

*I*SHBEL'S PUBLICLY-NOTED SORROW on leaving Ireland was genuine and well-founded. She was only twenty-nine, energetic, enthusiastic, and had found a new sense of mission. What was she to do now, back in England, where Gladstone was not only defeated but reviled, and mention of Ireland was greeted with weary derision? How could she find find the same sense of fulfilment that had been hers during the exhilarating few months in Ireland? The life of a wife and mother, mistress of two large households and active both in the social round and in charitable works, was simply not enough for her. She began to suffer from violent headaches, which a later generation would probably diagnose as being psychosomatic, caused by frustration and disappointment. The doctors advised the traditional Victorian remedy – travel. Aberdeen decided to take her on a world tour and the couple set out for a trip to India, Australia, New Zealand and Tasmania, and then across the Pacific to the United States and Canada. Ishbel was not a good traveller on this occasion, and was still in a gloomy and restless mood. She had hoped that the sea voyage would help her to make some plans for a rewarding future but the serene pale beauty of the Taj Mahal led her to write despairingly in her journal that 'it seemed to hold out an unattainable perfect pattern, and therefore to bring a sense of one's own dismal failure'.[1]

Letters from home did not bring cheering news. Gladstone was still under fire, and Lady Tweedmouth, Ishbel's mother, told her about noisy scenes in Parliament over Ireland, and the constant abuse of the ex-Prime Minister by the Press. 'Gladstonians', she wrote, 'are eyed with scant favour in high quarters, and you are well out of the way for your own sakes'. Dudley, Ishbel's father, was particularly vehement in his criticism of his one-time friend and leader, and Lady Tweedmouth added, 'he is so violent I have to keep absolutely mum'.[2] Ishbel too had had 'to keep mum,' not only in her father's house, but elsewhere. To Henry Drummond she had confided:

The mention of Ireland sets me on fire, yet I must drill myself not
to speak, not to look. It seems impossible for anyone here to
comprehend that one can really CARE about the Irish people,
whether they be good or bad.[3]

In Australia, however, her spirits lifted and she was delighted when
Irish organisations presented addresses of welcome to Lord Aberdeen in
recognition of his work in Ireland. They had not been forgotten, and even
so far away they were being fêted by Irish people. There was a brilliant
gathering at Sydney Town Hall, where they were given 'a genuine Irish
welcome'. It was the same story in the United States, where the
aristocratic couple were hailed as 'Home Rulers' by emigrant groups and
societies. There were discomforts to be borne on the long journey across
the continent (where she visited her exiled brothers) but when the
Aberdeens reached Niagara they were joined by Henry Drummond,
whose company always cheered and invigorated Ishbel, and the rest of
the trip became enjoyable. In New York they met more Irish groups, and
on their last night they were treated to a surprise serenade outside their
hotel by a choir drawn from all the Irish-American societies in the city.
Next day the Aberdeens sailed for England, and the *New York Herald*,
describing the scenes of 'genuine affection and enthusiasm' as the couple
departed, observed that Lord Aberdeen was 'perhaps the most popular of
British statesmen ever to have visited the United States of America'.[4]

Back in England, the Aberdeens involved themselves in work for the
Liberal party, badly shaken as it was by the defections of the Liberal
Unionists over the Home Rule issue. Ishbel now emerged as a talented
public speaker as well as a skillful organiser. She organised a three-day
conference in Aberdeen on behalf of a Ladies' Union, and spoke to a
large audience to such good effect that she was invited to speak at the
annual Liberal party gathering in Birmingham Town Hall in November,
1888, on the subject of Home Rule. She was almost ill with nerves
beforehand – understandably so, for it must have been extremely
daunting to face an audience of about five thousand, many of them
practised political speakers. It was still rather unusual in those days for a
woman to address a large public meeting (although the Moody and
Sankey revivalist gatherings had been addressed by very accomplished
women such as Geraldine Hooper, Jessie MacFarlane and Catherine
Booth) and her appearance caused much interest. She spoke well, a
journalist reporting with great condescension that her address 'had no

suggestion of the blue stocking or of hysterical rhetoric,' and that it 'was delivered in a clear sweet voice which thoroughly fascinated the audience and was heard perfectly everywhere'.[5]

After this success Ishbel was greatly in demand as a speaker and she became more and more accomplished. Her appearance was attractive – always an asset on a platform – and a reporter in Dundee described her as being:

> ...tall, generously-proportioned, with a frank, mobile face which lights up with a capital sense of humour, vivacious dark eyes and wavy brown hair.

She took her politics seriously, and in her journal she wrote that she had heard talk of a coming revolution, adding:

> The upper classes are defiantly determined to keep all they can ... Many of the best people withhold from what they feel is the contamination of politics. Yet in them lies the one hope for the country if they will only come forward as a duty, mixing with the working men, fighting their battles, leading them in the right way.[6]

Ishbel herself was ready to mix, and she thought of herself as a working woman, even saying so in public to a group of Glasgow mill girls when addressing them on behalf of a Benefit Society. She did work, and worked hard, organising the women's wing of the Liberal party – the Women's Liberal Federation, and its Scottish counterpart, the Scottish Women's Liberal Foundation, and later became President of both. She and Lord Aberdeen were involved in numerous charities in London and in Scotland, and spent both time and money on them. They overspent both in fact, and his lawyers had to warn the Earl to cut back on expenditure, as reduced rents from his estate would not be enough to cover his spending.

The couple had a position to keep up in society, especially in London, and entertaining made big demands on them. According to her daughter, Marjorie Pentland, Ishbel took great interest in the welfare not only of her servants, but in that of her guests' coachmen and set up for them a refreshment stall outside her house so that they could have hot drinks while waiting for their employers to finish the festivities. No doubt it was appreciated, but one wonders what the workmen engaged on the refurbishing of the house in Grosvenor Square thought of Ishbel's habit of reading them improving books or lecturing them on Home Rule when they broke off for their midday meal.

Although she was busy, this was not a happy time for Ishbel, made worse by her mother's illness towards the end of 1887, and a long convalescence afterwards. She confided to her journal that she wished her mother would die and be spared further suffering:

> And now as the fever rose and the doctors warned me there could be no hope, how I thanked God that the misery was over for her. The others thought me strange and cold, but how could I feel otherwise who had seen more than they of her life-long trouble, of her hourly self-sacrifice – I too who, as she came slowly, painfully back to life, saw the look in her eyes as she asked me, 'Will he [Dudley] be different?' [7]

Ishbel's later biographer, Doris French, sees this as a subconscious wish to punish her mother:

> … who had put her into corsets at the first sign of pubescence, imposed the rigidity of proper behaviour, taught submission to the dictates of society and the church', [8]

… but I see it more as resentment at being pulled back into that unhappy household from which she had escaped on marriage. She was now being forced once again to confront the miserable reality of her parents' relationship and was being reminded that the ties of family are so strong that one can only get so far away without being pulled back again.

She also suffered some sort of spiritual crisis around this time and was beset by doubts. These were so grave and caused her so much anxiety that she wrote in her journal:

> It was terrible to go on day after day as if all were the same. I thank God that that blackness, with all its horrors, has passed. Henceforth I accept nothing but the truth, no standing still, no fresh truth. How that scorches a past life, honest enough but superficial, trivial; when it seemed easy enough to rush forward without knowledge and help to put the world straight. The scars of battle remain, and though I would not have it otherwise the youthful happy confidence has gone. Perhaps it may be given to me to help others to a new freedom. [9]

Her introspective view of herself was unnecessarily gloomy – the 'happy confidence' returned and she continued to try to 'put the world straight'. That longing to tidy up what she saw as the muddle and mess made by others remained a feature of her character up to the end of her days, and it sometimes exposed her to justified accusations of meddling in affairs that were not, strictly speaking, her concern.

Ishbel's unhappiness, now as before, took a physical form and she suffered greatly from migraines. In 1889 she collapsed and her doctor prescribed complete rest for a year but inactivity only made her more restless, unhappy and unwell, so the familiar panacea, travel, was prescribed. The Aberdeens first went to Italy, but Ishbel was not impressed by the wonders they saw there, so, in complete contrast, the couple travelled to Canada in 1890. It wasn't a simple matter of two people setting sail – they brought with them a secretary, doctor, valet, maid, governess, nurse and six young women as servants for the house they were renting in Canada. An important item of Ishbel's baggage was the newly invented Kodak camera and roll film, and she was such an enthusiast for this new hobby that she took innumerable 'snapshots' all the way across Canada which were later published in a collection called *Across Canada with a Kodak*. On the ship she was upset by the lack of consideration shown to emigrants. They were not allowed sleep in their hammocks during the day, but no chairs were provided for them, so 'the poor ill ones lay about the deck anyhow, in abject misery'. With her usual briskness she added, 'The thing to do would be to get chairs for them and lots of amusing books and games'.[10]

The fate of emigrants generally was one of Ishbel's concerns during this trip, and later. Earlier in her married life she had been President of the Ladies' Union of Aberdeen, an organization concerned with the welfare of young country girls who had come to the city in search of work. The Union encouraged suitable young women to emigrate, and most of them selected Canada. Many married farmers and settled out on the lonely prairies. Ishbel, on her travels, saw how they lived and was horrified by their isolation, not only physical, but mental, or intellectual, and with the help of sympathetic women in Winnipeg, set up an association for the distribution of books and magazines to these almost-forgotten families. She lobbied her influential friends for help and collected from them books, magazines, puzzles, games – anything that would brighten the hard life of the emigrant women and their families. The editor W T Stead was a great ally in the undertaking and appealed to readers of his new monthly magazine *Review of Reviews* for parcels, and Ishbel herself had a letter in the December 1890 issue, asking readers to imagine what it would be like to 'live in a shanty on a vast plain where one's postal address is LOT 2, Section III, W'.[11]

Contributions poured in, and Ishbel persuaded railway and steamship companies to carry the literature for free. The scheme – originally known as the 'Lady Aberdeen Association,' but later shortened to the 'Aberdeen Association' – was a great success and brought happiness to many lonely homes, and a reassurance that those who lived and worked there were not forgotten. Ishbel insisted that the credit for the scheme belonged to the women of Winnipeg, but in reality it was her imagination that inspired the Association, and her powers of persuasion that got it running.

Back in England, the Aberdeens found that Liberal prospects were brighter, as the government had lost one by-election after another and it looked as if the Liberal party was on its way back to power. However, in 1890 the news from Ireland was not good. The Conservative government's policy of repression and coercion, although allied with conciliation in the shape of reforming the Irish land system, was not successful in bringing peace to the country, and the demands for Home Rule were as insistent as ever. Parnell was now as popular with the Liberal party as he was in Ireland, having been cleared by a Commission of Inquiry of the accusation of having written letters to *The Times* inciting his countrymen to murder. The case was a *cause celébre* and both Ishbel and Lord Aberdeen were in court when the true author of the letters – Richard Pigott – was unmasked. Ishbel was sorry for the man, and wanted to visit him, but was persuaded that it would be unwise. (Pigott later got away to Madrid where he committed suicide.)

There seemed to be every chance of a successful alliance with the Irish members of Parliament that would break the power of the Conservatives. What no one could have foreseen was that human emotions would wreck this hope. Parnell was cited in a divorce case by Captain O'Shea, the Irish member for Galway, who claimed that his leader had had, and was having, a liaison with his wife. Parnell did not rebut the charge because it was true, and on 17th November, 1890 the verdict was given against him. The Liberals were shocked, especially the Nonconformist element, and Gladstone refused to continue the Irish alliance while Parnell was head of the party. The Irish party itself split on the issue, and Parnell died, defeated, in 1891, aged 45.

The fall of Parnell was a blow not only to his own party, but to the Liberals. Gladstone wrote, 'the blow is the heaviest I ever received', and the Aberdeens shared his sorrow and disappointment, but interestingly enough, no reference is made in the Aberdeen memoirs to their feelings or views on the matter. Marjorie Pentland, however, quotes a letter from Lady Tweedmouth to Ishbel in which she speaks of being 'so sorry' for her:

> ...having to speak just now, for the Parnell fiasco seems likely to ruin the Home Rule cause and break up the party. Waverers will be all too glad to cut and run.[12]

Ishbel, it seems, was speaking at a meeting of the Scottish Women's Liberal Federation and her daughter quotes her as saying:

> It seems as though the supporters of justice to Ireland have again and again to be tested for fire. Those who know the Irish can understand the passionate loyalty with which they sprang to defend their leader. Let us show them that we will not join their opponents in railing at the man who is fallen; that we shall stand by them come what will. Let us not be discouraged: when misfortune overtakes a private home it is the woman's place to cheer up the man. So now, cast down but not destroyed, let us take the same part in public affairs.[13]

Although no longer living in Ireland, Ishbel considered that she did indeed 'know the Irish' for she was active in the affairs of the Irish Home Industries Association, which she had founded during her time as Viceroy's wife.

A London branch of the Association had been started in 1888, and Lady Aberdeen had undertaken to promote sales of Irish art and craft work there. The first offices of the London branch were in Victoria, but later Ishbel persuaded her husband to buy premises in Motcomb Street in the West End, and the Association, now known as the Irish Industries Association, leased them from him for use as a depôt. The shop was the subject of a fulsome article in an Irish journal, *The Lady of the House*, in September 1891. The writer, 'Our Special Lady Commissioner', was entranced by the 'hooded cloaks of fleecy wool … lined throughout with silk' that were available in russet, scarlet, blue, etc. They came from the Douglas Mills in Cork and 'on account of their lightness and warmth', were 'received with great favour'. Torchon lace that came from County Carlow and from Golden Bridge Convent near Dublin was 'long-wearing and very inexpensive' and the festooned curtain at the window was 'an exact copy of old Greek lace and was manufactured at the convent in Newtownbarry'. Needle point and rose-point crochet were very popular, especially with French women: 'one Parisian had just bought twenty guineas worth to adorn a dinner gown.' Hand-knitted socks for babies sold well, but although 'long shooting stockings for gentlemen were much in demand at the Edinburgh Exhibition' London sales were not so good. Table covers were greatly admired by the writer, and she was most impressed by how the colours harmonised. The manageress, a Miss Keating from Wexford, agreed, and commented:

> One peculiarity we find, namely, that the people in the middle and south of Ireland have more aptitude in combining colours than those in the north. When we get embroideries from the latter they glare at one another.[14]

In Dublin, the Irish Lace Depôt, a wholesale market agency for Irish lace workers, and a general centre for home industries, had been taken over by the Irish Industries Association after the death of its owner, Mr Ben Lindsey. It was Ishbel who was responsible for the take-over, insuring her own life for enough money to buy the business. There had been a rumour that a Jewish syndicate was going to buy it, and the anti-semitism of the times was such that people feared the workers would be exploited. It was vital so, that a native Irish group should step in and safeguard the future of the enterprise, and Ishbel acted quickly and successfully. The Irish Industries Association became a limited liability company with Ishbel as its President, and she was more than ever determined to promote Irish goods abroad. A big new international showcase was being planned – the Chicago World's Fair of 1893 (or to give it the alternative title, 'The 1893 World's Columbian Exposition') – and she turned her energies to planning an Irish exhibit there. Her committee was agreeable, but was rather taken aback when they realized that instead of their modest proposal of a showcase she was planning something much more elaborate – 'a full-sized model bride with wedding presents, alongside a full-sized Irish cabin, with live workers making the goods'.[15]

Her enthusiasm and her success in persuading the famous Chicago store Marshall Field to buy the bridal lace outfit won them over, and almost before they knew what was happening the cabin was extended to become a full Irish Village. This project happily occupied Ishbel for almost eighteen months and the next Aberdeen trip to the United States and Canada was in part a fundraising one as they travelled about seeking out Irish-American groups who would sponsor the grand project.

The idea of an Irish village at the World's Fair was not, in fact Ishbel's own, but was the brainchild of Alice Hart, who, with her husband, Ernest, had formed the Donegal Industrial Fund in 1883-84 to encourage craft workers in that county and to market their work. At the Irish Exhibition in Olympia in 1888 Alice Hart had set up a model Donegal Industrial Village, designed by herself and the Earl of Leitrim. It featured thatched cottages, an Irish cross and a round tower, and workers gave demonstrations of their crafts in the cottages. Ishbel admired the work done by Alice Hart's craftspeople, and ordered at least two dresses from her as well as woodcarvings, but she was not prepared to let Alice Hart take over the running of the Irish Village in Chicago. Instead, she suggested, sensibly enough, that the Donegal Industrial Fund and the Irish Industries Association engage in a joint venture, sharing both expenses and profits. This plan did not work, however, probably due to what is delicately called 'personality clashes' between the two strong-minded women. Horace Plunkett, politician and pioneer of the Irish Co-operative movement, described Alice Hart in his diary as 'an active, useful, vulgar, egotistical woman,'[16] terms which were later used by critics of Lady Aberdeen, so it is hardly surprising that a joint venture didn't work. In the end there were two Irish Villages at Chicago, one of them known as 'Lady Aberdeen's Irish Village'. Ishbel's motives in setting up 'her' village in Chicago were set out by her in her introduction to the official guide. Her eagerness to promote Irish goods was, she said, born of her wish to help the people of Ireland, 'that most distressful country' which had suffered because of 'English misgovernment'. Every year young people were forced, for economic reasons, to emigrate. There was nothing at home for them in a country where there was 'a lack of all other employment except that connected with agriculture', and although they prospered abroad in 'new lands so full of hope and opportunities' and never forgot the homes and families they had left, what about those who did not emigrate, and 'what of the country which thus loses the flower of its children?'

This need not be. The future, with proper development of natural resources and with improved communications could indeed be bright, and, she said:

> ...those of us who are Home Rulers are inclined ... to the belief
> that Ireland's full industrial development can only come under a
> complete system of self-government.

In the meantime it was not enough to sit by and hope for better times. Already there was 'ample proof of what might arise from small beginnings' and Ishbel cited the success of the shirt trade in Londonderry where:

> ... although now an enormous industry, it still employs, as it did from the beginning, women working in their own homes. The same can be said of the knitting industry, and in both cases the money brought in by the united work of mother and daughter small though it may be, makes all the difference...[for] it can be depended on, and will keep the wolf from the door.

With the success of these two industries as encouragement, the Irish Industries Association was:

> ... to watch over the beginnings of all industries likely to become permanent and to train the workers so that they may be able to meet the demands of the trade so soon as regular trade connections can be made for them.

Machinery had 'wrought mighty changes' but there were still areas where it could not compete with the work of skilled human hands, a fact that was now fully recognized. However, in face of competition, craft workers must be alert to the demands of the market. Not only must the work be of the highest quality – the designs must reflect changes in taste and be fully in the fashion of the day. This is where the Irish Industries Association could help, by sending out skilled teachers, new designs and information about market trends, and by making sure that all proceeds on 'sound and business-like methods'. Ishbel wrote:

> The work of teaching and organizing is obviously essential, but it requires money, and a large number of yearly subscriptions of $25 are needed to keep the Association going, and to expand, as it wishes to do, into poultry raising and the growing of early flowers and vegetables for the market. To this end, too, any profits made at the World's Fair will be donated.[17]

Much hard work went into organising the Irish Village and Ishbel visited Ireland frequently. One of her most important tasks was that of choosing the girls who would demonstrate their craft skills in the cottages. She was helped, of course, by local committees, and she recalled in her memoirs how the men always wanted to pick out the prettiest girls. They may have been successful, for visitors to the Irish Village remarked on the beauty of the girls there, and on her return from

Chicago Lady Aberdeen reported that they looked so well that visitors asked if 'their cheeks were artificially tinted'.

The venture was put on a business-like footing by the appointment of a manager for the Village – Mr Peter White, who had been manager of Michael Davitt's Woollen Company. Horace Plunkett was also heavily involved, but when Peter White died suddenly Ishbel and Aberdeen went themselves to oversee matters in Chicago. White's widow took his place later, and made an excellent job of it, but the presence of the Aberdeens added to the attractions of the Irish Village. The Fair opened early in May 1893, and President Cleveland paid a visit to the Irish section where, according to the *Irish Times*:

> ... he received the Earl and Countess of Aberdeen and a deputation of Irish lace-makers and dairy maids ... Lord Aberdeen gave the President a bunch of shamrocks, a blackthorn stick and a lace handkerchief for Mrs Cleveland.[18]

It wasn't as dignified a ceremony as it sounds, for the President was in a hurry and didn't wait for the official presentation. Ishbel sent her husband in pursuit but Aberdeen failed to make contact. When he came back, reporting lack of success, Ishbel said briskly that they would take six of the best-looking girls with them and would catch the President before he left town. The party dashed across Chicago in cabs and made it to the railway station where Mr Cleveland was standing alone on the rear platform of his private train. Here the Aberdeens thrust the Irish items at him and were duly thanked for their trouble. The six good-looking girls were presented and were able to tell their parents at home that they had shaken hands with the American President. Lord Aberdeen later described his rôle at the World's Fair as 'being a sort of nondescript position, combining that of manager, policeman, agent, guide, inspector and other offices', and perhaps he had that Presidential chase in mind.

On May 12th 1893, the Irish Village was officially opened and Lord and Lady Aberdeen each made a speech referring, according to the *Irish Times*, to the 'philanthropic nature of the project, and the commendable purpose of the Irish Industries Association'. The speeches were followed by a programme of Irish music and a formal reception was given by the Earl and Countess at *Lyre-na-Grena* ('The Sunny Nook'), 'a true, little Irish cottage, neatly furnished,' which was to be the Aberdeens' headquarters during their time there. Visitors could then enter the village, on payment of 25 cents, and for their money they saw what could only have been an idealised version of an Irish community. According to the official Guide, the entrance had been copied from the north doorway of Cormac's chapel on the Rock of Cashel, and led into a reproduction of the cloisters of Muckross Abbey. A Celtic cross stood in the corner of the village square, which was surrounded by cottages, but the outstanding feature was a model of Blarney Castle (on a scale of two-thirds), complete with its famous stone. The interior was set aside for living and sleeping rooms for the Village workers, but an exterior staircase allowed visitors to ascend to the battlements, kiss the stone and get a 'view of All-Ireland',

Back at ground level they could refresh themselves at the 'Tigosda', or inn, before visiting the shops, the Village Music Hall:

... where Miss Josephine Sullivan, the youthful professor of the harp, from the Dublin Academy of Music, discourses sweet music on the national instrument with a sympathetic touch such as would surely bring joy to the spirit of her patriot father, the late A M Sullivan.

Also to be seen was Tara's Hall, where reproductions of the Tara Brooch and other Celtic jewellery were being made, and the village museum. It was the craft workers, however, and their demonstrations who aroused the most interest, working in the cottages, where pots of potatoes cooked over turf fires, and blackened kettles steamed upon the hobs. Ellen Aher, trained at the Presentation Convent in Youghal, made needle-point lace; Kate Kennedy illustrated the making of Carrickmacross appliqué lace, Mary Flynn demonstrated the fine crochet work from Clones and Ellen Murphy showed how Limerick lace was made. In the next cottage Bridget McGinley spun her old-fashioned wheel to produce the wool for Patrick Fagan, the Donegal weaver of 'delightful homespuns'. Maggie Dennehy 'who talks real Irish,' sat near by and showed how the women of Valentia Island earned a living by their knitting.

A working dairy fully equipped with up-to-date utensils was staffed by three girls, Johanna Doherty, Kate Barry and Maria Connolly, who showed 'all the delights of a well-trained dairy maid's profession'. These girls had been trained at the Munster Dairy School near Cork, 'an excellent institution where all branches of scientific agriculture are taught, to the great benefit of the people'. Bog oak carving was also on display as was wood-carving and metalwork and 'in another of the cottages with their quaint old-fashioned furniture and open roof' there was to be found a photograph store 'from whence many a memory of Ireland and its beauties can be carried away'. Mrs Peter White, in Lady Aberdeen's absence, lived in *Lyre-na-Grena*, which was furnished with 'specimens of beautiful old Irish furniture, a lovely mantelpiece from an old Dublin house, old Irish prints and books on Ireland'. The guide concluded by suggesting that every visitor with Irish sympathies should carry away 'a native blackthorn as a memento of this bit of "Ould Ireland" in the New World'.[19]

Marjorie Pentland described the reactions of Irish emigrants when they beheld this representation of the homes they had left and lost:

Ishbel had watched the pathetic pleasure of old Irish people as they went through the cottages and saw the familiar settles and dressers of their youth or were persuaded to join again in a crossroad's jig, or an Irish reel.[20]

Horace Plunkett had a more realistic approach. He wrote in his diary in October:

It was direly gotten up, not Ireland, but a taking show enough as the turnstiles testify. Mrs Peter White presides over 100 and more shop girls, lace makers, spinners, weavers ... Money recklessly spent but seems to be coming back[21]

Indeed, the final figures showed a profit of £50,000. Andrew Carnegie, one of the guarantors of the Irish Village, had also been worried about the cost and had been sceptical about the pulling power of Irish cottages etc, and had written to Ishbel while matters were in the planning stage, expressing his doubts:

When I see what you are committed to ... I find myself hoping that you ... will decide to let the whole matter go. A facsimile cottage may not appeal to people, at least to the extent of an admission fee. If I were you, I should drop it.[22]

She had ignored his advice and had been proved right – not only did the Irish Village make money (one of only three attractions at the fair to do so – the other two being the Ferris Wheel and Cairo Street) but Ishbel secured fresh outlets and orders for Irish goods because of it.

Plunkett had been on good terms with Ishbel when they worked together in the Irish Industries Association, and his earlier diary entries are admiring and pragmatic. For example in 1891:

Lady Aberdeen is a good woman, but rather scattering. Still, she is rich and attracts wealth into the sphere of usefulness.[23]

Some months later he recorded that he had had:

> ... a good talk with Lady Aberdeen about Home Rule. She thought my line [social and economic development rather than political agitation] would have worked six years ago, but now it was too late. The trend to wards Home Rule was too strong.[24]

By the autumn of 1893, however, Plunkett's view of his co-worker had changed and was now tinged with irritation. He did allow that:

> ... one great secret of success [the village] is the way which Lady Aberdeen is advertised. Her name is all over the village – it is her village – the IIA. Jim Power, [James Talbot Power, President of the Committee] and the rest of us – I'm not jealous – have given our work and money to make Lady Aberdeen the best advertised lady in the world. Well, she works hard herself, and her work is mostly good.[25]

Clever Ishbel, who, as the wife of an ex-Viceroy known to be in favour of Home Rule, realised that the Aberdeen name would have pulling power, and used it liberally. Americans, too, although citizens of a democratic republic, were intrigued by a title, and she shrewdly played on their interest. By the following week Plunkett was seriously aggrieved and wrote in his diary:

> Went to village and found Lady Aberdeen and also her staff (including Lord Aberdeen). She is most difficult and makes my position so too.[26]

As he himself recognised, Ishbel's husband was quite obviously in second place to his wife, but as Plunkett had earlier observed, he was 'a bit of a muff, a good amiable creature, but physically weak'.[27]

There was a potentially dangerous incident at the Irish Village later in the year when a group of young men climbed the steps of 'Blarney Castle' and hauled down the Union Jack from its flagpole. In the earlier months of the Exhibition a plain green flag had been flown – in order not to give offence to Irish-American sentiment – but when in November, Lord Aberdeen, recently appointed as Governor-General of Canada, was on a visit to the Village, the Union Jack was flown in his honour. The young men were captured by the police, and some of the Irish party wanted to press charges but Horace Plunkett persuaded them not to, and his diplomacy was so effective that there were no further national demonstrations.

The Aberdeens travelled to Ireland at the end of May, 1893, to report on the 'chances' of the Irish Village, and to seek out more craft work for display there. They were greeted with great enthusiasm at Queenstown, where Ishbel reported on progress so far. Large crowds lined the route to the Queen's hotel where the aristocratic couple were staying, and the Saint Colman's band played for them when they appeared on the balcony. A declaration of support from the Mayors of Ireland for Lady Aberdeen's work was presented to her at a large meeting in Cork on the 2nd of June and shortly afterwards she set out on a tour of the West in connection with the work of her Association. Priests, nuns and bishops greeted her, and the *Irish Times* reported, 'Wherever she goes she is received with open arms and the people hail her as a benefactor'.[28]

Her fame inspired Davy Stephens, the newspaper seller at Kingstown, a familiar and well-loved character who greeted all distinguished travellers as they landed on Irish soil, to mention her in his 'Davy's Kolum'. In the July 1894 issue of *The Kingstown Monthly* he:

> …congratulated the Countess of Aberdeen on the great success of her benevolent tour through poverty-stricken districts of the West and North West.[29]

Her energy appeared to be inexhaustible, and people marvelled at how she seemingly could travel for days, have innumerable meetings, conduct serious business without ever flagging. On the way to Letterfrack, in the remote wilderness of Connemara, crowds of schoolchildren lined the route 'boys and girls alike wearing red flannel petticoats'. There were wild whoops of joy as 'the Lady' passed by and bonfires on the hills as she made her way to Donegal and Derry. In Donegal at that time there was much unrest due to some particularly heartless evictions, yet the parish priest of Killybegs was moved to write to Ishbel expressing his admiration for the excellent qualities that adorned her 'beautiful and noble character and particularly her energy and activity in promoting everything which had 'the public good for its object'.[30]

Ishbel thoroughly enjoyed the journey around Ireland, the way made smooth for her by her friend James Talbot Power (Chairman of Power's Distillery, a Catholic, a Conservative and later Sir James) who organised all her trips – 'special trains, barouches with beautiful horses, wagonettes or side cars' or even 'his own coach and four grey horses', for transport, accommodation in private houses or hotels arranged in advance, and groups of interested individuals ready at each stop to help her with local knowledge. Talbot Power even saw to it that she had a selection of small gifts for everyone, 'framed photos, sweets, pipes, cigarettes, needle cases, work bags, and silver thimbles of various sizes with [Aberdeen] initials on them'. There were also Irish-made waterproofs and hoods ready at hand for the inevitable rain. It was a jolly party, and Ishbel recalled that:

> Henry Drummond was in high spirits and insisted on our all
> playing rollicking games at the places where we stayed for the
> night, whether country houses or hotels.[31]

Ishbel had every reason to be happy with the Chicago venture, and the Irish Industries Association was in a healthy position – its finances were sound, and its influence was growing – but its very success must, in a way, have been galling to her for she would not be in Ireland to manage and guide it. The Chicago Village scheme had been predicated on the Aberdeens being back in Dublin in the Castle and the Viceregal Lodge. A Liberal election victory in 1892 had brought Gladstone back into power and Lord Aberdeen, the popular Viceroy in Ireland six years previously, quite naturally assumed that he would be returning there. It is dangerous to make assumptions, particularly in politics, and the shock and disappointment felt by the Aberdeens when he was passed over in favour of Lord Houghton, was compounded by disbelief. It transpired that John Morley, the new Chief Secretary, charged with the responsibility of furthering a Home Rule policy, had refused to have Aberdeen as Viceroy, and Gladstone had yielded to him. The Prime Minister explained to the Aberdeens that:

> ... when Mr John Morley accepted the Chief Secretaryship of
> Ireland he said that, if he were to be responsible for piloting the
> Home Rule policy through the House of Commons, he wished to
> have a new Lord Lieutenant as he felt it was essential for him to be
> boss, and that could not be with Aberdeen, as they had been in
> Ireland before on an equality, and that would not do now. He alone
> must be responsible.
> Mr Gladstone tried to persuade him that we only wished to do the
> non-political side of the business – to work for public health and
> promote industries, etc – and that the affection and confidence
> manifested in us by the Irish all over the world would be a real
> asset. But Mr Morley was adamant.

No hint of resentment towards Gladstone appears in the Aberdeen memoirs, however, although the disappointment is made clear, and the references to him are bland and non-contentious. They recalled:

> Mr G. said that at his age he felt he could not press his own views on those who undertook the charge of the various departments and he tried to console us by saying that after all there were other openings.[32]

The Governorships of Canada and India would soon become vacant and Aberdeen could take his pick. Canada was the obvious choice, given the family links there, so Canada it was. Ishbel felt the death of the Irish dream very deeply and letters from Ireland regretting that she would not be returning upset her.'Each post,' she wrote, 're-opens the wound.' So far, her daughter said in her biography, her life had been a success story, but now, at thirty-five years of age she 'had learnt that colleagues may distrust energy and popularity'.[33]

One wonders if it was Ishbel rather than her husband whom Morley did not want in Ireland - there are hints to that effect in the Aberdeen memoirs and the daughter's biography but from what one can learn of Morley's character and career it is doubtful if personal motives can in this case be ascribed to him. Ishbel herself was very keen to dispel all rumours of bad feeling between them and in her memoir she described a meeting she had with Morley, at her instigation, in the Shelbourne Hotel in Dublin in 1893. He told her that he had 'absolutely nothing' against Lord Aberdeen but 'that he felt *himself* (JM) responsible for this Home Rule policy, that it was a desperate venture and that he and he alone must lead'. That was not a very satisfactory explanation of his refusal to have Lord Aberdeen as Viceroy, but Morley's assurance that Gladstone 'fought like a lion' for his friend's appointment was some consolation. Nevertheless, Ishbel showed her feelings of resentment 'too plainly', so much so that she later wrote to Morley saying she was sorry and that both she and her husband could bear their disappointment, knowing that the new Chief Secretary was 'only acting as he thought *right*, and for the best interests of the country.' Morley replied to her letter in a missive of surpassing sweetness, promising to show interest in her work in Chicago and in any other venture connected with Ireland. He professed himself 'cut to the heart' by her words about the luncheon. He had walked away that day in great distress, for he had not realised how much pain he had caused. Her letter was 'most magnanimous' and he was the Aberdeens' friend for as long as they wished him to be.[34] In his *Recollections* Morley makes no mention of the incident, and his only reference to the appointment of the new Irish Viceroy is a eulogy of Lord Houghton's qualities of good sense and reliability.

In September 1893, the new Governor General of Canada, Lord Aberdeen, accompanied by his wife, stepped ashore at Quebec, to take up his appointment. Ishbel realized that all thoughts of the vanished Irish appointment had to be put out of mind, and she settled down to life in Canada. Some of it was fun – she enjoyed sightseeing with Henry Drummond, who had concluded an American lecture tour and had come to meet them, – and later the winter sports of skating and tobogganing were greatly to her taste and her *Canadian Journal* contains many references to the enjoyable times she had with her children on the snowy slopes and ice-bound lakes and rivers. Dances and balls were also enjoyable (she still loved dressing-up and as her daughter recalled 'she took great pleasure in ceremony and picturesque effect') but formal occasions were as dull as ever and she detested the 'stifling official artificiality'[35] which required her to wear 'a perpetual smirk'. There was also a great deal of criticism voiced in the Press, most of it of a personal nature, and Ishbel's Canadian biographer, Doris French, says that 'barbed comments, along with distorted tales of democratic antics with her servants'[36] put her under great strain. She was accused of being too much of a politician, and of outshining her husband, and of being too philanthropic. Ishbel indeed was a politician by nature, but the only way she could enter the political arena was by courtesy of her husband. Fortunately for her, but not perhaps for himself, Aberdeen was easily led, and Doris French quotes a former Canadian Prime Minister, Sir Charles Tupper, as complaining that Aberdeen was 'a weak and incapable governor, under the controll [sic] of an ambitious and meddlesome woman'.[37]

It was generally felt that Ishbel was the driving force, and while admirers may have been happy with this, her behaviour was inappropriate. She never had enough guile to conceal her meddling or hide her influence under the cloak of diplomatic wifely submission. She was an excellent example of the enthusiastic amateur, unelected, and uncontrolled by the restrictions and conventions of a political party structure and responsible to no one, who rushes ahead unaware of the damage that can be done.

Nevertheless, the five years in Canada were happy ones, and her occasional visits to Ireland in connection with the affairs of the Irish Industries Association kept alive the links with Ireland. Her attachment to that country was a constant one, and in a lecture given by her in Toronto at the request of the Catholic Young Ladies Literary Association, she spoke passionately about Irish history and literature under the title of the 'Celtic Literary Revival'.

Ishbel described an ancient Ireland, well governed by Brehon Laws, where men and women alike had rights and redress for wrongs. She spoke of the coming of Saint Patrick, and told how the saint was so impressed by these laws that he did not try to rewrite them or put Roman law in their place. Then she moved on to list the Irish authors, men and women, past and present, who made up the glory that was Irish literature. She quoted from Thomas Moore, William Carleton, Charles Lever, Maria Edgeworth, Douglas Hyde, Emily Lawless, Samuel Ferguson, Jane Barlow, Pamela Tynan Hinkson and W B Yeats – an impressive and eclectic assortment.[38]

Ishbel was introduced to the listeners by the Archbishop of Toronto, John Walsh, who reminded them that she had 'endeared herself in a special manner to the Irish race at home and abroad'. Her efforts to 'ameliorate the condition of the Irish labouring classes' were enlightened ones, for she did not 'pauperise and degrade them' by doling out alms, but by 'stirring up within them a spirit of self-respect and self-reliance, and by bringing within their reach the means of earning an honest livelihood'. Just what Ishbel liked to hear, and she took the opportunity to advance the cause of the Irish Industries Association and to seek new members for it. Action, particularly involvement in matters of social welfare, was what Ishbel thrived upon, but Canada was too vast for the deeply personal sort of work she had done in Ireland. There were many problems to be solved – the ill treatment of immigrant domestic workers and the exploitation of women workers for instance – but she could not tackle them on her own. Fortuitously, she had help at hand.

While she was in Chicago in May 1893, Ishbel had been elected President of the International Council of Women, an organisation founded by the American suffragists, Elizabeth Cody Stanton and Susan B Anthony, as a base for social reform. From its beginning in Washington in 1888 it had grown rapidly and now had branches in most European cities. This was the era of women's clubs, as middle-class women, better-educated, with more leisure, looked outside the home for enjoyment, companionship, and stimulation. The more serious-minded involved themselves with social problems, and in doing so, often found that they were facing one of the huge paradoxes of the age – if women were capable of dealing with difficult and challenging issues, why then should men deny them the right to gain the political power which was the ultimate resolution of such issues? Indeed, the rise of women's clubs, and the subsequent politicisation of many of their members was looked on by some observers as a very dangerous development, but in spite of male opposition and derision, clubs continued to flourish. By 1905 Ex-President Grover Cleveland was so concerned by the increase in women's activities outside the sacred circle of home and family that in an article 'Woman's Mission and Woman's Clubs' published in the American *Ladies Home Journal* in May 1905, he solemnly stated his belief that such clubs were not only harmful but a menace to society. 'The best and safest club for a woman to patronize', he declared, 'is her home.' Her duty was to teach her children who were 'to become rulers', lessons of 'morality and patriotism and disinterested citizenship'.[39] It was, of course, only the male children who were to become rulers.

As President of the ICW Ishbel was now in a position to exploit its full potential for change and reform. Her own attitude towards women's suffrage was then, at best, cautious. In her earlier years in London, in 1889, she had made inquiries about standing for election to the first London County Council. By the terms of the Local Government Act of 1888 women rate-payers could vote, but it was not clear whether they could stand for election. Ishbel, it transpired, could not even vote – she was not a ratepayer. Instead, she became President of a new society to secure the return of women to local councils – the obvious place where women could use their influence on matters that were of special concern to them. Her daughter quotes remarks Ishbel made at the first meeting; 'What do we find will be under the control of these Councils?' she asked.

> Why, asylums, reformatory schools, music and dance-hall licenses, baby-farming, artisans' dwellings, open spaces – cannot women help in all this? This is not a plan for obtaining Women's Rights – a most unfortunate term. I, for one, would not lift a finger in it just for the glorification of women. The right we claim is to be allowed do our duty ... We begin to understand that we must go back to the causes of poverty, and think for the hard-pressed working woman who has no leisure for thought, no chance for action, yet upon

whom comes the hardship caused by defective laws, soul-crushing competition, low public standards.[40]

A woman as clear-sighted and as shrewd as Ishbel must have been aware of the power that possession of the vote would give to women and she could surely see the rewards for an energetic and able woman such as herself who could harness that power to achieve the reforms she so badly wanted. Yet there was an important factor that held her back from commitment – her devotion to the Liberal party, exemplified as it was by Gladstone. Although Liberals, piously echoing the sentiments of their founder, John Stewart Mill, who had been an open advocate of women's suffrage and had nevertheless been elected to Parliament, had always professed to be in favour of women's suffrage they had never done anything to promote it. Gladstone was evasive and unhelpful when Ishbel asked him about the issue, saying in his letter of reply:

Undoubtedly the addition of Women's Suffrage to my cares in connection with the masculine part of creation has been a little less than convenient; but I feel and think more of the real and urgent weight which you have had to carry in your intermediate position, and from the genuine sympathy which flows out and around you on behalf of all sections with which you are in contact.[41]

Gladstone was referring to the fact that there were divided views on the matter within the Women's Liberal Federation, and it is possible that Ishbel feared a complete split if she pushed for a declaration of support for women's suffrage. That would deprive the Liberal party of one of its greatest props, and that was unthinkable. She referred to this possibility in a letter to John Morley in May, 1889, saying, 'I wish the concession to be delayed in case it affects the interests of Liberalism', a clear enough statement of her belief in the paramount importance of the Party. Yet in the same letter another, more personal, belief is voiced:

I detest "Women's Questions", pitting men and women against each other. I shrink from them all, and long for the time when the law will recognise no sex.[42]

In later years her attitude changed and she pressed the leaders of the party to commit themselves to granting the vote for women. Her efforts failed, and it was not until after the 1914-18 war that a limited vote was granted and full suffrage for women was not available until 1928. Needless to say Ishbel did not approve of the aggressive methods used by Lydia Pankhurst's Women's Social and Political Union, for she was opposed to all forms of violence.

In Canada Ishbel organized a Council to be affiliated to the International Council of Women and she became its first President. Local Councils followed and she was kept very busy criss-crossing Canada to help in their foundation. By sending her private secretary, Teresa Wilson, to Europe, Ishbel kept up her contacts with the ICW and she attended the second Quinquennial meeting of the council in London in 1899. There, as President, she called for arbitration as a means of settling international disputes, and chaired meetings on the legal and social issues that concerned women. The assembly called for the unimpeded entry of women to the professions, equal pay for equal work, a state-paid maternity allowance, etc. The big question of votes for women was avoided, in spite of intense interest among the delegates, by leaving it off the agenda. As with the Women's Liberal Federation, Ishbel was afraid of a public rift, which would lessen the power of the organisation, and she devised a curious solution to the problem. The main assembly would not debate the question, but a second forum would be set up under the aegis of the Women's Suffrage Society of Great Britain where discussions could take place. Strangely enough, the tactic worked, no schism followed, and the council displayed a united front.

The desire within the International Council of women was, however, for women's suffrage and at the Fourth Quinquennial Meeting in Toronto in 1909, Ishbel's views were that of the majority, clearly and unequivocally expressed. She repeated what she had stated years before, that women should exercise their rights in order to do their duties as citizens:

> ... remembering the loss that accrues to every city and country
> where the women are not in the position to give it all the
> contribution which lies in their power to give to the life and work
> of the community.

Very much aware of the social composition of her audience, she went on:

> We must remember that one of the main reasons why women
> workers must desire to hasten forward this movement is not so
> much on account of those who like ourselves ... in our sheltered

homes, have much power and influence, but it is for the sake of the working women on whom all such social legislation bears so severely and so harshly that we desire especially to claim the power of voting.[43]

In 1898 the Aberdeens left Canada, in debt because of overspending on official functions, Lord Aberdeen claiming that 'family claims and interests' called him home, but it is possible that politics in London had something to do with his return. There had been rumours of friction between himself and Joseph Chamberlain, the Colonial Secretary, and although these had been denied, it was significant that the new Governor-General, Lord Minto, was a 'Chamberlain man' and many of the rumours about Ishbel's so-called unconventional domestic arrangements while in Ottawa were circulated by the Mintos.

When Ishbel looked back on her years in Canada she could be proud of some of her achievements, notably the foundation of the Canadian National Council of Women and the establishment of the Victorian Order of Nurses, a system of district nurses for the sick poor. She had had to contend with much opposition in the creation of this body, particularly from the medical profession, so her satisfaction in success was great.

On a personal level Ishbel had greatly enjoyed the vacations in the Aberdeen holiday retreat in the Okanangan where she could relax in the company of her children. Marjorie Pentland looked back on the holidays as a truly happy time, full of simple country pleasures, and Aberdeen, basically a shy man, was completely at ease in that undemanding atmosphere. A change, however, had taken place in Ishbel's appearance – she had put on weight. She had always been tall and, as they said, 'well-built', but flesh had settled on her, giving her a matronly appearance. This change is recorded in photographs taken in the Canadian years. In an early one, Ishbel, in riding costume, is beautifully proportioned, a large well-shaped bust set off by a small waist, but in one of the latest she is well on the way to being the bulky figure familiar to the Irish public. Ishbel herself attributed the weight gain to the lack of exercise available in Canada (an odd comment, considering all the winter activities), but it was more likely to have been caused by the non-stop consumption of food at official dinners and the erratic eating on those uncomfortable trips to local groups and associations. The flowing gowns she wore did not flatter her, nor did the fussy accessories – the feathers, fichus, capes, wraps, stoles and the large veiled hats that overpowered her face.

A huge sorrow had befallen her in 1897 – the death of her dear and devoted friend Henry Drummond. Although he had been ill for a year with bone cancer, Ishbel had not realized the nature of his illness and he himself had made light of it, so that his death was a great shock that almost paralysed her. The Aberdeen's great hero and mentor, William Gladstone, had died in 1896, but although they were saddened by his passing, he had been an old man and had had a long and fruitful life. Henry was only forty-six and so much of his life and work was still ahead of him. Although Ishbel herself was only forty, her youth had vanished and with it so much of hope and faith in the future. In her *Canadian Journal* she wrote:

> … there is one event which crowds out all the others and which
> will ever be remembered as the dying out of a great light and joy in
> our lives – and that is the death of Henry Drummond on March
> 11th at 11.15 a.m. It would be useless to write of this – it seems to
> us that it can have been granted to but few to have known so full
> and so perfect a friendship with one whose character and nature
> ever seemed to reveal new riches and new perfection the closer one
> came to him. None can know what it has all meant to us except
> himself and ourselves. It has all been so perfect and there has never
> been a shade over our relationship since that first evening when he
> came into the drawing-room at Holyrood and when we seemed to
> know one another right away.[44]

A memorial to Drummond was erected in the chapel at Haddo House and Ishbel went on alone without the confidant who had so inspired her and helped her through her darkest moments as well as bringing so much gaiety and laughter into her life.

Back in England, Ishbel was received by the aged Queen Victoria and arranged for the Queen to hold a reception at Windsor Castle for all the delegates to the 1899 International Council of Women, a triumph of personal persuasion considering the Queen's detestation of women's suffrage.

On the political scene both the Aberdeens soon became active. Ishbel again took up the Presidency of the Scottish and English Liberal Federations and spoke at meetings and conventions all over the island. She was a Liberal through and through in the Gladstonian sense, and was uneasy about the war then being waged in South Africa against the Boers – a war which Gladstone with his distrust of imperialism, would have deprecated. Liberal party opinion was divided on the question of the war, but the Aberdeens adopted a middle position – the war, they felt, should have been avoided, but since it had not been, they supported the cause of the English armies in South Africa, while hoping that in victory they would display magnanimity.

Ishbel's interest in Ireland had never diminished and she was saddened by the fact that Irish unrest was still widespread. The country had not been pacified in spite of the Chief Secretary, Arthur Balfour's strong coercive measures and bitterness seemed to have intensified rather than lessened.

Further personal sorrows clouded those years; her brother Archie, who had been a semi-invalid for years, died in 1900, and there were rumours of suicide. Her elder sister, Lady Mary Ridley, had died in 1899, and in 1904 her sister-in-law, Fanny Tweedmouth, to whom she had been particularly attached, died of cancer. Ishbel's own son, George, Lord Haddo, was a continuing source of worry, for he suffered from epilepsy, and it was doubtful if he could lead a normal life. The defeat of the Liberal party in the elections of 1900 was a heavy blow, and although Ishbel continued to work for the sacred Liberal cause, she turned more and more of her energies to the International Council of Women, and was re-elected President in 1904. It was satisfying and rewarding work and she was stimulated by the company of intelligent, interesting and well-educated women from all parts of the world and whose friendship she retained for life.

In 1905 an even more exciting opportunity to be of service presented itself. The Liberals won the General Election that year, and the new Premier, Henry Campbell-Bannerman, asked Lord Aberdeen to be Lord-Lieutenant of Ireland. John Morley, who, as Irish Chief Secretary, had caused Ishbel such pain in 1893 by his refusal to tolerate Aberdeen as Lord-Lieutenant, had been appointed Secretary of State for India, and James Bryce, the new Irish Chief Secretary, was happy with Aberdeen's appointment. Ishbel, of course, was delighted to be returning to a land which, emotionally, she had never left. All her dedicated work for the advancement of Irish industries had been inspired by this romantic attachment, and she remembered with nostalgic pleasure the happy times she had had there, not only when she was in state as the Viceroy's wife, but when she had travelled the country in search of Irish crafts and craftworkers. There were the official receptions in the towns and cities, the addresses of welcome, the gifts given with love and respect, the torchlight processions, the bands serenading her in the morning and the evening, and above all, there were the humble women and girls in their small, dim cottages who looked on her with such affection and gratitude as their benefactor. There was so much more she *could* do, and *would* do, and the years ahead looked bright – with the ever-glittering prospect of Home Rule on the horizon. Such were her dreams and although in many ways, the reality turned out otherwise, she discovered in Ireland what was to be her final crusade.

The final crusade begins

HEN LORD AND LADY Aberdeen left Ireland in 1886 they had done so with sadness, not only because they were leaving a land which they, and especially Ishbel, had grown to love, but because that land's future looked bleak. The high hopes for Home Rule had collapsed and nothing seemed to lie ahead but a period of Conservative coercion and repression. Now, in 1905, they were coming back to a country where optimism was again in the ascendant, for the prospect of self-government seemed to be a possibility. In personal terms the Aberdeens were pleased to be returning to a country where they had both been extremely popular, and with which they had retained close links. Their stay in Ireland, where earlier violence had diminished, promised to be a pleasant and untroubled one. In this they were mistaken. The Ireland to which they returned was not the Ireland which they had so reluctantly left twenty-one years before but a country which had been changed by events and happenings of those years. The Aberdeens were aware of the new spirit of nationalism but were charmed by its romantic elements and overlooked its political implications.

The fact was that there was a decline of popular interest in Home Rule and in the efforts of the Irish members of parliament at Westminster to obtain a measure of self-government. The struggle had been going on for too long and without any apparent success. Minds were turning to other methods of achieving independence. The old militant Fenianism still existed but more in its negative sense of anti-British sentiment than in a positive philosophy. Two other movements, however, supplied philosophies of struggle. There was Sinn Féin (simply and tellingly translated as 'Ourselves'), the movement founded by Arthur Griffith, which preached neither violence nor parliamentary agitation, but non-co-operation. The Irish members, Griffith advised, should withdraw from Westminster, and set up an Irish government. The British would then peacefully withdraw and Ireland would enter an era of industrial achievement. Unlike Horace Plunkett, pioneer of the Co-operative Movement in Ireland, Griffith did not view the future prosperity of Ireland as lying in agricultural development.

Then there was the Irish Socialist Republican Party, led by James Connolly, who saw Britain as the embodiment of capitalism and imperialism and who dreamt of a Workers' Republic in Ireland. Only in an Ireland free of a British presence could a socialist state come about, so that talk of Home Rule (with its attendant subservience to Westminster) was totally irrelevant.

To these two forms of nationalism was added a third based on a consciousness of an independent Irish race and culture. From the early years of the nineteenth century there had been a romantic interest in the past and the work of writers, historians and archaeologists had continued throughout the century, leading to a conviction that what Ireland had was unique and should be so valued. This form of nationalism was the one with which Lady Aberdeen identified, and, in truth, she made her own valuable contribution to it by means of her support for Irish arts and crafts.

Respect for native Irish culture however, went further than Lady Aberdeen could ever imagine when Douglas Hyde, who founded the Gaelic League in 1893, called for 'the de-Anglicization of Ireland'. This was to be achieved mainly by the revival of the Irish language as the medium of everyday speech and writing. A sturdy supporter of this ideal was the Gaelic Athletic Association, established 1884, which revitalised native Irish football and hurling and banned what its founder, Archbishop Croke, called 'fantastic field sports [such] as lawn tennis, polo, croquet, cricket and the like'.

Redressing the linguistic balance somewhat was the emergence of what came to be called 'the Anglo-Irish' writers, chief among them William Butler Yeats, who wrote in English of the glories of their native land. These also contributed to the new sense of Ireland as a place sufficient unto itself, no longer dependent on Britain. The sum total of these teachings, political, economic and cultural, was that everything British should be cast aside. In this climate what reverence could there be for a representative of a British monarch and his establishment? All the trappings of Viceroyalty became alien; the military rituals, the social round, the entertainments, the garden parties, and the cricket and polo matches, all were foreign to the idea of an independent state. Even the

Viceroy's concerned and charitable lady, tirelessly working 'to improve the lot of the Irish people', was an object of suspicion, and during her time in Ireland, Ishbel was to experience fully what she had had a foretaste of in Canada, criticism in the newspapers, as well as in private.

There was another factor in the Irish equation which was to make life difficult for the Aberdeens in their nine-year term of office in Ireland. This was the problem of the Ulster Unionists, and what a problem it was, not by any means new, but now more of a worry than ever before. Putting it simply, many of those living in the nine counties of Ulster did not want to break with Britain. There were historical, social, economic and religious reasons for this and paramount among these was the religious one. The Protestants of Ulster (many of them Orangemen harking back to their hero, the seventeenth-century Protestant British king, William of Orange) did not want to live under what they perceived would be a Roman Catholic government ushered in by a Home Rule Bill. Cultural aspirations such as the revival of the Irish language and the banning of foreign games added to their feelings of exclusion from the rest of the island. They felt safer in a union with Britain, where they believed their lives, their property and their culture would be respected.

In earlier days, as in 1886, when it looked as if Home Rule would be granted, Protestant unease had expressed itself in serious rioting and sectarian violence in Belfast, and there was always a chance that not only would this be repeated, but that it would be on a larger and more serious scale. In fact, the developments were even more dramatic, and what was seen from the Liberal government's level as a noisy and defiant group in 1906 became a potent threat to that government and the peace of the whole island by 1914. Alarmed by the Liberal Party's stated intention in the General Election of 1905 of giving Home Rule to Ireland, the Ulster Protestants organised themselves for resistance. They set up a network of clubs all over Ulster in readiness for the hour of danger, and they mounted a propaganda campaign to influence the British electorate. The organization became strong and powerful and the propaganda took effect, especially in Conservative (and in time, even in some Liberal) circles. In January of 1912 the Ulster Unionists began openly to raise a military force – the Ulster Volunteers – with a double purpose, to support the 'provisional government' which the Unionists would set up in Ulster if Home Rule was introduced, and to control possible public disorder.

This militancy was matched by the rise of a similar spirit in nationalist

Ireland and in 1913 a movement to launch an Irish Volunteer Force was set up in Dublin. This was under the aegis of the Irish Citizen Army, the body set up by James Connolly to protect workers during the great strike and lock-out of 1913, a strike which ended with victory for the employers in January 1914 and which increased bitterness not only against the employers but against the authority which supported them.

From then on, both sides, Unionists and Nationalists, were on a collision course, not only with one another but with the British government. In Ulster the Volunteers openly flouted British authority and their leader, Edward Carson, challenged the government to arrest him.

Failure to do so was looked on as weakness, and eventually the Prime Minister, Herbert Asquith, decided on a show of force to eliminate opposition to the Home Rule Bill that was now about to become law. In March 1914, orders were given for naval and military movements to strengthen the position of the crown forces in Ulster. The General in Command – Ireland, acting on the authority of the War Office, asked officers if they would be willing to serve in Ulster and pointed out that refusal would mean dismissal. Fifty-eight cavalry officers stationed in the Curragh made it clear that they would prefer to be dismissed rather than fight against Ulster Volunteers and plans for Government aggressive action in Ulster were abandoned. Public confidence in the army was shaken and the prestige of the government suffered greatly.

Then, in April, the Ulster Volunteers smuggled in a large consignment of arms at Larne, in County Antrim, a move which was followed in July by similar gun-running by Irish Volunteers at Howth in County Dublin, in broad daylight. Troops were sent from Dublin to confiscate the arms, but failed, and were jeered by a stone-throwing mob. Panicking troops opened fire and three civilians were killed. The prestige of the Irish Volunteers promptly rose and it looked as if the two anticipated collisions with crown forces, north and south, were imminent.

In an effort to negotiate a peaceful settlement, King George V called a conference at Buckingham Palace for 21st July. The question at issue was 'should Ulster, or part of it, be excluded from the Home Rule Bill'. Neither Carson for the Ulster Unionists, nor John Redmond, for the Irish nationalists, could yield on this issue, and the possibility of war in Ireland, when the Home Rule Bill would pass into law within a few weeks, was a very real one. In August, the issue was postponed, not solved, by the outbreak of war between Britain and Germany, when both

Carson and Redmond agreed to throw their whole weight into the war effort and to put national problems to one side for the duration. The Home Rule Bill passed into law, but with a suspensory act postponing its operation until the return of peace.

This then, was the background against which the Aberdeens were to play out their Viceregal roles, but, like their political masters in London, they were not prepared for what was to come. Aberdeen himself was indeed in favour of Home Rule, and his wife even more so, and both hoped to be the last Viceregal pair in Dublin, but they could never envisage a complete breakaway from the Empire. The *Freeman's Journal* on Monday, 5th February 1906 in its report of the 'cordial welcome' extended to Lord and Lady Aberdeen on the occasion of their State Entry to Dublin on the previous Saturday said that:

> ... it was made plain that the mass of Dubliners remember 1886 and entertain the hope that the "spirit and aims of Mr Gladstone", may prove to be the spirit and aims of the new Administration.

There was no doubt of the goodwill of Lord and Lady Aberdeen but the reception indicated the hope that his Viceroyalty would be marked 'by more significance than his personal good intent alone could stamp it with'.[1] The *Irish Times* in an editorial on the same day, referring to the death of Lady Grey, wife of the Foreign Secretary, Sir Edward Grey, noted that:

> ... in the presence of Death how petty appear the squabbles and intrigues of ordinary political life and how insignificant its functions and ceremonials.

In the circumstances the paper:

> ... need do no more than record the entrance into Dublin of the new Lord-Lieutenant and Lady Aberdeen and express the hope that their sojourn ... may be agreeable to themselves and beneficial to Irish people of all classes.

Then came the warning (not unexpected from a newspaper with Unionist sympathies) to Lord Aberdeen not to become involved with Irish internal affairs:

> ... If he carries out the intention attributed to him and takes no part in politics, he will go a great way towards making his Viceroyalty successful.[2]

Elsewhere in the paper there was a news report of the State Entry, which took place after a rough sea crossing from Holyhead to Kingstown that caused many of the distinguished passengers to suffer seasickness. The Earl and Countess had recovered sufficiently on landing to receive an address of welcome from the Kingstown Urban District Council in which the Councillors remembered 'with special pleasure the deep interest shown by Her Excellency ever since her residence here'. Some sections of the crowd shouted 'Welcome back,' but the reception in the city though cordial, was respectful rather than enthusiastic.

However, in College Green and Dame Street, which were thronged with people, the Countess was 'accorded quite a remarkable demonstration on her own accord,' and there was 'a loud cheer for Lady Aberdeen and the Irish Industrial Revival'. The writer concluded that:

> ... the welcome which was extended to Her Excellency bore striking testimony to the fact that the friendships which she established during her former stay in Ireland have not grown cold during the score of years which have since intervened.[3]

This sentiment had been prefigured by a cartoon in the *Leprechaun* magazine of January 1906, bearing the caption 'Should Auld Acquaintance Be Forgot'. The drawing showed Lord Aberdeen in a kilt, Lady Aberdeen in evening dress (looking very young and pretty) surrounded by ladies scattering flowers at their feet. A cheering crowd looked on, and a banner in the background read 'Céad Míle Fáilte'.[4]

Ishbel had come back to the adulation which always warmed her heart and was ready to continue her work for the Irish people, no longer as an outsider, albeit a very special one, but as a resident in the centre of power, able to influence individuals and events. She told a meeting of the Irish Kennel Association later in the week when they presented her with an address of welcome that it had seemed a good omen that an Irish terrier should have followed her carriage all the way from Westland Row to the Castle when the Viceregal party made its State Entry.

The first businesses to be attended to were sociable, and charitable. The Castle season had to go ahead, having been postponed due to Court mourning following the death of King Christian IX of Denmark, father of Queen Alexandra, Consort of King Edward VII. (For the State Entry Lady Aberdeen had been dressed entirely in black, 'rich black mantle, with black feather and toque to match'.)

An insight into the problems of dressing for Viceregal functions is given by the announcement in the *Irish Times* of February 12th, by the Lord Chamberlain, that 'by gracious permission of the King,' ladies who had already ordered coloured dresses for the Viceregal Drawing Room on March 7th were allowed to wear them. The Drawing Room turned out to be, literally, a sparkling affair, with gaily bedecked clothes 'outshone,' said the *Irish Times* report, 'by the diamonds of the Marchioness Conyngham, Countess of Annesley, Lady Holmpatrick, Lady Pirrie, Lady Gwendolen Guinness, etc'. Coiffures were special features of the evening, although less exaggerated than usual. There were no huge chignons, but every other style of hairdressing for the last fifty years was on display, adorned with ostrich plumes which were 'used with picturesque effect'. Bouquets, although very beautiful, came in for some criticism. They were large, heavy, soiled the gloves, and the 'heavy perfume of lilies, gardenias and tuberoses' was almost overwhelming in the heat of the rooms. Some ladies had revived the fashion of carrying just a sheaf of lilies or a posy of three or four large blooms tied with silver ribbon or a chiffon scarf, and the writer felt that that fashion was bound to be popular. It was 'an advanced hour' before the guests left, but they had been refreshed by the tea or coffee obtainable at the buffet – 'a welcome innovation at the Drawing Rooms',[5] and one for which the credit went to the ever-practical Lady Aberdeen.

Tea had also been served at the afternoon reception in the Castle on March 5th, where Lord and Lady Aberdeen moved among their guests without ceremony. The State Ball on the 10th March attracted between eight and nine hundred guests, who danced in St Patrick's Hall and in the Throne Room. The St Patrick's Day festivities followed the usual pattern – parades, military displays, etc and the Season concluded on the 21st March with an evening party at the Castle. This was a musical and dramatic entertainment, and the guests were treated to an all-Irish programme, organised by Lady Aberdeen, and including a short Irish play, Irish songs, and Irish jigs. Not everyone appreciated the entertainment; Lady Alice Howard, daughter of the Earl of Wicklow, wrote in her journal 'We all went to a party at the Castle. Irish music and an Irish play. All too horrid and vulgar for words'.[6] In general, Lady Alice did not enjoy Castle hospitality. Of a dinner party there on the 20th February she had written 'There was a large dinner party – very common lot',[7] and of another big dinner on the 21st February she wrote 'there was hardly a soul we knew'.[8] This was a change of heart since the March of twenty years before when she had written of her stay as a house guest in the Castle, 'the Aberdeens are very nice and kind'.[9]

Tory and Unionist supporters did not attend Castle functions and those whose official positions forced them to be there were extremely uncomfortable, as they testified in their reminiscences. Page L Dickinson, whose father was Dean of the Chapel Royal, recalled in his memoirs *Dublin of Yesterday* how with the installation of a Liberal Lord-Lieutenant:

> ... social amenities were flung to the winds, and the rag tag and bobtail of Dublin went to Court. After a few years of the Aberdeens' term of office many people of breeding gave up going to the Castle, and social life in Dublin underwent an amazing decline. Man after man of my own generation who would, as a matter of course, have gone to the Court functions avoided them and laughed when the Castle was mentioned. Without being a snob, it was no pleasure and rather embarrassing to meet the lady at dinner who had measured you for your shirts the week before.[10]

Dickinson made the point that the only rationale for:

> ... such a court was that it should be the imitation or reflection of that of England ... During this time it became merely grotesque, and indeed, offensive, to those of a Tory habit of mind while being anti-Irish in political aim to those of the extreme Nationalist view. [It was popular so] only with middle-class folk who liked to think they were dressing up in feathers and trains, and strutting in rarely-worn evening suits and swimming in a dashing social life entirely foreign to their upbringing, but congenial to their worldly ambitions.[11]

Dickinson was right about the anomalous position in which the Aberdeens found themselves socially. The Tories did not wish to attend the Castle functions for political and snobbish reasons, while the Nationalists laughed the whole idea to scorn. The patriotic Countess Markievicz, it is true, was once an attender at Castle functions, but ceased to accept invitations as her Nationalist convictions grew in intensity. There were still, of course, a great many people, especially of the business and professional classes who were extremely happy to be honoured with an invitation to a Viceregal function, and nowhere is there a report of very poor attendances. On a personal note, it was a great sadness for Lady Aberdeen that her long-time friend and co-worker in the cause of the Irish industrial revival, Lady Arnott, could not come to court. As Lady Arnott wrote in an undated letter, on the subject of a proposed Old Dublin Ball (date unknown):

> Most gladly will I help you in any way I can, but as Unionists we shall be unable to attend any official entertainment at the Castle. You wrote so kindly last September that one's personal relations need not be affected by political warfare so I venture to accept this offer and know you will understand. Yours affectionately.[12]

The Aberdeens were sincere in their attempts to widen the Castle guest list to include a greater variety of people, but Neville Wilkinson, Ulster King at Arms, in his autobiography, *To All and Singular*, published in 1925, wrote of this 'laudable intention of widening the popular support of the [Viceregal] institution' that it had the opposite effect:

> A few months after the arrival of Lord and Lady Aberdeen, blue reefer coats and brown boots made their appearance at Castle receptions, an innovation which could have offended no one had their wearers treated his Majestys' representative with the traditional respect. But this laxity gave the opponents of the existing regime the opportunity of advertising their contempt for the high office of the Lord Lieutenancy and its holder.

His conclusion was that overall, there was 'very little effort made to uphold the dignity of the ceremonial at Dublin Castle'[13] The same criticism was made in his autobiography *The Brimming River*, by R F Brooke, member of a prominent Unionist family, published in 1961. He accused Lord Aberdeen (whom he described as having been 'a rather unsuccessful Lord Lieutenant for a few months in 1886') as 'having an utter lack of dignity'. The Viceroy had always been a nervous type of man, and during his stay in Dublin he seemed to become more and more agitated. As Brooke tells it:

> ... he gave an impression of continually hopping from one leg to the other, his hands were never still for one moment and he seemed always to be jerking his head from one side or the other as if afraid he might miss something. When he arrived at the Horse Show he took off his hat and put it on again, then quickly repeated the operation, rather like an artiste about to do a music hall turn.[14]

These nervous twitches of Lord Aberdeen, in conjunction with his frantic leaps around the dance floor earned for him the nickname of 'Jumping Jack,' while Lady Aberdeen was 'Blowsy Bella' (attribution unknown, but more likely to be a jeer from the Unionist rather than the

Nationalist side).

Maurice Headlam, the Treasury Remembrancer and Deputy Paymaster for Ireland 1912-1920, was untroubled by the matters which seemed to be upsetting other officials, as he recalled in his *Irish Reminiscences*:

> It was the fashion to sneer at the Aberdeens' entertaining and possibly it was not so well done as under his predecessors. Of this I had no knowledge. But Lord Aberdeen confided to me that he never spent less than £6,000 per annum in addition to his annual salary of £20,000 – in many years more than £6,000. When I told this to an unsympathetic Dubliner she said that he ought to spend another £20,000 – like his predecessors!
> The Court Balls were perhaps not "smart," as the big Irish peers, all Unionists, did not attend the Court of the Home Rule Aberdeens. There were only, therefore, a few of the Irish peerage and their daughters, the rest of the company being judges, officials, doctors, etc, and soldiers who were commanded to go. But there were plenty of people to dance with. I liked dancing to a good band, and did not know or care if they were the right people.[15]

The criticism of the Aberdeens for their supposed shortcomings in entertaining was relentless and continued throughout their stay in Dublin. A comment in the *Irish Society and Social Review* in February 1910 expressed disappointment that the rumour concerning Lord Aberdeen's possible resignation (following Cabinet changes in London) was untrue. He was to remain as Lord Lieutenant in spite of 'the collapse of Castle hospitality'. Those who did avail of the hospitality, such as it was, were pilloried in the November issue of *Irish Life* in 1912. Under the heading 'The Irish Social Ladder', the writer sneered:

> Since the present top-rung was installed in its high position, the popularity of it has been paltry. Few hoped to reach it. Those who did, too easily did so, no matter what their claims to social distinction might be.[16]

The *Irish Times*, a relentless critic of the Liberal Aberdeens, took a more high-minded stance and editorial comment, politically inspired, affected to be worried about the disrepute into which the Aberdeens brought the Viceroyalty, and the consequent fall off in trade among Dublin businesses. An article in the paper, pseudonymous, in February 1912 encapsulated the *Irish Times* attitude when the writer, 'A Man With A Memory,' asked why the Castle season had been interrupted (owing to

Court mourning for the Duke of Fife, brother-in-law of the King) while Court functions were going on as usual in London. It was very bad for business and poor people were suffering.[17] A letter published some days later, and signed 'Scrooge from Rathgar', expressed total agreement, and went further, referring to the 'partial eclipse of the Castle under the Aberdeen régime'. It was the duty of all Irishmen to see that the social prestige of the Castle was maintained and the writer ended on a militant note:

> If we are not getting value for money then it is the duty of the Irish members to bring matters before Parliament when the Irish estimates come up for discussion, as the question is a serious one for Dublin traders.[18]

A further letter, from Sir Anthony Weldon, the State Steward and Chamberlain, pointed out that the Court procedure in Dublin was the same as in London and that it was inaccurate to say that there were fewer entertainments during the Aberdeen régime than there had been previously.

> Entertainments closely correspond with those of other Viceroys and the number of people partaking of hospitality is greater than at any season since 1895, when records were first kept.[19]

In spite of this official correction, the criticism continued and a question was asked at Westminster (not by an Irish member) about the expenses of the Viceregal Court, the implication being that Lord Aberdeen was skimping on hospitality in order to save money for himself. According to the report in the *Irish Times* the member, Mr Newman, asked the Chief Secretary:

> ...whether owing to the reduced scale of entertainment that has been customary for some years past, he will, before Clause 3 (a) of the Government of Ireland Bill is discussed, prepare a statement showing the actual annual expense incurred by the holder of the office of Viceroyalty, any easement derived from the sale of garden or other produce, or rent received for grazing being taken into consideration.[20]

The *Irish Times* printed the reply of Chief Secretary, Mr Birrell on April 6th, but made no editorial comment. In answer to Mr Newman's question Birrell said that the Viceregal expenditure always exceeded income, and that the surplus produce of the gardens was given, as usual, to charitable institutions.[21] The report of the matter in the *Irish Times* evoked a letter from 'An Irishwoman' who objected to 'the spirit of meanness underlying the question asked in Parliament.' She called for 'fair play' citing the 'untiring devotion and unostentatious generosity of Lord and Lady Aberdeen'.[22]

The *Freeman's Journal* came to the support of the Aberdeens. In an editorial comment at the end of April the suggestion of money-saving was deemed 'mean and unworthy,' and the questioner, Mr Newman, was described as:

> An Irish landlord sitting for an English constituency, evidently inspired by one who wished to withhold having to mention his identity … The fact is that the salary is not enough. It was once £30,000 but the Duke of Northumberland [an earlier Viceroy] had it reduced to £20,000. It is still that, and at least £10,000 more would be needed for expenses.[23]

The Aberdeens had foreseen this problem of expense. Canada had been a drain on their private purse, and they had confided to Horace Plunkett, as he noted in his diary in 1904, that if Aberdeen were to be appointed again in Ireland, they 'feared the expense, especially after the spacious days of Cadogan and Dudley'.[24] Lady Aberdeen, in a letter in January 1905 to Henry Campbell-Bannerman, the Prime Minister who had appointed her husband to Ireland, said unequivocally that they 'could not attempt' to keep up the magnificence of the Dudleys and the Cadogans but would try to keep the expenses within income as much as possible, but feared that they would not have a marked success. She went on to say that perhaps simplicity of entertainment might be a good thing, given the circumstances of life in Dublin.[25]

She was wrong, of course, because she was more interested in the bread than in the circuses, and was unaware of the importance people placed on the superficial glitter of life. She was ready and willing to do all that was required of her in social terms but in her scale of values other matters were more important. Of course, given the temper of the times, the Aberdeens were damned whatever they did. As they were, they were accused of meanness, but if they had done otherwise the cry, raised by Tories and ultra-Nationalists alike, would have been 'heartless extravagance'.

In any event, social life went on and Lady Aberdeen graciously carried out her duties. The *Irish Independent*, in direct contrast to the *Irish*

Times, reported in May 1912:

> The scene has certainly changed, and for the better. Now the season
> is one incessant round of private dances and dinners, "At Homes,"
> concerts, evening parties, entertainments for young and old, in
> addition to the regular State Functions. The Viceregal hospitality
> has been extended beyond "the Season" for Lord and Lady
> Aberdeen are not absentees and remain all year.[26]

On at least two grand occasions Lady Aberdeen managed to combine
her social duties with her broader interests. In March 1907 she organised
an Irish Lace Ball at the Castle. This, as the *Irish Times* reported, 'was a
scheme whereby an artistic industry which lies very close to her
Ladyship's heart would derive considerable benefit'. Earlier in the winter
she had made it known that a ball would be given at which:

> ... ladies would be expected to wear Irish lace or crochet or Irish
> embroidery on their toilettes, for which Irish poplin might be
> appropriately used. Gentlemen were requested to appear in Court
> costumes, Highland dress or hunt coats, with cravats or ruffles of
> Irish lace.

This announcement was a great boost to the Irish lace-making
industry, which Lady Aberdeen had supported for so many years not only
by wearing Irish lace herself on every important occasion, but by
regulating its design, production and sale. The result of her patronage
and encouragement could be seen on the night of the Ball, for although
many 'proud possessors of rare old Irish lace were only too pleased to
have so unique an opportunity of displaying their filmy treasures' the
greater part of the lace on display was of modern manufacture. This
proved, said the reporter:

> ... an object lesson in the vast improvement effected in the art of
> lace-making, since good designs, carefully-selected materials, and
> advanced instructions have been brought within the reach of the
> workers, who now can challenge comparison with the famed
> Continental lace-makers, whose wares at one time absorbed the
> whole custom of the English market. Little by little Ireland has
> been winning back some of this lost trade, and there is cause for
> celebration in the success of last night's entertainment.[27]

This was a night of triumph for Ishbel, but she was not able to join in
the dancing. A bad attack of rheumatism had confined her to bed for
some time and it had been doubtful whether she could even attend the

function. Her medical advisers, however, gave permission for a brief appearance, and she arrived in a wheelchair which was placed on the dais. As usual, she had paid careful attention to her toilette and was magnificent in deep blue velvet trimmed with Irish point lace, made in Youghal. She had a tiara and necklace of diamonds and wore a stole of white ostrich feathers around her shoulders. Lord Aberdeen was wearing the Gordon tartan, with a scarlet and gold waistcoat, and 'a profusion of magnificent stars of Orders glittering on his coat'. From the dais the official party watched the quadrilles and the Irish eight-handed reels, danced by gloriously arrayed men and women who included Count Casimir and Countess Markievicz, the latter wearing:

> ...an emerald green chiffon over silk, entirely veiled with beautiful
> Limerick lace, caught with black velvet rosettes, and finished off
> with a black velvet sash.

Every description of Irish lace was to be seen; 'old fashioned flounces meeting the new and up-to-date panels and corsage trimmings'. Lady Grenfell's 'berthe and sleeves were composed of superb old Carrickmacross guipure' while Mrs George Pim's:

> ...maize chiffon robe topped by a shaped coat of lace embroidered
> in pearls and crystal and raised roses, was a lovely creation, and the
> lace was specially supplied by the Royal Irish Industries
> Association.

A few words and phrases were enough to describe the men's fashions – Limerick lace ruffles and cravats, black velvet Court suits, old-fashioned waistcoats and jabots – but they wore as much lace as their limits allowed.

The big event of 1907 was the International Exhibition held in Dublin from May to November. It was organised by a group of Dublin businessmen and Lady Aberdeen dearly wished to become involved. Horace Plunkett, now head of the newly-established Department of Agriculture and Technical Instruction, advised her to be cautious. He himself had doubts about the wisdom of having yet another Exhibition, following on those of Cork, Glasgow and St Louis (in all of which the Department had had an input) but she gave her support to the plan and made preparations for the involvement of the Irish Industries Association in the Exhibition. They would show what they had done for native industries, arts and crafts in the Home Industries section. A big incentive for the organisers was the prospect of a royal visit in connection with the exhibition and King Edward duly promised to attend. Nationalists seized upon this, stating that the whole purpose of an 'International Exhibition' was to have the King over and get knighthoods from him. 'Why not a National Exhibition?' asked the Nationalist paper, the *Leader*. [28]

In February a permanent building would be erected that could house a permanent, though ever-changing exhibition of Irish goods. There could be an annual exhibition there, and space could be allotted to the Gaelic Athletic Association for displays of Irish games. No attention was paid to this cry and plans went ahead for what the *Leader* insisted on calling 'Humphrey's Dump' (after the chief contractor, Colonel Humphrey,) in Herbert Park and the great International Exhibition duly opened at the beginning of May. There was a State Opening by the Lord Lieutenant who read a gracious message from His Majesty the King. In his telegram from Paris where he was on a State visit, the King said 'Trust that the Exhibition you are to open today may prove a success and demonstrate International progress made by Ireland'. According to the *Irish Times* the 'manifest spontaneity and genial sincerity' of this brief message:

> ... appealed directly to the warm sympathy of a representative Irish audience, and the genuine heartiness with which it was acknowledged was undoubtedly to be regarded as a guarantee of the welcome which the Sovereign would receive should he later visit his Irish subjects.

The Countess of Aberdeen accompanied her husband in the third carriage of the Viceregal Procession and it was noted that she 'bore only the faintest trace of her recent illness' (a bad attack of rheumatism).[29]

The buildings included a Central Hall, Palace of Mechanical Arts (with working models), Palace of Fine Arts, Palace of Industries, an Irish Industries building and a Concert Hall. There were also Canadian and French Pavilions, and amusements that included a water chute and a helter-skelter. One of the sideshows that attracted a great deal of attention was the replica of a Somali Village, with native-style mud huts and genuine Somali natives. The *Irish Times* called it 'a feature of remarkable interest ... the peculiar-looking villagers going through their simple life with delightful Somali aplomb'.' They were 'a thin lot ... but by no means unprepossessing'. The crowd was entertained by their singing and dancing – 'a weird Somali version of a cake walk', and impressed by 'the vigour with which they clapped hands at every step'.

Three 'small-headed members of the tribe addressed all in faultless Somalian and extended a hand for the grip of friendship'. The reporter was moved to wonder how 'natives of a torrid clime can stand the Irish climate in such scanty attire' for not only was there torrential rain and thunder in the opening days of the Exhibition but it was unseasonably cold.[30]

A worry of a more spiritual nature disturbed the reporter from the *Leader* who was upset by the dances performed by the villagers. He objected to people:

> ... performing their religious worship as part of the value for the sixpence paid to enter a side-show. The worship of God is sacred and is not a fit subject for a "turn" ... . If the Somalians, or alleged Somalians, are sincere it is an outrage on these poor people that they should be asked to earn money for a ... side-show by placing their worship of God on exhibition for the amusement of Rathmines Johnnies and frequenters of music halls.

If, on the other hand, these dances were not genuinely religious then the whole thing was a farce.[31]

Whatever the case, the Somali village was one of the most popular side-shows in the Exhibition, and curiously, its name lives on in North Dublin. There, on the south side of the Hill of Howth, stands a group of houses known locally as 'the Somali Village' or 'the Somali' for short. The story goes that when they were being built in 1907-8, an old resident of the area snorted contemptuously that they were as badly built as those in the Somali Village, and the name stuck.

Arthur Griffith's paper *Sinn Féin* was implacably opposed to the Exhibition – 'the Anglo-Jewish bazaar' – and its account of the opening ceremony set the tone for all further comments. The writer referred to the 'extraordinary display of armed force' in connection with the opening ceremony (two regiments accompanied the State procession) and pointed out that this was necessary in view of the fact that the bulk of public opinion was against the holding of such an exhibition, listing no less than eight organizations that objected to it.[32] In May the paper criticised the Canadian Pavilion, stating that it was nothing more than an elaborate scheme to encourage emigration, and in a passing reference to the King's visit in July it asserted that he had come in order to give 'a lift' to the Exhibition which was not proving popular. Neither, it asserted, was it good for business. The *Leader* had forecast that Bray and Kingstown would be badly hit, as would city restaurants because people would spend all their spare money on the entertainments at Donnybrook. However, in an article on the Exhibition in the *Dublin Historical Record* in 1973 the amateur historian F E Dixon records that 'various firms and companies in their reports for 1908 explained the fall in profits as due to 1907 having been an exceptional year for them'.[33]

Overall, the Committee of the Exhibition, or rather their guarantors, were out of pocket (partly because of a legal dispute with the Pembroke Township Council over a claim for alleged damage to the site) to the tune of £100,000, but as always with such enterprises there were probably invisible profits.

Whatever the financial outcome, and in spite of criticisms, the visitors to the Exhibition seem to have enjoyed themselves. It was easy to get to Dublin because the railway companies laid on special trains, and once there, an excellent tramway service, augmented for the occasion by the Chairman of the Dublin United Tramway Company, William Martin Murphy, proprietor of the *Irish Independent*, and a major guarantor of the Exhibition, brought the visitors to Donnybrook.

There they could view exhibitions of paintings, sculpture, drawings and photographs, admire Irish glass and silver, and marvel at the 20-foot long model of the Battle of Waterloo which was included in the Napoleonic collection. In the Palace of Mechanical Arts and the Palace of Industries there were working models on view, including sewing machines, oil heaters, electrical items, and a cinematograph. The French Pavilion gave a glimpse of what life might be in that land of fabled culture, but the Canadian Pavilion with its photographs of a ruggedly beautiful land, and its examples of native wild life (stuffed) appealed to more adventurous spirits.

For sheer enjoyment the Amusement Park was worth visiting, not only for the Helter-Skelter and the Water-Chute, but for Tofts' Hobby Horses and Swing boats, the Indian Jugglers, a Crystal Maze of distorting mirrors, a cinematograph, and a Shooting Jungle with life-size models of animals in their natural habitats. Bands played throughout the day and evening, many of them military (including the Royal Irish Fusiliers, the Grenadier Guards and the Dublin Fusiliers), and musical programmes included selections from Gounod, Verdi, Wagner, and the ever-popular Gilbert and Sullivan.

Refreshments of all kinds were available (catering by the English firm of J L Lyons, another source of Irish grievance) in the many restaurants and cafés in the grounds. At night there were firework displays, watched over by the volunteer corps of fire-fighters that had been formed for the occasion. Entry to the Exhibition cost one shilling per day per adult, sixpence per child, but some individual shows cost extra (sixpence to the Somali village, threepence for children). Visitors were generally well-behaved, although there were reports of arrests for pick-pocketing, and presumably they took heed of the notice which warned 'Visitors found smoking or spitting in the building will be liable to expulsion'.

Lady Aberdeen's chief interest in the Exhibition, apart from State visits for the opening and closing ceremonies, the Royal visit in July, and the visits of various foreign dignatories, was in the Home Industries section. As President of the Organising Committee, which included the Countess of Mayo, Sir Horace Plunkett, William Murphy, Reverend P J Dowling, C M and Mr W T Macartney Filgate, she was responsible for what the *Irish Times* called the 'magnificence and comprehensive character of the collection'. There were two industrial halls, one for home-based industries, the other for manufactured goods. In the first there were examples of linen, lace, embroidery, tweeds, rugs, crochet etc, all of which were created by workers at home. In the second there 'could be seen, in full working order, a number of industries some of which' as the *Irish Times* said, 'already exist in Ireland, and some of which might profitably be introduced into this country'. Toothbrush manufacture was being revived, and the pottery industry looked as if it could become profitable. The section included a village hall, hospital, and two model labourers' cottages, complete with village green on which step-dancing competitions took place.

A *Handbook of Irish Rural Life and Industry* was published in connection with the Home Industries display and contained over fifty articles on lace-making, tobacco-growing, beekeeping, straw hats, embroidery and so on. There were also articles on Irish folklore, Irish dancing, ancient Irish Industries, the Arts and Crafts Society of Ireland, and the scheme for district nurses. Contributors included Lady Dudley, Horace Plunkett, P W Joyce, and Dermod O'Brien, RHA, and the foreword was written by Lady Aberdeen. She first praised the:

> ... well-arranged and attractive exhibition produced by the skill of trained cottage workers who have been supplied with good designs and brought into touch with the demands of the market ...

– the two points which she had been stressing since the setting-up of the Irish (now Royal) Industrial Association – and regretted that she and her committee had not kept the collection of exhibits they had sent to the International Exhibition at Edinburgh in 1886. If they had done so, the public could now see what progress had been made, especially in design. For the future, though, consider what a transformation there would be in Irish life if:

> ... we could find in every parish in Ireland
>
> 1 Subsidiary industry which could be carried on at home.
>
> 2 Cottages designed for the comfort, health and convenience of their inhabitants.
>
> 3 A miniature Cottage Hospital where emergency cases could be treated and from which district nurses could carry on their ministrations.
>
> 4 A Village Hall, which could be made the centre of social life, and where all manner of gatherings could be held for the education and amusement of the people, quickening their interest in music and art and literature, as well as in social questions.
>
> 5 A public thoroughly alive to the importance both of encouraging native industries and of caring both for the education and the health of the people.[34]

Readers of the book, and visitors to the Exhibition could help realise this dream in several ways, firstly, of course, by supporting native industries but also by joining one or more of the concerned organisations. These included her own newly-formed Anti-Tuberculosis Society, the Women's National Health Association, Lady Dudley's scheme for establishing district nurses in the poorest parts of Ireland, the Royal Irish Industries Association, the Arts and Crafts Society or the Art Companions.

It was clear from this foreword that Lady Aberdeen had greatly matured in her attitude towards Irish life. It was no longer a scheme for the advancement of industry that she was describing, but a plan for the revitalising of the rural community. In her travels around Ireland Lady Aberdeen had probably seen more of rural life than many of her class and background. She had visited workers in dark, cramped cabins, had seen the beautiful handicrafts they produced and had experienced first-hand the exquisite courtesy which was always shown to the visiting stranger who came with goodwill and good intentions. The limits of rural life were known to her – not only the lack of material benefits, particularly medical ones, but the absence in so many places of a chance to broaden intellectual horizons. She had obviously thought deeply about social problems and had applied to the Irish situation what she had learned from her experiences with the International Council of Women. It was a thoroughly modern vision, non-political and European in concept, but doomed to failure because it came from the wife of the English Viceroy.

The *Irish Times*, praising the Home Industries section, reported that visitors were both impressed and delighted by what was on view, and that many expressed their astonishment that so much native talent was to be found in Ireland. It concluded that earlier fears about the undesirability of an 'International' as opposed to a 'National' exhibition were unfounded, for

> ... the general characteristics of this section are alone sufficiently
> obvious to refute the ill-timed, unworthy fears of those who
> imagined that Irish industries had something to fear, that their very
> existence even was threatened by being placed alongside the
> products of other countries.[35]

Reports in the *Leader* on visits to the Home Industries section indicated a change of editorial heart, which seems to have taken place within a week. On the 25th June 1907 the correspondent, admiring the Somalian villagers, opined that their methods of making shoes and pots were more advanced than those of the Irish, but on the 29th June, a writer commented that the International Exhibition depended on Irish manufacturers for half its attractions, and that the Home Industries section was 'particularly attractive'. On the 13th July readers who intended to visit the Exhibition were advised to pay special attention to the Irish exhibits which covered a very wide range and were well worth inspection. Further praise came in the 27th June issue when the 'most orderly arrangement' of the Home Industries section was commended and special admiration was expressed for the little model of a tobacco plantation, and 'a pair of Limerick gloves so fine they fit into a walnut shell'.[36] This recommendation can not have pleased the Gaelic League which had forbidden its members, under pain of expulsion, from attending the Exhibition, a fact which *Sinn Féin* reported with shrill satisfaction.

The undoubted success of the Home Industries section was not due alone to Lady Aberdeen and her committee, hard-working though they were. Three public bodies had been involved in the preparations – the Department of Agriculture and Technical Instruction, The Congested Districts Board, and the Local Government Board, all of which were concerned with rural matters. The overall growth in Irish cottage industries, for which Lady Aberdeen is due an enormous amount of credit, both for her setting up of the Irish Industrial Association, with its subsequent participation in Exhibitions, especially the 1893 one in Chicago, and her personal support of native work, cannot be attributed to her alone. She was influenced in the 1880s by the international revival of interest in handicrafts which was, in part, a reaction against the increasing mechanisation of industry. In England this led to the formation of a group concerned with improvement in taste and in design, loosely known as the Arts and Crafts Movement. The chief influences on this group were from an earlier day – the writings of John Ruskin, critic and social reformer, and those of the architect Augustus Welby Pugin. Ruskin advocated individuality rather than standardisation and deplored the results of machine work rather than manual work in the finished article, while Pugin's advocacy of medieval design led to an interest in its revival.

Equally important in forming the taste of the times was the establishment of government schools of design, which under the direction of Henry Cole, writer, artist, civil servant, developed the concept of art being applied to industry. This idea was given vivid expression by the life, work and writings of William Morris, poet and artist, who married art and industry by setting up a firm that specialised in the applied arts, carrying out ecclesiastical and domestic commissions in painting, carving, furniture, metal work, stained glass, tapestry weaving and hand woven carpets from designs by, among others, Burne-Jones, Rossetti and Ford Madox Brown. Morris made crafts respectable and the movement known as Arts and Crafts was under way, never to look back. It spread quickly throughout England and thence to Ireland where the Arts and Crafts Society of Ireland was initiated in 1894 by Lord Mayo, who had been in touch with William Morris and received his blessing. The Royal Institute of the Architects of Ireland was particularly supportive of Lord Mayo's plan, because they had great difficulty in finding Irish craft workers for stained glass, encaustic tiling, terracotta work, mural decoration and wallpaper design and printing, and money that should be going to Irish workers was instead leaving the country.

The Arts and Crafts Society of Ireland held its first exhibition in Dublin in November, 1895, and among the exhibits were some specimens of lace work from Lady Aberdeen's Royal Irish Industries Association. Further exhibitions followed, all advancing the cause of the Arts and Crafts movement, and Lady Aberdeen showed her continuing interest by opening, with her husband, the fourth exhibition of the Society in 1910. Ireland was found to be rich in talent, and some enterprises became internationally famous - Sarah Purser's stained glass workshop, *An Túr Gloine*, Evelyn Gleeson's Dun Emer Guild rugs and tapestry and Oswald Reeve's enamelled work. When King Edward visited the International Exhibition in July of 1907, he was so admiring of a Reeve's box that he wished to buy it, but it had already been sold to Lady Aberdeen and the King had to be content with another souvenir. Craft classes were established in the Irish schools of Art in Dublin, Belfast and Cork, and tuition was given in mosaic work, enamelled metalwork and pottery. Lord Mayo, as President of the Arts and Crafts Society, was responsible for the organisation of the sub-section of the Home Industries display at the Exhibition, and it was obvious, as the *Irish Times* put it, that there had been 'a marked advance' in the artistic merit of the goods produced by Irish craft workers.

The Department of Agriculture and Technical Instruction and the Congested Districts Board had both played an active part in the revival and renewal of Irish crafts and had taken part not only in the larger exhibitions such as those in Glasgow and St Louis (to which the Congested Districts Board had sent two carpet weavers and a loom to accompany an exhibit of Donegal crafts), but in the many provincial exhibitions round the country, mainly industrial, but with sections for crafts. A voluntary organisation that encouraged and publicised Irish industries was the influential Gaelic League which organised exhibitions at home and abroad, especially in the big English cities where there were large Irish populations and the pages of the Nationalist papers are full of advertisement for these events.

A particularly interesting venture by a member of the Gaelic League, Captain Otway Cuffe (at whose house the Aberdeens were once entertained) was the establishment in 1907 on his estate in Kilkenny of a colony called the Kilkenny Woodworkers, who produced many pieces that were both elegant and sturdy and of contemporary design, rather than copies of Georgian work. Lady Aberdeen so, was very much in tune with the artistic mood of the times, with its insistence on a separate Irish identity, modern in design and execution, but inspired by the example of the past. Her organisation of the Home Industries section in Herbert Park was probably her largest public contribution to the cause of the Irish home craft revival, but in 1909 she put on another display that would further it. This took the form of a Pageant of Irish Industries and it was held in St Patrick's Hall where the *Irish Times* reported in its issue of March 16th 'cinematograph equipment had been set up to record the proceedings', and where 'the powerful electric light from the lanterns made a great addition to the lighting of the hall.' This was not the only time the cinematograph was used, and according to Neville Wilkinson, its use was not popular because of the revealing properties of strong electric light. He recalled how the lights had a bad effect on complexions – 'rose petal' cheeks turned a 'livid purple' and so-called diamonds were revealed as paste. The film of the particular State procession he attended was, he said, banned by London because it made everyone look so ugly and artificial.[37]

At 10.30 pm a fanfare announced the arrival of Lord and Lady Aberdeen, the Viceroy in Highland costume, and his wife in a gown of saffron Irish poplin, embroidered in cream and gold in a Celtic design incorporating the Irish goods trade mark. Her full Court train of Irish poplin was heavily embroidered in gold in a design from the Book of Kells, and it was borne by two pages. Then, to the opening bars of the Festival March from Tannhaüser the Pageant commenced. Groups representing the various Irish industries slowly proceeded past their Excellencies.

Pride of place was given to the linen and flax industry of Ulster and, said the *Irish Times* in its lengthy report:

> … it was worthily represented by twelve ladies and gentlemen
> attired in costumes illustrative of the various products of the hand
> and power looms.

Then came the wood workers, the ladies carrying carpenters' tool baskets. Lady Pirrie, wife of the Chairman of Harland and Wolff, the Belfast shipbuilders, headed the shipbuilding group, carrying a silver model of a full-rigged ship. Agriculture was illustrated by 'prettily-gowned maidens and milkmaids, carrying milk, cream and butter', while others showed the processes of sowing, reaping and milling corn. Poultry-keeping was ingeniously represented by 'maidens with wings cunningly constructed of variegated shades of linen'. Horticulture, bee-keeping, fruit-bottling and fishing were all duly depicted, as were the textile industries, which included cottons, woollens, carpets and Connemara curtains.

A striking appearance was presented by the tobacco group:

... the ladies' gowns being of brown and green, showing the big brown leaves of the plant, ingeniously-contrived ornaments of matches and pipes adding considerably to the general effect.

The soap group was also very attractive: the ladies carried candelabra of soap and had white hats like candle extinguishers,' while the ladies of the peat group 'carried small creels on their backs and baskets of turf in their hands'.

Art had its place in the procession, where a beautiful group of ladies wore fourteenth century costumes:

... illustrative of lace-making, enamelling and jewelling, stained glass and mosaic, art leather and metal work'. Humbler industries, knitting, basket-making, artificial flowers, brushes, etc. 'also found their representatives, the whole Pageant forming an elaborate picturesque and highly effective spectacle.[38]

Lady Aberdeen certainly knew how to stimulate interest in Irish crafts within Castle society, whatever about her efforts in a wider field, and there is no doubt that her patronage gave employment to designers, dressmakers and jewellers in Dublin and elsewhere in Ireland. The constant claims by *Sinn Féin* and other critics that the Aberdeens did nothing for Irish workers seem to have little foundation in fact, even if we take only the Castle entertainments into account.

Visits to Ireland by royalty always meant extra official entertainments – and more employment – and the expected visit of King Edward and Queen Alexandra in July of 1907 was eagerly awaited. The organisers of the Exhibition were in a high state of anticipation, for it was rumoured that His Majesty would bestow a knighthood or two in appreciation of their efforts. The Aberdeens were, of course, the official hosts, but Lady Aberdeen wasn't happy with the arrangements, particularly the suggestion that the Royal couple should spend two nights on their yacht in Dublin Bay and only one night in the Viceregal Lodge. This, she felt, was so short as not to warrant the upheaval it would cause, and on May 30th 1907, she wrote to the Prime Minister, Campbell Bannerman, expressing her 'despair' at the plan. A longer stay in the Park, yes, but not just a single night. The other arrangements were suitable, a garden party at the Viceregal Lodge (where 'all Ireland' could be entertained) and a big dinner in St Patrick's Hall. She particularly approved of the plan to make use of the Royal Yacht, because Dublin people were very proud of Dublin Bay, and would be delighted to have the chance of seeing Their Majesties embarking and disembarking. In a candid aside she added, 'I know full well the King cannot abide me, although he tolerates Aberdeen',' but concluded with a message of cautious welcome, 'We are willing to do all in our power to make the visit a success, but we cannot go to *unlimited* expense'.[39]

In the event Their Majesties made the Royal Yacht their headquarters, returning there each evening after the day's engagements. Their stay in Dublin was brief – giving rise to some grumbling among their loyal subjects – but it was very busy. The Royal party, which included the Princess Victoria, arrived at Kingstown at 8 am on Wednesday, the 10th July, and came ashore at 11 am to be greeted by Lord and Lady Aberdeen. A loyal address was presented by the Kingstown Urban District Council and the party then drove along the decorated streets lined with cheering crowds to the Exhibition grounds at Donnybrook. A quick tour of the Exhibition (with special attention paid to the Home Industry section) and then it was on to the Viceregal Lodge for a garden party.

The weather had turned fine at last – "King's weather", was the phrase being smilingly exchanged on every side – and the sun shone from a cloudless blue sky. According to the *Irish Times* the entire route to the Park was festooned with flags, bunting and streamers, and the thousands of spectators who had waited for hours to see Their Majesties cheered lustily in 'a most enthusiastic demonstration, spontaneous and cordial'. At the Viceregal Lodge the King was presented with no fewer than eleven addresses of welcome from various societies, which may, or may not, have diverted his attention from the fact that the Corporation of Dublin had voted not to accord him the traditional civic welcome. The scene was a brilliant one, 'the ladies ... arrayed in bright summer costumes and carrying dainty coloured parasols'. Queen Alexandra wore white silk, striped in black, over which was draped a boa of black and white feathers, and on her head she wore a green straw hat, trimmed with roses and osprey feathers. Lady Aberdeen's toilette was even more elaborate – rich golden brown satin, trimmed with ivory lace, a large spray of roses fastened on her bosom, a stole of green and brown feathers, and a toque of brown crinoline, topped with maize-coloured ostrich feathers. The other female guests wore gowns of equal splendour, and Their Majesties moved graciously amongst them with practised royal courtesy. Neville Wilkinson recalled a moment of kingly composure during the visit when a lady 'well known for her endeavours to present the mould of form' made her curtsy to the Royal pair in Dublin Castle. At the moment when 'the tortured silk of her gown strained to breaking point', by some mischance one of the motors parked below the windows of Saint Patrick's Hall back-fired.[40] The King kept a straight face, although some of the onlookers were not so successful.

In 1911 there was another Royal visit – that of King George and Queen Mary, and the Royal Party was enthusiastically greeted, both officially and unofficially. When the King and Queen visited Lord Iveagh's Play Centre in the Liberties, the cheering crowd had to be held back by a detachment of soldiery. There was a huge military parade (over 16,000) in the Phoenix Park, an Investiture of Knights of St Patrick at Dublin Castle, and the Aberdeens had a big house party that lasted a week. There were garden parties, regattas, levées, and all the usual entertainments associated with a Royal visit. The citizens of Dublin were entertained by illuminations and the city was bright with flags and flowers. The weather was ideal, and most suitable for the pleasure cruises run from Kingstown around the Home Fleet in the Bay where the great dreadnoughts were at anchor. Overall, as the *Irish Times* reported, the occasion 'transcended that of any previous Royal visit'.

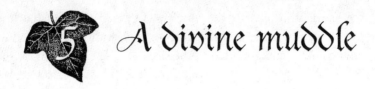# A divine muddle

HE ROYAL VISIT OF King Edward and Queen Alexandra in July 1907 seemed, on the surface, to go smoothly. There were cheering crowds, loyal addresses of welcome, social functions and no untoward demonstrations. There was, however, an unpleasant and deeply embarrassing incident that made all the bowing and smiling, nodding and greeting that the Aberdeens were forced to do, a tremendous test of social and personal skills. This was the theft from Dublin Castle of the Irish Crown Jewels.

Their loss had been discovered only a few days before His Majesty arrived in Dublin, and it was the Viceroy's embarrassing duty to tell the King that they were missing. Not the easiest of tasks – telling your guest that his valuable property had disappeared. Unfortunately, there is no record of the conversations between the King and his Irish representative, though Lady Aberdeen must have written about it in one of her missing journals (see Introduction) – such a catastrophic occurrence couldn't have been ignored.

The missing items were part of the Insignia of the Order of St Patrick, which had been founded by George III in 1783. The Viceroy of the day was Grand Master of the Order, and as such was entitled to wear the jewels on formal occasions. These were the Star and Badge, presented by William IV in 1830, both set with emeralds, rubies and diamonds, and together valued in 1907 at around £50,000. With these, supposedly in the safekeeping of Sir Arthur Vicars, Ulster King of Arms, and 'Registrar of and Knight Attendant on the Order of St Patrick,' were the jewelled collars of the Knights of the Order. These valuable jewels were kept in Dublin Castle in a large safe in a library in the Office of Arms. There was a strong-room, specially built for the purpose in 1903, but when it was finished it was found that it was too narrow for the safe to fit in. The Board of Works blamed Sir Arthur Vicars for not giving the correct dimensions of the safe, and Sir Arthur blamed the Board of Works for not doing their job properly. There was no money available for alterations, so the safe remained outside the strongroom for the time being. It was still there in 1907, in a library-cum-waiting room to which many people had access.

During the week before the Royal visit, when Sir Arthur Vicars was frantically busy with arrangements, two unusual incidents took place. The charwoman, Mrs Farrell, arrived at the office early on Wednesday morning and found the front door already unlocked. On the following Saturday morning the front door was locked, but the outer door of the strongroom was open. Quite properly, she told Vicars about it, but he took no notice and did not report matters to the police.

On the Saturday afternoon, the theft of the Crown Jewels was discovered when the safe was opened. Also missing were valuable items belonging to Sir Arthur Vicars, including a Charles II silver bowl. The police were called in and investigations began. There was no sign of forced entry to the building, the safe had not been tampered with, and most curious of all, the tissue paper wrappings which had protected the jewels were neatly folded, back in the boxes, and a ribbon which had been attached to the Badge of the Order had been very carefully detached, an indication that whoever had rifled the safe had been able to do so at leisure. The crime had all the signs of having been committed by an insider, and although nothing was ever proved suspicion fell on those connected with the College of Arms.

Sir Arthur Vicars, of course, stood accused of carelessness, if not worse, and when the King grew impatient with the lack of success in the police investigations he demanded that Vicars should be dismissed and told Lord Aberdeen so. There was to be no public scandal and Sir Arthur should be allowed to resign. This he refused to do and demanded a public inquiry, but his request was refused. Eventually a Commission of Enquiry *was* set up but it was held in private, and its terms of reference were simply to enquire whether, as custodian of the jewels he had 'exercised due vigilance and proper care'. Not surprisingly, the Commission found that Sir Arthur had not been properly vigilant, and he was dismissed as Ulster King of Arms.

During all this time and for years afterwards the wildest rumours were circulating in Dublin; there were hints of homosexuality, depravity and orgies in the Castle. A more innocent theory said to have been put forward by a Dublin jarvey was recalled by Sir Henry Robinson (Vice-President of the Local Government Board) in his book *Memories, Wise and*

Otherwise. According to this theory the King himself was the culprit for:

> ... he lost a lot of money at cards to the Duke of Devonshire, so he
> sent round Lord Aberdeen wan [sic] night to take them out of the
> safe and bring them to him, and say nothin' at all about it. Sure they
> were his own and hadn't he as good a right to clame them as he
> would have to see his own gould watch and chain?[1]

The unfortunate Aberdeens were connected with the unsolved crime in a very public way in 1912 when a weekly paper, the *London Mail*, published a scurrilous article asking, among other questions:

> ... why did Lord and Lady Aberdeen display such extraordinary and
> inhuman vindictiveness against Sir Arthur Vicars, when their son,
> Lord Haddo, did all he could to vindicate the accused man?[2]

This unfair and untrue attack on the Aberdeens also revived the old rumour that Lord Haddo was in some way implicated in the theft, although he wasn't even in Ireland at that time, but worse was to follow.

Because of other assertions in the article, Sir Arthur Vicars was forced to take out a writ claiming damages for libel, and the newspaper prepared to defend the case in court. Among particulars of justification stating the grounds on which the defence would be based was an extraordinary document, the chief points of which were, as quoted in the newspapers of the day, that a key of the safe, or a duplicate, had been obtained by a woman known as Molly, who was the mistress of Sir Arthur Vicars and who had become jealous of the 'great intimacy and friendship' Sir Arthur enjoyed with Lady Haddo, daughter-in-law of Lord Aberdeen. On the night before the jewels were stolen, this woman, Molly, was in Dublin Castle and with others was playing cards with Vicars. She spent the night with him but left early the next morning and fled to Paris. It was contended that Vicars in his evidence to the Commission of Inquiry had suppressed the fact that the woman had been his mistress and that she had been with him on that night. The implication was clear, that the unknown lady had stolen the jewels in an act of revenge but that Sir Arthur had lied to protect her.

The case was opened on July 4th 1913, but the newspaper made no attempt to justify what was said in the original article and Sir Arthur was vindicated and awarded £5,000 in damages. Lady Haddo was called upon to give evidence, but stated that she had no more than a social acquaintanceship with Sir Arthur Vicars. The judge expressed his sympathy with her and his disgust that her good name should have been traduced. Wisely, the Haddos took no legal action, although they would have been entitled to do so, and eventually the sensation died down, but there was left in the public mind, in Dublin at any rate, a perception that the Aberdeens had had some connection with the mysterious and unsolved theft of the Crown Jewels, epitomised by the remark made by a Dublin woman as she watched the ex-Viceroy and his wife leave Ireland, and quoted by Sir Henry Robinson, 'There they go, with the microbes and the Crown Jules in their baggage'. A Dublin ballad, composed in 1910, and critical of Lady Aberdeen, concluded with the verse:

> They'd wonder at our thoughts if we'd reveal them,
> We're neither deaf nor dumb,
> But our only word is "Mum"
> When there's talk of Castle jewels and those who steal them![3]

All in all, it was a most unfortunate affair which gave joy to satirists, ammunition to enemies of the Castle crowd (on either side of the political divide) and must have brought great private grief to the Aberdeens, although neither mention of nor comment upon the theft and its consequences was made by the pair in their book of reminiscences.

The suspicion cast on Lord Haddo and his wife was only one of the personal troubles to beset the Aberdeens in the early years of the twentieth century. In 1899 Ishbel's elder sister, Lady Mary Georgina Ridley had died, aged 42, and in 1900 her brother Archie also died. He had been in poor health for some time, and there were rumours of suicide. Then, in 1904, Ishbel mourned the death of her sister-in-law, Fanny, Lady Tweedmouth, to whom she had been very close. Lord Haddo, Ishbel's eldest son, was always a source of worry because of his epileptic fits and the Aberdeens feared for the future of the Gordon dynasty. The young man had wished to get married, but there was always the danger that his condition might be hereditary, and his parents did not wish him to produce an heir. The problem was solved by his marriage in 1905 to a widow, Florence Cohane, mother of a college friend, and roughly the same age as his own mother. Ishbel reputedly encouraged the match – it solved the whole problem of what to do about Haddo – and the wedding in London was a splendid affair in spite of the fact that it was held on the August Bank Holiday when London was empty of Society. However, as the *Irish Times* pointed out 'Lord Haddo, being delicate in health, has never had the desire to make a society display'.[4]

There were no children of the marriage and the second son, Dudley, eventually inherited the title. Dudley married Miss Cécile Drummond in London in March 1907. The ceremonies were carried out with great pomp and splendour but unfortunately Lady Aberdeen was unable to attend, because of a bad attack of rheumatism. However, as a personal gift to the bride, she sent her a beautiful full length veil of Carrickmacross lace. Ishbel's widowed mother, Lady Tweedmouth, whose husband had died in 1894 was a prime mover in the match-making, and was involved in all the family affairs. Then, in 1908, she died after a short illness and was deeply and publicly mourned by Ishbel who arranged an elaborate funeral for her beloved mother.

More family troubles assailed Ishbel, and they were of a public as well as a private nature – inevitable when a family is in the political arena. Her brother, Teddy, Lord Tweedmouth, had been appointed First Lord of the Admiralty in 1906, but was ineffectual in the position and was eventually compelled to resign because of some unwise correspondence with the Kaiser. His private wealth had dissipated, and he was forced to sell Guisachan, the family home in Scotland, and the bulk of his father's art collection. Ever-loyal to her family, Ishbel invited Teddy to Dublin, and cared for him through an unspecified illness until he died in the Under-Secretary's Lodge in the Phoenix Park in September 1909.

With Haddo safely married (and never was the adverb 'safely' more suitably used), Dudley, a total non-academic, happily working as an apprentice in the Aberdeen Shipyards, and Marjorie a happy wife and mother (she had married John Sinclair, later Lord Pentland, a man nearer in age to her mother than to her, in 1904) there was only Archie, the youngest, left to worry about. In fact there wasn't anything to worry about in his case. Unlike his two elder brothers he excelled in his studies, and had graduated from Oxford in 1906, with an Honours Degree in History, and had later worked in banking in Berlin, Paris and London, with occasional stints as ADC to his father in Dublin. Archie was not only intelligent, he was good-looking and charming. One of those whom he charmed was Violet Asquith, daughter of the Prime Minister, and a romantic relationship grew up between them. We don't know what Ishbel thought of it – her mother, the formidable Lady Tweedmouth, had disapproved of Violet, and of her stepmother, Margot Tennant – but there was no reason why she should not be happy with the possible match. Archie was twenty-five and was showing interest in a political career, and other considerations aside, the Asquith connection would be a valuable one. Archie had brought Violet to Haddo House some years previously and the occasion had gone off quite well although Violet confided to her diary that she was rather frightened of her hostess the whole time. She felt, however, that she had won approval, for Lady Aberdeen had admired the Worth gown that the eighteen-year old Violet had worn at the tenants' and servants' ball. 'I was so amused', wrote Violet, 'that the first little feeble élan of her heart towards me should be provoked by a Worth dress of all things.'[5]

Approval, or disapproval, it was all irrelevant, for on the last Sunday in November, 1909, Archie Gordon was fatally injured in a road accident outside Winchester. His Daimler was in collision with another vehicle on a crossroads, and Archie was the only one to be seriously hurt. He was brought to hospital in Winchester where he lay in terrible pain. His parents were sent for and kept vigil over him for two agonising weeks. On the 15th December it was clear that he was going to die and Violet Asquith was allowed to see him. She wrote in her diary of that emotional reunion and parting – 'the greatest day in my life' – when she told him that she loved him and that they should announce their engagement.[6] They did so and were congratulated by the assembled family who had to act as if indeed there were a future, in spite of the fact that Archie was near death. Violet, Ishbel and Aberdeen were with him when he died at twenty minutes to seven on the morning of Thursday, the 16th of December.

Much sympathy was felt in Ireland for the Aberdeens in their grief and expressions of condolence came from many public bodies. Many referred to the work of Lady Aberdeen, 'the amiable and warm-hearted spouse' of the Viceroy, and noted that she had always taken a 'gigantic interest in everything appertaining to Ireland' and the Dublin County Council regretted that 'she should have met with more than one affliction in recent times'. Her missing journals would no doubt have told us in her own words of her grief, anguish and heaviness of spirit, but it does not require much imagination to know what she felt, and what sorrows lay behind the brave public face.

When the funeral ceremonies were over the bereft parents put together a memorial volume dedicated to their beloved son, and across the divide of the years comes the reality and immediacy of their pain. The volume was prepared, says the introduction, by Archie's parents 'for themselves and their children, and for those friends whose wealth of affection and friendship was the crown and glory of their dear boy's sunny life'. Those friends added their tributes to the family ones, and a picture does emerge of an attractive young man, who, as his college tutor said, had 'a bright, affectionate, engaging personality – impossible to think of it extinguished by death'. One of the many friends quoted described him as 'the most vivid human being I ever knew' and the surgeon who attended him said that he 'had never witnessed such heroism' as Archie had shown during his last hours. According to his mother, as he lay dying, and the nurses congregated by the open door of his room were softly singing 'Abide With Me', Ishbel bent down and whispered 'My Benjamin, who never brought anything but joy to his Mother'. His face brightened, she wrote, and 'lit up with his own brilliant smile, as he said "Oh, Mother, what a wonderful thing for a mother to be able to say"'.[7]

The funeral services are described in detail, the memorial in the Temple Church in London, where Brahms' Requiem was sung and the old Scottish version of Psalm CXXI – 'I to the hills will lift my eyes' and the ceremony concluded with the Funeral March by Handel. Then the funeral party went by train to Scotland, and a service took place in the private chapel of Haddo House. Ishbel described the day, 23rd December, as 'beautifully fine and calm', although snow lay on the ground, and the large crowd of mourners, including the tenantry, were able to stand outside the house. After the service, which concluded with the singing of 'Oh God, our help in ages past,' the oldest employees carried the coffin to the private burial ground, and lowered it into the grave, which was lined with ivy leaves, the badge of the Gordons. Violet Asquith threw in a wreath of violets inscribed simply 'To my beloved', and it was over.

The memorial volume is illustrated by photographs and a painting 'Two little Home Rulers,' painted in 1886 by Madame Starr Cansiani, showing Archie and his brother Dudley as idealised Irish peasant boys. Photographs include one of Archie, as a very little boy, watching Mr Gladstone planting a tree at Dollis Hill (the Aberdeen's home outside London) in 1889, and another as a page in attendance on Queen Victoria at the unveiling of a statue in Kensington Gardens in 1893. As a young man he appears at Bisley, rowing at Balliol, and as Siberius in the Oxford University Dramatic Society production of 'As You Like It.' Two final photographs show him in his coffin which is draped with and surrounded by flowers, the first caption 'Thanks be unto God who giveth us the Victory.' and the last, a close-up of his dead face, with, written beneath it,

'For so, He giveth His Beloved Sleep.'

Archie's death did not sever Violet's connection with the Aberdeens. On the contrary, they became very close and grieved together. Violet's diaries and letters were published in 1996, and edited by her son Mark Bonham Carter in conjunction with Mark Pottle under the title *Lantern Slides*. In Violet's early diary she for some time had the rather disconcerting habit of addressing Archie directly, as if he were still alive and would read her entries as she records visits to Dublin and time spent with his parents.

The first of these is dated Thursday 21st April 1910 and is from the Viceregal Lodge. Addressed to 'My Own Darling', it tells of her arrival at Dublin Castle:

> ... past the sentries and into the courtyard...Up the stairs and through $1/4$ of a mile of passages and rooms into a long narrow drawing room where people were having tea ... then a sudden fanfare of trumpets & several outriders – & in drove your Mother and Father in a wonderful carriage on high springs covered with postillions and wigs and crowns and every sort of grandeur.[8]

Later that evening Violet was presented to the Viceroy and Vicereine.

> You would have laughed, Dearest, at hearing my name bellowed by the last of a long row of ADCs and seeing me curtsy to your Mother and Father.' After the Procession the guests entered St Patrick's Hall 'very big & brilliant – quite full of glittering uniforms & swords & medals & hideous women covered in feathers of every colour.

Violet danced with Lord Aberdeen – the first time he had danced since Archie's death – and she was moved by the suffering he, like herself, was trying to conceal. Lady Aberdeen saw her to bed and helped her remove her Court dress. Violet stayed on in Ireland until the 10th May and described the visit to her friend Maurice Bonham Carter (whom she later married) in a letter from the Viceregal Lodge, dated 6th May as:

> ... 3 days of great pomp at the Castle – trumpets & postillions & sentries outside the bathroom & a band at breakfast, – then a peaceful week at Abbey Leix [home of Lord de Vesci] ... then back here – where the Viceregal ritual is somewhat modified.

That evening she wrote in her diary of the King's death, telling Archie how she and his Mother were sitting talking in the bedroom when a secretary told them the news. She recalled how she and Archie had danced before at the last Court Ball: 'Who could have dreamt then that *you* and he were destined to have the same strange adventure within a few months.'[9]

In that 'delicious house in the middle of the Phoenix Park' Violet had the status of honoured guest and almost-daughter-in law, and she grew to appreciate Lady Aberdeen's good qualities. On the earlier visit to Haddo House she had mocked her in her diary, calling her 'heavy and heifer-like,' and lacking in a sense of humour:

To her life offers two vocations, suffering – and ministering thereto. I fall between both those stools – I am neither maimed nor hurt nor do I do anything to help anyone who is.[10]

Now, after Archie's tragic death, Violet was indeed 'maimed and hurt' and she found some solace in Lady Aberdeen's ministering. Their roles were occasionally reversed, as Violet confided to Archie via her diary on 10th October 1910. The Chief Secretary, Augustine Birrell, had come to tea that afternoon in the Viceregal Lodge, and Violet, conscious of Birrell's contempt for the Aberdeen's lack of wit and sophistication, recorded that she was:

… terrified of what he is going to say next when he is with them – & torn in half between a desire to protect them from him & a passionate appreciation of his jokes.[11]

She was also drawn in to Lady Aberdeen's many charitable activities but was rather overwhelmed by her. In a letter from Dublin in November 1912 to a friend (Hugh Godley, son of 1st Baron Kilbracken), Violet said that Lady Aberdeen's life really 'stupefied' her with wonder and admiration – 'one thankless (but infinitely fruitful) task undertaken after another out of sheer love and humanity'.[12] This made Violet feel 'criminally idle & frothy & superfluous,' but, perhaps in an effort to show that she did have a social conscience she accompanied Lady Aberdeen to America in the following month. This trip was officially a visit to the British Ambassador to Washington, James Bryce, one-time Chief Secretary to Ireland, but it was also a fund-raising enterprise in aid of Lady Aberdeen's organisation, the Women's National Health Association in its fight against tuberculosis in Ireland. Violet showed some enthusiasm for this cause, and had already travelled with Lady Aberdeen on some of her many trips around Ireland on WNHA business. Her presence in America, given her youth, good looks and position as British Prime Minister's daughter, attracted much publicity, and was a great boost to

Lady Aberdeen's campaign.

On the personal level, great warmth seems to have grown up between the older woman and the younger one, and Violet, in a letter to Maurice Bonham Carter, tells a rather touching story of how as they crossed the Atlantic, she woke in her cabin on Christmas morning to hear 'a stocking crackling at the foot of my bed' placed there by Lady Aberdeen. She was amazed by the older woman's way of dealing with the reporters – 'a crowd of the most howling cads' – who accosted them on their arrival at New York, telling her father that while she, Violet, remained silent.

> Lady A…received them with the utmost benevolence and suavity – "chatted" to them for several minutes – was docilely photographed whenever asked, etc.

Ishbel understood the uses of publicity, and the power of the press, and, unlike Violet, she wanted something. Her natural and effective skill in public speaking was now even more polished, as Violet noted in her diary address to Archie:

> Your Mother made the *most* excellent speech [in aid of the WNHA]… she spoke for almost an hour & the most marvellous response followed – everyone rising & offering everything they could give with the most extraordinary directness, spontaneousness and lavishness.[13]

The Asquith connection may have had a direct effect on the Aberdeen's tenure in Ireland. In 1911 the Premier, for reasons that are unclear, considered removing Lord Aberdeen and replacing him with another Lord Lieutenant (the *Irish Times* confidently stated that the Duke of Connaught was to take over) but Violet intervened on Aberdeen's behalf. She wrote to Archie in her diary on 2nd October, 1911:

> I have just written a long letter to Father about the removal of yr. F & M. from Ireland. How I pray it can be stopped. Anyhow I have stretched every sinew.[14]

Whether it was Violet's plea that saved Lord Aberdeen we do not know, but he remained as Lord-Lieutenant until 1915, when, family connections or no, Asquith dismissed him.

Family connections hadn't helped in January of 1912 either, when Lord Pentland, the Aberdeens' son-in-law, was removed by Asquith from his post as Secretary of State for Scotland and sent off to be Governor of Madras. Violet, though 'amused that the axe had at last fallen on

Pentland' was sympathetic towards Marjorie, his wife, and the children (beloved of their Aberdeen grandparents), who would have been better off in New Zealand (a possible posting) than in India. 'I am anxious,' she wrote to Archie in her diary, 'about how much your M. will mind,'[14] and in a later entry, February, 1912, she refers to a sad letter from Lady Aberdeen about Pentland's departure from Scotland.

There must have been times when Ishbel wondered about the men she had known in her life. Her father a bully, her brothers failures, two of her sons lacking in academic ability or political drive, her husband gentle but no more than adequate, and now her son-in-law failing to achieve high office. Ironically, the two men in whom she had placed her trust and her faith in an intellectual sense – Henry Drummond and her own younger son, Archie – had died before their talents had come to full fruition. Henry had achieved a lot, but he could have achieved more and could have given her so much, while Archie had showed promise of a life that would have enhanced her own. One hopes that her religious faith remained strong enough to make some sort of sense out of what seemed a Divine muddle of creation.

6 ᄐᅠe wჸite pᆰague

ONTEMPORARIES WERE ASTONISHED BY Ishbel Aberdeen's stamina and physical energy. *Crown* magazine reported breathlessly in its issue of July 12th, 1906:

> Some people retain their energy under all circumstances and of those Lady Aberdeen surely is one. On Tuesday Her Excellency went through a programme which merely to read about makes one feel exhausted.[1]

She had caught the mail train early for Castlerea, there attended a reception given by the High Sheriff, then on to Loughglynn where, amid elaborate ceremony, she opened a bazaar. She inspected schools in the area, including a housewifery school established by the Franciscan Missionaries of Mary, made another speech, then travelled to Athlone where she had lunch, opened another bazaar, made a third speech, then travelled back to Dublin by train. This was, in fact, a typical day for the Viceroy's wife. Opening bazaars, inspecting schools, attending sales of work, and visits to hospitals and lunatic asylums, these were all part of her duties.

In addition, Ishbel took an interest in several organizations and associations – for example the committee of the Police-Aided Children's Clothing Society, the Hibernian Bible Society and the Central Bureau for the Employment of Women. To this last-named group she made a speech in March 1906, on the subject of education, showing very clearly where she stood on the controversial subject of education for women. 'There seemed to exist,' she said, 'an idea that so to train a girl was to assume that she was to be an old maid', but she believed that it was 'the bounden duty of parents to equip their daughters as well as their sons for the battle of life'. Educated women who went into domestic service would raise its status and 'make it recognised as the honoured profession it was, demanding skill, training and brains'.[2]

The desirability of education for women was also the theme of the address Ishbel delivered to a meeting of Presbyterian women in Belfast when she and Lord Aberdeen made an official visit there in June of 1906. To the Presbyterian women she said that it was :

> ... essential that ... leading workers in Churches should help women in their Churches, especially their younger sisters to train themselves so that they should be ready in the fullest possible manner to take advantage of any openings that presented themselves.

This did not mean, she added, forestalling possible criticism, that wider opportunities would win women away from their homes. She concluded:

> [They] ought to be what God intended them to be in their own homes, but must they not also understand the difficulties in the world outside?[3]

There is no doubt that Ishbel was sincere in her call for education for women and for further opportunities for them in the world of work, but by a terrible irony, those women whose rights she was supposedly championing were being oppressed by the Belfast bosses who were entertaining herself and her husband. There was a strike of women workers in the textile industry and the women were locked out. Perhaps they had heard of Ishbel's 'advanced' views as well as the Viceroy's reputed kindness, but, for whatever reason, a deputation had waited upon Lord Aberdeen in the Viceregal Lodge in Dublin, and had put their case to him. He had received them sympathetically and had learned how low their wages were – nine shillings and sixpence (47½p) was the highest weekly rate for weavers and winders, while seven shillings (35p) was the more usual rate. They had pointed out to him how his hosts of the following week in Belfast belonged to the same Christian church as he did but, in the words of the paper *Labour Leader*, which reported the matter on June 16th, 'they were the most notorious of sweating employers'. According to the report, the women came away 'hopeful that Lord Aberdeen would intercede for them'.[4]

When the Aberdeens arrived in Belfast:

> ...over 10,000 women and about half as many men made silent avenue for them to pass through on their way to the General Assembly Hall.

Lord Aberdeen held a conference with the leading textile employers in the Town Hall, and later at lunch in the Harbour Office he showed his sympathy with the employers by advising the workers to go home. This, said the *Labour Leader*, was Lord Aberdeen's 'betrayal' of the textile workers, but what Ishbel thought of the whole affair we will never know. While a Socialist-inspired paper was condemning Lord Aberdeen, a society one was damning him with faint praise but extolling the virtues of his wife. The *Onlooker* reporting on the Belfast visit, said:

> The Earl is one of the best of men, but no one will say that his personality is precisely that likeliest to captivate the light-hearted Irish, yet on Wednesday men and women of all classes cheered him heartily when he appeared. Lady Aberdeen is more expansive in her graciousness and her bow and smile are charming; and when at the launch, after having been presented with a handsome shawl of Irish lace, she gracefully threw it round her shoulders and then rose to express her thanks, the hall's handsome roof fairly shook to the shouting. The Countess is already the most popular lady in Ireland.[5]

Ishbel had become an accomplished public speaker, not just of gracious nothings, but of well-researched, serious comments on matters of public interest. She was prevented by her husband's position from taking part in politics *per se*, but her experience as President of the International Council of Women, a position which she had held from 1893 to 1899 and again from 1904, had schooled her not only in the manoeuvring that goes with the holding of office in any organisation but in platform oratory. She was no longer an appendage, the wife of a man in high office, but a person in her own right. She had worked extremely hard for the International Council, chairing meetings, proposing resolutions, preparing reports and editing accounts of the Council's proceedings, and her work had been recognised and valued.

The International Council was itself growing and extending its influence with more and more National Councils becoming affiliated to the parent body. Delegates were coming not only from European countries, Canada and the United States but from Australasia. The exchange of ideas broadened Ishbel's horizons and developed her thinking on the pressing matters of the day. The Council was concerned with matters as diverse as public peace and arbitration, education, public health, the protection of birds, use of an international language, and the suffrage for women.

It was on this last subject that the development of Ishbel's thinking was most clearly seen. It was a potentially divisive one, as she had discovered during her Presidency of the Women's Liberal Federation, and again during the International Council's Quinquennial meeting in London in 1904. At that meeting, in order to avoid what looked like being a split in the organisation, Ishbel had side-stepped the issue. However, at the 1909 Quinquennial, held in Toronto in 1909 and attended by delegates from twelve countries, Ishbel spoke out on women's suffrage. She started her speech by boldly admitting that while her husband occupied the position he did, it was not considered desirable that she should speak on any subject of public controversy. However, as President of a Council which bound together women workers of the world, who had 'reiterated their conviction that the basis of all progress lies in the granting of Political Suffrage to women,' she felt that she could not remain altogether silent. Her speech was a model of common sense and sweet reason but diplomatically unthreatening.

> It has always seemed to me that it is a most understandable thing why it [women's suffrage] should be made such a terrible bogey. I think it is a pretty safe prophecy to say that within the next few years suffrage will be granted to women in most countries of the world having a representative government, and it is also safe to say that when that time comes we shall look back and wonder what in the world caused all this shindy about so simple and elementary a privilege of citizenship .... It is the object of this movement that women should exercise the rights that have been alluded to by speakers here tonight, which means that ... we may be in the position of *doing our duty* for the sake of the home, city and country, remembering the loss that accrues to every city and country, where the women are not in the position to give it all the contribution which lies in their power to give to the life and work of the community.

Ishbel then went on to deride the commonly-held belief that the aim of the suffrage movement was to claim equality with men, saying:

> Oh, my dear friends, is it not really time that this phrase should be given up? Is it not enough that we should realize that *as women* we have a great and wonderful mission to perform? And it is just because *we are women* that we want to be able to fulfil that mission in its fullness, *side by side* with men. Often we hear of wonderful pictures being drawn of a time when women will, as a body, vote against men. Can you fancy that, ladies? Do you think that human nature would ever sanction such a proceeding?[6]

When the disbelieving laughter had died down, Ishbel went on to praise those men – husbands, brothers, fathers, sons – who supported the women in their aims, but added that, of course, there were still men, who from notions of 'mistaken chivalry,' wished to keep their womenfolk safe from 'soiling' their hands with the business of politics and government. Did not this argue that perhaps these menfolk had not got a 'very exalted' view of politics? If this were indeed the case, would it not be to everyone's advantage that women should take part in politics, and indeed bring up their children 'to look forward to the time when it would be their high privilege to serve their community in some direction or other'. When women had obtained the suffrage they would have it in their power to raise the whole ideal of Government, be it local or national. The Resolution was then put to the House 'That the International Council of Women reaffirms its belief in the desirability of women having a right to vote in all countries where a representative Government exists'. It was carried unanimously.

Official duties, family life, charitable work, involvement with the Royal Irish Industries Association, and the Lace Depôt (which was an on-going success), foreign travel in connection with the International Council of Women – one would have thought that this was more than enough for a woman who was no longer young, but Ishbel's most taxing work was yet to come. This was her campaign against tuberculosis, which she called her 'crusade.' A good choice of name, for the disease was an evil and stealthy enemy that demanded every effort on the part of those who fought it.

Known popularly as 'consumption,' it was by no means a new disease but little had been known of its origins until the end of the nineteenth century, although its effects were only too obvious. It knew no boundaries, neither of nation nor of class but its victims tended to be mostly young people, either in childhood or in their late teens and early twenties. The most commonly-observed form of the disease was that in the lungs – pulmonary tuberculosis – although it could strike anywhere in the body, especially in the spine, where, in the words of a medical historian, Frank Ryan, in his study of the disease *The Greatest Story Never Told* said:

> ... it gouges large holes ... destroying their bodies and causing the spine to collapse in the upper back. This "hunchback" is very suggestive of tuberculosis. [It] also ulcerates the ends of the long bones, causing painful and disfiguring changes.[7]

Tuberculosis can affect any of the organs of the body, bowel, bladder, kidneys, brain, even the skin. Tuberculosis of the lungs acquired an air of romance, as its victims appeared to waste away, often assuming an ethereal look as they were 'consumed' by the disease.

The sufferer's typical pallor was sometimes dyed a deep and hectic red, an outward sign of the consuming fire within, and her customary languor gave way to feverish activity. A racking cough exhausted her from time and the handkerchief she brought to her lips came away stained with her life blood. The supposed romance of the illness was enhanced by the fact that well-known poets and artists – Keats, Shelley, Chopin, for instance – suffered from tuberculosis. By association then, it came to be seen as the disease of sensitive and refined persons, and for a time it was actually fashionable to cultivate an air of tubercular illness.

In fiction, the romanticizing of tuberculosis went much further. The disease provided a useful deathbed scene for Alexander Dumas' *La Dame aux Camellias*, later made even more poignant in Verdi's opera, *La Traviata*, which was matched in sentimentality only by Mimi's death in Puccini's *La Bohème*. Little Eva in *Uncle Tom's Cabin* died from tuberculosis, as did Milly Theale in *The Wings of a Dove*, Smike in *Nicholas Nickleby* and young Paul in *Dombey and Son*. In the lower reaches of literature there were countless little moral tales where the heroine (the protagonist here was usually feminine) succumbed to 'consumption' and by her resignation and fortitude turned others away from a life of vice.

Indeed, as Susan Sontag has pointed out in her essay 'Illness as Metaphor,' death from tuberculosis in fiction went with:

> ... the inveterate spiritualizing of TB and the sentimentalizing of its
> horrors. Tuberculosis provided a redemptive death for the fallen,
> like the young prostitute Fantine in *Les Misérables*, or a sacrificial
> death for the virtuous, like the heroine of Selma Lagerlöf's *The
> Phantom Chariot*. Even the ultra-virtuous, when dying of this
> disease, boost themselves to new moral heights ... . Little Eva
> during her last days urges her father to become a serious Christian
> and free his slaves ... Milly Theale, after learning that her suitor is a
> fortune hunter wills her fortune to him and dies ... Paul [Dombey]
> "felt a gradually increasing impulse of affection, towards almost
> everything and everybody in the place."[8]

Resignation to one's fate was also a feature of the fictional treatment of tuberculosis. Heroes and heroines accepted the onset of death, becoming more and more passive as the end approached. The redemptive quality of the disease was most notable in the case of Violetta, who was the *Lady of the Camellias* and *La Traviata* – the lost one. She was a courtesan (the disease was believed to increase one's sexual appetite), a fallen woman, and given the *mores* of the times, she *had* to die. Her profession, that of the woman who prostituted herself, was, as David Pountney noted in his essay on Verdi's opera, (contained in programme notes for the English National Opera's production of *La Traviata* in 1989) the mirror image of the disease. Since no one understood how it was caught or how it could be cured tuberculosis was the classic miasmatic disease.

> It 'rose up' like a mist out of the slums, and with it came an amazing complex of associations. The prostitute was virtually described by the associations of TB … It was associated with speed – with hectic and frenetic activity – hence a 'fast' life style often went with 'galloping' consumption. It was associated with deceit, for it dressed itself up and painted its face. The victim looked healthy, but her rosy cheeks were the result of fever; she seemed vivacious, but the vitality was illusory and self-destructive – often the prelude to death. It was associated with contrast – instability, violent changes of mood – emphasising the prostitute's function as a participant of disorder and chaos. It was also an erotic disease, a disease of passion, arising, some thought, from an excess of sexual desire, and bestowing an exceptional power of seduction.[9]

Virtuous or otherwise, nobody was safe from the dread disease, and the mystery of its origins gave rise to numerous theories. It was certainly thought to be hereditary – witness the recurrence of the disease in some families (among the famous ones are numbered the Keats, the Brontës and the Trollopes) – and although the illness was not confined to those who lived in poverty it was commonly believed that the slums were its breeding grounds. A standard medical textbook (quoted by Susan Sontag) listed the causes of tuberculosis as: 'hereditary disposition; unfavourable climate, sedentary indoor life, defective ventilation, deficiency of light, and "depressing emotions"'. The textbook appeared in 1881, a year before the German bacteriologist, Robert Koch, discovered that tuberculosis was caused by a bacillus, or bacteria, and was, therefore, infectious.

Although this discovery solved the mystery of the origins of the disease, it took quite a while for old beliefs to die out. Still clinging to the old notion that tuberculosis was a 'wet' disease, that caused moisture in the lungs, medical men advised sufferers to travel to high, dry places, – mountains or deserts. If travel did not cure the patient, at least it might alleviate his sufferings and would psychologically be of benefit – Robert

Louis Stevenson's dictum that 'it is better to travel hopefully than to arrive' takes on a deeper meaning in the light of his own illness. Only well-to-do people could afford to travel, of course, and such advice was useless to the poor. The only palliative a doctor could offer (if a poor sufferer could afford the services of a physician) was a mixture to soothe the cough that was the prime symptom of pulmonary tuberculosis. There was a brisk trade in such mixtures – lung tonics, cough syrups, elixirs – mostly containing morphine in the form of laudanum, and all available over the chemist's counter if one had the cash to pay for them.

Koch had a job convincing doctors of the validity of his discovery, especially his claim that the bacilli causing tuberculosis were transmitted by sputum. Eventually his perseverance paid off and consumption officially became known as tuberculosis, shortened in popular speech and writing to TB. The diagnosis of the disease was one thing, but its treatment was another. Surgical intervention (the collapse or removal of a diseased lung) was a possibility in some cases, but it became clear as time went on, that generally speaking, the disease was incurable. There were cases where the body seemed to heal itself and patients recovered completely, but usually the best hope seemed to be that the progress of the disease might be arrested. This could be achieved, it was thought, by a régime that included a nourishing diet, fresh air and rest. In the homes of the well-to-do this régime presented no problem, supervised as it would be by the family doctor, and where the inevitable burden of caring for the patient would be eased by the employment of professional nursing staff. Alternatively, the well-to-do patient could receive treatment in one of the new sanatoria that catered exclusively for TB sufferers.

In each case, given that the infectious nature of the disease was now fully recognised, precautions against its spread must be taken. It was easier to do this in a sanatorium, where strict rules of hygiene could be observed and imposed but it could also be done at home. The patient's crockery and cutlery were kept apart from everyone else's, bed-linen was washed separately and the sputum bottle (sufferers in advanced stages coughed up as much as half a pint of phlegm in twelve hours) was thoroughly disinfected. He or she was kept in isolation, as far as possible, preferably in a custom-built châlet in the garden, open to the fresh air, as were the beds in sanatoria, wherever possible.

Private home treatment of this nature was not possible for the sufferers who came from poor backgrounds. Privacy, washing facilities and good

The Marquis and Marchioness of Aberdeen and Temair, photographed during retirement at Cromar

John Campbell Gordon, pictured as a
student at St Andrew's, 1864

Ishbel Marjoribanks, aged three, 1860

Haddo House, Aberdeenshire

Lady Aberdeen in court
presentation dress in
1878, the year after her
marriage

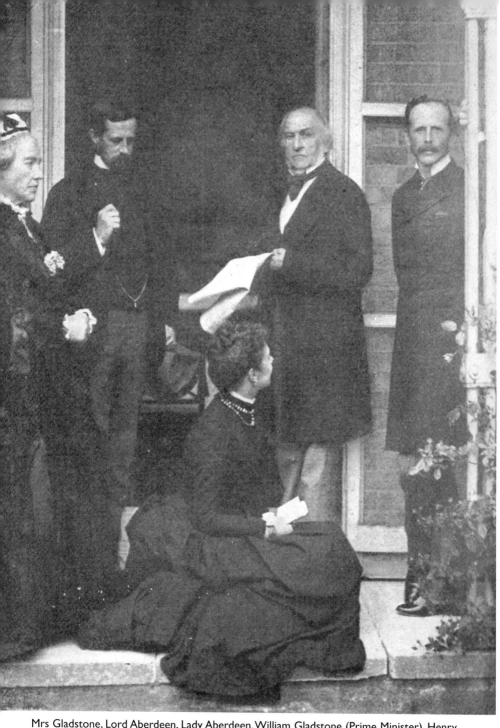

Mrs Gladstone, Lord Aberdeen, Lady Aberdeen, William Gladstone (Prime Minister), Henry
Drummond at Dollis Hall.
"Sometimes Mr and Mrs Gladstone would come down on Friday night after the House of
Commons had risen ... however late the hour, the first thing was a cup of tea ..." *We Twa*

Photo, by the Countess of Aberdeen.

Mr. and Mrs. Gladstone bidding adieu to Lord and Lady
Aberdeen as they were leaving for Liverpool
en route for Canada.

Photograph taken by Lady Aberdeen – "I am glad that my Kodak was faithful in preserving for us a picture of our beloved friends standing at the door … as we left with their 'God bless you and yours' on their lips. That photograph has always been near us wherever we have lived since."

We Twa

A drawing of the Irish Village at the Chicago World's Fair of 1893

The Aberdeen's four children in 1897 – Haddo, Marjorie, Dudley and Archie

The Countess of Aberdeen in court dress with her pages Lord Killeen and Master Thomas Arnott, Dublin Castle 1907

Visit of King Edward and Queen Alexandra to the International Exhibition, Dublin, in July 1907

The health caravan *Éire* starting her tour from the Viceregal Lodge. Note Lady Aberdeen pointing to the word 'WAR'. This caravan was destroyed by fire on the night of March 15th 1909

Éire in trouble in Donegal. " … one of the wheels of the caravan got stuck in a bog on a lonely road, the doctor had to walk some miles to get assistance … whilst the leader of the party waited on the snowy road." *More cracks with We Twa*

The replacement caravan for *Éire*, aptly called *Phoenix*, which started work at Fintona, Co Tyrone

King George and Queen Mary paid a coronation visit to Ireland in 1911. Here they are pictured with Lord and Lady Aberdeen at a garden party given at the Viceregal Lodge

'Two little Home Rulers'. Dudley and Archie Gordon, painted in 1886 by Madame Starr Cansiani. In 1909, Ishbel allowed this portrait to be used on a leaflet distributed throughout the country by the Women's National Health Association. Under the caption 'Brought up on stirabout and milk', the leaflet promoted the virtues of sunlight, fresh air, cleanliness, cheerfulness and temperance. This picture hangs on the main staircase at Haddo House

The Babies' Club stand at the *Uí Breasail* exhibition, Ballsbridge, Dublin, in 1911

The Ballymacarret Babies' Club in Belfast, the first Babies' Club in Ireland

Ormond Market, Dublin, before its development in 1912 – "a rookery of tenements and ruinous sites"

The Boy's camp at Ormond Market after its development

The site of St Monica's Playground, Augustine Street, Dublin, before development

The opening of St Monica's Playground in 1912. Lord Aberdeen is near the centre of the photograph in the top hat

The East and West Pavilions at Peamount Sanatorium

Prime Minister Asquith opening the Children's Pavilion at Peamount in July 1914. Lord and Lady Aberdeen flank the steps

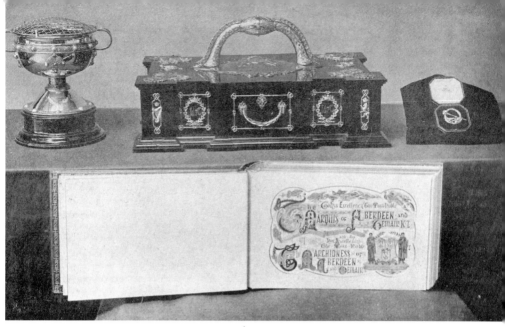

Some of the gifts presented to Lord and Lady Aberdeen at the Mansion House, before they left Ireland for the last time in 1915. The book is kept in the casket, which is now in the Library of Haddo House

One of Lady Aberdeen's own snapshots which she took from the State Barouche during the procession which took them through Dublin on their way to the boat in 1915

The *Connaught* leaving Kingstown (Dun Laoghaire) with Lord and Lady Aberdeen on board, at the end of their Viceroyalty

Still busy – the Marquis and Marchioness of Aberdeen and Temair in the kitchen at Cromar in the 1920s, helping to mix the Christmas pudding

food were unheard-of in the slums of the world where TB was most widespread and most deadly. Treatment in specially-built sanatoria was an option, but there were not many of these, and they were beyond the means of poor people. In some countries, in the absence of public funding, charitable organizations funded sanatoria – in England the Friendly Societies which were so much a feature of nineteenth-century workers' lives, had a good record in this regard – but they were too few in number to make any great impact on the problem.

As the years went by following Koch's discovery that TB was infectious, it became more and more obvious that the best way to fight the disease was to limit its spread – what was a private and personal fight against ill-health, must become a public one. Public health had become a matter of official concern, not, as it had first been perceived, the province of a few campaigners. The movement, a combination of successful Victorian engineering and administrative zeal aimed not only to contain but to prevent outbreaks of infectious diseases. Tuberculosis was to join cholera and typhus as a disease that had an identifiable cause and that, if not checked, could infect large numbers of the population.

Ireland was, it transpired, more vulnerable to the ravages of tuberculosis than was the rest of the United Kingdom. The death rate in the country from smallpox, typhoid fever, typhus, measles, scarlet fever, diphtheria, whooping-cough and diarrhoea (the last of these accounting for high infant mortality) declined from 2.8 to 1.5 per 1,000 between 1882 and 1906 (still appreciably higher than the rate in England), but that from tuberculosis did not follow the same pattern. In fact, it was the most common cause of death among Irish people – more than twice as many deaths as from all the other infectious diseases combined, and it showed no signs of following the long-term mortality from TB seen in England and Scotland. Most of its victims were in the 15 to 25-year age group, and as this was the group which was most likely to emigrate, many young people leaving Ireland carried with them the deadly bacillus, so that it was noted in the United States, for instance, that Irish immigrants were particularly susceptible to tuberculosis. It could, however, be argued, as it was in the nationalist paper *Sinn Féin*, that:

...the huge rise in mortality ... can be ascribed to the large number who returned from America in the worst stages of the disease. The American climate ... the strenuous life and the bad drinking water, undermines the health of thousands who leave Ireland with a light

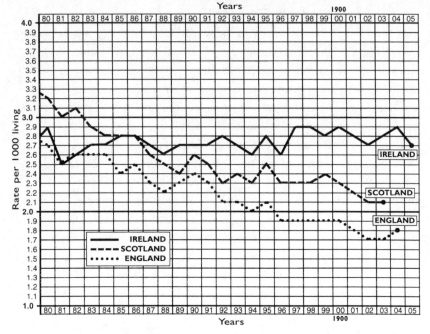

TUBERCULOSIS

The death rate from tuberculosis in Ireland compared with that for England and Scotland for the years 1880 to 1905. These figures are taken from the *42nd Annual Report of the Registrar General for Ireland* (1905). This report also gives the figures for deaths from tuberculosis in 1905 as approximately 11,800, compared to about 8,600 deaths attributed to old age, 8,200 to heart disease and 3,300 to cancer.

heart. Out there, there is no sympathy with the man of failing strength – they have no time to spare for mere sentiment. A simple order from the Medical Officer of Health means compulsory deportation of an incurable case. When the emigrant returns he brings the disease with him and it spreads through the community.[10]

At home the disease spread rapidly through institutions and the figures for deaths from TB in workhouses, lunatic asylums and prisons were shockingly high. Only two sanatoria, Crooksling in County Wicklow and Heatherside in County Cork, were built by local authorities for the specific treatment of tuberculosis, otherwise sufferers had to seek treatment in the fever hospitals. This was very much a last resort – only those in the last stages of the disease and without family members able to care for them would enter the fever hospital which was seen, rightly, as the prelude to death.

Hospitals were places to be feared at the beginning of the twentieth century, when the new discoveries of anaesthesia, bacteriology, radiology and pathology, were only beginning to signal the advent of modern medicine. Most people were born and died at home, and if, in the years between, they became ill, they paid for doctors and nurses to attend them there. Most women had their babies at home; only the very poor went to the maternity hospitals. Although the nursing homes attached to the voluntary hospitals were growing in popularity, in general people kept well away from hospitals for it was well known that the people who attended there were the poorest of the poor, reeking with dirt and disease. Only desperation would have brought them there, for illness was something to be concealed. In spite of the revelation that tuberculosis was *not* hereditary, but infectious, Irish people in general stubbornly held to the view that it was a family weakness, and, as such, must be hidden from censorious outsiders. This attitude, allied to apathy about preventive measures was perhaps the greatest threat to Lady Aberdeen's crusade against tuberculosis.

It was her work with the International Council of Women that sharpened Ishbel Aberdeen's interest in the prevention of TB. During her years as President, especially since she had taken office in 1905, she had learned a great deal about the subject from other delegates representing foreign countries, including those of Scandinavia, Germany, the United States, Australia and Canada. In an article in the Journal of the Irish Colleges of Physicians and Surgeons in July 1995, Professor Alun Evans, surveying Lady Aberdeen's crusade, suggests that the:

> ... Aberdeens' interest in tuberculosis can be understood when it is known that His Lordship's grandfather's first wife and three daughters all died of the disease[11]

But such deaths were common enough in families at the time and were removed enough from Aberdeen and Ishbel to be of little more than regretful interest. Ishbel knew of the ravages of tuberculosis on a world-wide scale and she could see that Ireland was particularly hard hit. The country was poor, people were apathetic and it was inefficiently governed. She recalled in her memoirs:

> ... the representatives of the medical profession, of the National Association for the Prevention of Tuberculosis and the Local Government Board and various women workers approached Lord Aberdeen and myself, with a view to institute an educational

campaign in regard to tuberculosis …

So Ishbel was eager to start her crusade. It was launched in Dublin on 13th March 1907 'to fight the appalling ravages of tuberculosis in Ireland'. To this end she founded an organisation – the Women's National Health Association – not, as Marjorie Pentland pointed out in her biography, the suggested Anti-Consumption Society, but a more all-embracing title that covered all aspects of health. According to Pentland:

> The idea was of a good-health service for all. A national service too, surely a rallying point for Government and Sinn Féin, Protestant and Catholic.[12]

The opening meeting was well attended and those present included the Reverend Dr Donnelly, Roman Catholic Bishop of Canae, and the Dean of St Patrick's Cathedral. Dr Walsh, the formidable Roman Catholic Archbishop of Dublin was unable to attend, but sent a letter of support, as did Dublin's Protestant Archbishop, and press comments were generally encouraging. They welcomed the Association's stated aims, which were three-fold:

1 To arouse public opinion, and especially that of the women of Ireland, to a sense of responsibility regarding the public health;
2 To spread the knowledge of what may be done in every home, by every householder, to guard against disease, and to eradicate it when it appears;
3 To promote the upbringing of a healthy and vigorous race.[13]

This last aspiration was greatly commended by the leader writer in the *Kerryman* who, in an article entitled, 'What Women Can Do' stated firmly that:

> … it was the elaborate directions of the Mosaic laws as to scrupulous attention to cleanliness and to diet that have made the Jews the most virile race on earth.

The paper welcomed the WNHA, led as it was by that 'humane and kindly lady' who had already shown her great concern for the welfare of the Irish people by her interest in industries and education. Readers were urged to follow the precepts of the new association, for 'although,' the writer pointed out:

> … truly we must be a virile race to have withstood for such a long time the terrible scourges of emigration and TB and their attendant

evils. Had we not been blessed with sound inherited constitutions the Irish race would have disappeared long ago ... but if drastic measure be not taken at once our people will, in a few years, be classed as one of the vanished races.[14]

The *Belfast Telegraph*, welcoming the new Association, also lauded the aim of racial improvement – a preoccupation of the times. Pessimism was expressed, however, by the *Northern Whig* which feared that:

... the outlook was not very encouraging [for, they believed] the poor have a rooted objection to fresh air and personal ablutions and ... in spite of lectures and teaching at school, they will not feed infants properly, or learn to do plain cooking.[15]

The education of the public began at once. Ishbel arranged for lectures to be given on every aspect of tuberculosis, and Sir William Osler inaugurated the series. These lectures were later published in a three-volume work *Ireland's Crusade against Tuberculosis*. Osler, Regius Professor of Medicine at Oxford, was the outstanding medical man of his day. He had been an adversary of Ishbel's during her struggle to establish the Victorian Order of Nurses in Canada but had later been won over by her passionate dedication to the fight against disease. Osler's support was a great boost to the new association and plans were made. A stand devoted to the causes and cure of tuberculosis would be taken in the Home Industries section of the International Exhibition which was shortly to be held in Dublin. According to the report of the opening day in the *Irish Times*, the idea was suggested to Ishbel by a professor from the John Hopkins clinic in the United States, who was staying in the Viceregal Lodge. He told her of the success achieved by such exhibitors in the United States, Germany and France and she seized on the idea, and his assertion that the Irish climate did not predispose Irish people to tuberculosis was extremely cheering.

The Chief Secretary, Augustine Birrell, also struck an optimistic note in his speech, opening one of the sessions when he recalled that in his youth typhoid fever was considered to be an act of God, but that now it was known to be preventable and the same could soon be said about tuberculosis. Professor Lindsay from Queen's University in Belfast, agreed that there was 'no foundation for belief that the Irish were specially prone to tuberculosis' and went on to say that since the facts of the disease were well known one could now fight it.[16] The weapons were 'the segregation of the infected, good food, good housing and pure air'.

The battle, indeed, was 'one for social betterment in general'. Hearing of the proposed exhibition, the *Evening Telegraph* of August 30th 1907 commented:

> The interest of such an exhibition is bound to be of a somewhat grim and unpleasant character, yet it will doubtless have a useful educational effect.[17]

It was certainly educational. The numerous visitors who visited the stands in the Home Industries section in Herbert Park, from October 1907 to November, paying one shilling (5p) each, were informed if not exactly entertained, by what they saw in the four sections of the exhibition. There were the statistics of mortality, illustrated by diagrams. These showed that of every 100 deaths in the country, 76 were caused by phthisis, or tuberculosis of the lungs. Maps revealed that tuberculosis was not prevalent in the Dublin and Cork Unions, but that in the Unions where lunatic asylums were to be found the death rate from tuberculosis was exceptionally high – more than 25% of the inmates dying from the disease.

The literary section contained works dealing with 'consumption' and its cause, and out-of-doors the buildings section featured temporary dwellings, cheaply available, and very suitable for use either in sanatoria, or at home. One of these was a revolving waterproof sunbox, which could be erected in a patient's own back garden.

It was the pathology section, however, which was the most arresting. Here was a diseased human lung, and various veterinary exhibits showing clearly how bovine tuberculosis was rife among the cows whose milk humans drank in untreated quantities. A Dr Birmingham from Westport had prepared models illustrating 'microscopic appearances of bacilli in human sputum when stained with aniline dyes and magnified'. It was explained how tuberculosis was spread by the common Irish habit of spitting. When the infected sputum dried the air-borne bacilli floated freely, to be inhaled by the unsuspecting public. Those known to have tuberculosis were, therefore, urged to use spitting cups (examples of which were on view), their own handkerchiefs, or, most ingeniously, a hollowed-out sod of turf which could, and certainly *should*, then be burned on the fire. In one of the lectures associated with the Exhibition a Canadian doctor described how the custom of spitting in public had been stamped out in the United States. It had once been considered 'an inalienable right,' but when heavy fines were imposed on offenders spitting became too much of an expensive luxury.

Lady Aberdeen presided at the meeting of the WNHA held in conjunction with the exhibition and on the platform with her was the Archbishop of Tuam, Dr Healy, who expressed the hope that the display 'would be an object lesson to everybody in Ireland', making them realise that the disease was preventable, and in a large number of cases, curable. He proposed a resolution that the exhibition be worthy of support, praised Lady Aberdeen for her efforts, and added that 'ministers of religion had a duty to inform their flocks of the terrible ravages of tuberculosis'.

That evening Sir William Osler gave a lecture at the Royal Dublin Society in Leinster House where he emphasised what was already known about tuberculosis – that it was *not* hereditary, but was infectious and came from both people and cows. Good living was essential, but so too were appropriate treatments. There were several things that needed to be done immediately – the campaign of public education must go on; the health services should be re-organised and should include compulsory notification of cases of the disease; treatment of sufferers should be carried out in sanatoria, whose buildings were constructed cheaply, so that they could be burned down every fifth or sixth year. This proposal was loudly applauded, an indication of the fears people had about places where the infection was concentrated. This attitude towards sanatoria was to surface again and again during the crusade, usually expressed as hostility fuelled by fear. Sir William concluded by reminding his listeners that the war against tuberculosis could be won – typhus was now overcome, and malaria was in retreat. With enthusiasm and perseverance the 'white plague' as Oliver Wendell Holmes, the American physician and writer, called it, could also be defeated.

It was agreed that the exhibition should become a travelling one, on the lines of similar exhibitions in the United States, and thus carry the message to remote parts of the country, as well as to large centres of population, and branches of the WNHA were to be set up wherever enough enthusiasts were to be found. One of the most vigorous of these was initiated in Belfast at the end of October 1907, and Lady Aberdeen addressed a public meeting in the City Hall there, speaking fluently and with passion. She was also extremely diplomatic, aware that she was in a city proud of its position as an industrial and manufacturing giant, and among people who were renowned for their energy and resourcefulness.

On the platform with her were local dignitaries and letters of support had arrived from leaders of the Roman Catholic and Presbyterian Churches and from the Roman Catholic Cardinal Logue. The Marchioness of Londonderry sent a telegram expressing her 'deepest interest in the health and physique of the Irish race'.

Lady Aberdeen started her speech by acknowledging that much valuable voluntary work in the field of public health had already been done in Belfast so that 'it must not, therefore,' she said, 'be thought that the WNHA arrogates to itself the credit of discovering that the care of public health is a duty'. She paid tributes to the pioneers of the public health movement, both officials and volunteers, but went on to speak of what still needed to be done. Extreme poverty, insufficient or 'impure' food and bad housing were all factors in the deteriorating health of the people. Infantile mortality, which was declining in Scotland and in England, was up in Dublin and Cork, and the report from the National Commission of Education spoke of schools which were in an unfit and insanitary condition. 'In them,' she said, 'ill-fed children assemble under conditions which can only promote ill health of body and of mind.' Newspapers, notably the *Belfast Telegraph* and the *Irish Times*, gave extensive coverage to Lady Aberdeen's speech, and reported her impassioned words as she spoke of the special mission of the women. The message that ill-health was preventable could only be got through by 'the awakening of the women – the women of all classes – the guardians of the homes of the people'. She asked:

> How have we carried out that mission? Does not the blame for those black figures [of mortality] be largely at our door, my sisters? We will not, however, accept the burden of it altogether, for the conditions under which women have to live and work in Ireland, as elsewhere, is the result of the legislation of men, and it is hard for a woman who has never been taught the elements of hygiene and sanitation to struggle to bring up her children in health under pressure of poverty, bad food and insufficient house accommodation.

This was fighting talk. Not only was she laying the blame where it truly belonged, but she was rallying women against another enemy – male indifference to female needs. It must have struck a chord in the hearts of the intelligent and educated women who were listening to her, and made them realize that there was a purpose for them, and a rôle which they were emotionally ready to fill – repairing the damage caused by male indifference, or worse, male ineptitude.

Lady Aberdeen had, as Professor Alun Evans has granted in his less than enthusiastic article about her quoted earlier, an understanding of the rudiments of public health (he cited her dictum "Public Health is purchasable. Within natural limitations a community can determine its own death rate") but equally importantly, she had also the power to inspire others with the fire of her own convictions. Lady Aberdeen was, however, no Suffragette, and later in her speech she made it clear that men, when properly influenced by women, had a vital part to play in the crusade. She spoke feelingly about the high infantile mortality and referring to the unnecessary deaths of small children that resulted from drinking infected milk, she hit at the prevailing resignation of bereaved parents.

> If we can once make the mothers – and the fathers too – realise that
> these deaths need never have been – that it was not God's will that
> these little ones should perish ... then the victory is ours. ... One of
> the Glories of this movement is that it can and does unite
> Irishwomen of every class, of every creed, of every party, and that
> in uniting them it unites also those men who ... may ever be
> counted upon to champion a cause to which their wives, their
> mothers, and their daughters devote themselves.

Ishbel's closing remarks referred to patriotism – and at this stage her listeners, Unionist and Liberal, Nationalist, Protestant and Catholic may have braced themselves for some gaffe from the Vicereine, but she made good use of that loaded word by remarking that it was always a test of patriotism to die for one's country, but that the Association was appealing to the men and women of Ireland to *live* for their country, and to do so in good health. She concluded 'Will you join me in our crusade, women of Belfast? I know I need not ask. You have done so already, and I thank you'.[18]

This personal appeal in its simplicity was typical of Ishbel's style. Her grasp of the relevant facts and figures was impressive, her eloquence was admirable, but it was that identification of herself with her audience that made her such a successful public speaker. She assumed that everyone shared her concern – and indeed, her indignation – and that all would march forth to battle together. She might be the leader, but she relied on her loyal and valiant troops to win the victory.

While the Association organized its branches around the country (eventually totalling over 100) arrangements were made for the travelling exhibition to tour Ireland. A horse-drawn caravan, christened *Éire*, was bought with the help of a grant of £500 from the Pembroke Irish Charities Fund and set off on a trial run through County Wicklow early in 1908, visiting Kilcoole, Newcastle and Newtownmountkennedy. It carried, as reported in the third volume of *Ireland's Crusade against Tuberculosis*:

> ...diagrams, charts, pictures, literature of various kinds for distribution, pathological exhibits, a limelight lantern with slides for illustrating lectures, and a gramophone which was intended not only to give musical selections to enliven the proceedings, but also wise and pithy lecturettes on matters of health.

The caravan was adorned with health slogans, in Irish on one side, and in English on the other. It was drawn by two horses, and its company:

> ...consisted of Mr J. O'Connor, a young medical lecturer, who spoke Irish and English; Miss Manderson, a cookery teacher and demonstrator, Mr Fitzpatrick, the custodian, who slept in the van, and Cunningham, the driver.[19]

The trial run in Wicklow having been a success, the caravan set off for a tour of the north-west of the country. It was conveyed first by rail to Killeshandra in Co Cavan, and then onwards by road to counties Fermanagh and Tyrone. This tour was officially launched in Trillick, County Tyrone, by Lord and Lady Aberdeen, and in her speech, reported in the *Strabane Weekly News*, December 5th 1908 and quoted by Professor Alun Evans, Ishbel said that

> ... another important point in these exhibitions and lectures was the unification of Ireland. All political ties, and all creeds and all classes were at one in the movement.[20]

This sentiment drew applause, and the caravan set out on its travels, while Ishbel went ahead to organise meetings in Donegal and to meet up with it there. The *Fermanagh Herald*, 28th November 1908, quoted by Professor Evans, displaying that distrust of the Aberdeens which was so deeply felt among Unionists, reactivated an old ill-founded slur, saying that the reason for Ladyship's 'peregrinations through the country' was to get a clue as to the whereabouts of the Crown Jewels.[21]

The caravan's tour of Donegal was a great success, although the roads were so bad that travelling was extremely difficult at times, especially around Glencolumbkille. The people of Carrick feared they were not going to get a visit, and when it was learned that the caravan was indeed coming, the town was illuminated. The coming of the travelling show was a big event in small country towns and villages where there was very little to break the monotony of long winter evenings. Lantern slides, music, cookery demonstrations, these were all novelties, and if people had to listen to lectures telling them how heedless they were of their health, and how much better they could order their lives, then that was a small price to pay for entertainment. Best of all, the whole show gave the locals something to talk about for the rest of the winter, and perhaps a few people were sufficiently impressed to take the good advice they were given.

The gramophone selections were particularly popular and in some places local musicians also entertained the crowds. Donegal had a high incidence of tuberculosis, possibly due, as in other western districts of Ireland, to the miserable conditions in which seasonal workers dwelt while in England and Scotland. First signs of the disease were often seen soon after the migrants' return from harvesting there and in Westport tuberculosis was known locally as 'the English Cold', so it was essential that *Éire* visit the smallest and most remote villages, no matter how tough the going. The caravan criss-crossed the county (and got stuck in a hole in a lonely snow-covered road near Mount Errigal) before visiting Strabane and Derry and then back to Lifford. Here, a truly unfortunate accident happened – the caravan was destroyed by fire on the night of March 15th 1909.

In the official record in *Ireland's Crusade Against Tuberculosis*, Vol III, no details of the calamity are given, but Professor Evans speculates that the burning may have been deliberate. He cites a number of possible reasons – a 'natural antipathy to health promotion in these islands,' political opposition to the Aberdeens (both Nationalist and Unionist), Lady Aberdeen's fostering of the Tuberculosis Bill of 1908 which would have made tuberculosis a notifiable disease, but whose relevant clause was vetoed by the Irish party at Westminster, antipathy to the WNHA as a suffragette-type organisation, and fear of the infection that might be relayed by the caravan.[22] It was supposed to have had, for demonstration purposes, slides and cultures of various bacilli, and Sir Henry Robinson, Vice-President of the Local Government Board, in his memoirs recalled people saying that the van was dangerous, as "some of them microbes might escape ... and attack quiet people when it was too dark to see them and get out of their way".

The best way, in the popular view, to deal with infected clothes or premises was to burn them (as was done with Keats' clothes and belongings when he died of tuberculosis in Rome) and it is a possibility that cleansing by fire took place. Only a possibility, no proof, and Professor Evans does not say otherwise, quoting instead from local newspapers of the day which described the blaze. The fire was evidently caused by an oil stove that either overheated or overturned, almost totally destroying the van and its contents. Mr Cunningham, the driver, and Mr Fitzpatrick, the custodian, suffered minor burns and cuts in their attempts to contain the fire, but there were no other injuries. It was a merry spectacle for the townspeople of Lifford and a local photographer who quickly appeared on the scene captured some good shots of the blazing vehicle. These appeared two days later in the *Belfast Evening News* and were subsequently reproduced and sold as postcards.

That was the end of caravan *Éire*, but by that time it had brought the exhibition to three hundred and seventy meetings in the northern counties, and had been visited by over 74,000 people. Another caravan, initially named the *Phoenix*, was obtained, and the show went on visiting not only the northern counties but also the southern and western ones and after two years' hard travelling, *Phoenix* was replaced by another van, the *Blue Bird*, that made its maiden voyage through County Down.

The success of the travelling exhibition was due to many factors – not least its entertainment value – but chief among them was the growth of the WNHA and its organisation of the meetings. Branches were formed in almost every district to be visited and local people were, generally speaking, very helpful. Protestant ministers and parish priests co-operated by recommending the exhibition and praising the aims of the Association and local doctors usually showed enthusiasm. These doctors knew first hand the terrible toll of lives taken by tuberculosis and were not only anxious to help but grateful to the WNHA for its help.

Among doctors who had already fought the disease, Dr Seamus O'Beirn of Galway was outstanding in his efforts. He was an enthusiast for the Irish language, and was scornful of the current practice of appointing doctors who spoke nothing but English to dispensaries in Irish-speaking districts. Having qualified in 1905, and survived a spell as locum in Spiddal during a typhus epidemic (where five doctors had died of typhus during the previous ten years), he started an Anti-Consumption Campaign in Kilmilkin, Oughterard in June of 1907. It began with a series of twelve lectures on 'The Body and How it Works,' covering Disease, Infection, Consumption, Sanitation. Each week's lecture was followed by an examination and prize-giving – all in the Irish language. The programme was so successful that the Oughterard Board of Guardians, his employers, asked him to repeat it in two other centres in south Connemara.

O'Beirn identified ignorance as the main cause of the spread of tuberculosis. In this his thinking was on the same lines as that of Lady Aberdeen, and like her he tried to 'educate, educate, educate'. His proposal for a comprehensive educational scheme in Connemara, involving teachers and doctors, was not, however, approved by the Board of Guardians, so he looked elsewhere for help. In an article in the *Freeman's Journal* on November 7th 1907, the writer Stephen Gwynn described Dr O'Beirn's work 'in the heart of the Joyce Country mountains'. The doctor travelled 'five miles out to Kilmilkin, and five miles back, over a wild mountain pass'[23] but such was the great interest in his lectures that he was happy to do so. O'Beirn told Stephen Gwynn that the people were not, as some said, fatalistic about tuberculosis, but were worried and uneasy and were looking for help. Ignorance was the chief cause of the spread of the disease, and there was an extra problem with returned emigrants. In November 1908 he wrote a letter to *An Claidheamh Soluis* (the magazine of the Gaelic League), describing the conditions in Connemara, outlining his proposals for their amelioration, and concluded by asking 'Is the Gaelic League for work or for talk?' It could take a countryside in hand, he wrote, especially when that countryside was Gaelic-speaking. In addition to educational lectures, he pointed out that home improvements were necessary, so that people could 'put in good cement floors, windows, roofs, etc. and to build outhouses'.[24]

The Gaelic League responded at once, and started a fund which enabled O'Beirn's educational work to go on. In Lady Aberdeen's Preface to the first volume of *Ireland's Crusade Against Tuberculosis* she referred to O'Beirn's work in the West of Ireland and noted with approval that the Gaelic League had given money to him to allow his educational programme to go ahead. A committee had been set up, 'to sustain his efforts' and the WNHA was represented on it by one of its prominent members, Dr Michael F Cox.[25] By the time it closed in February 1909 the

Fund had almost £300 in hand (£25 of which had been donated by Lady Aberdeen) and the Home Improvements Fund was opened. This was not so successful, notably in its efforts to get official money.

Dr O'Beirn was a member of a deputation that waited on Sir Henry Robinson, Vice-President of the Local Government Board to ask for a grant to improve housing and sanitation in South Connemara. Others with O'Beirn in this group included J Cox, secretary of the Gaelic League, P H Pearse, editor of *An Claidheamh Soluis*, and Mrs Rushton, Secretary of the WNHA, but all they got from Robinson was a half-promise to consider the matter. *An Claidheamh Soluis* then organized its own nation-wide fund and O'Beirn went back to his educational work. Unfortunately he became ill, and had to travel abroad for the sake of his health. By the time he returned to Ireland some months later, things had changed. Tuberculosis Officers were being appointed and Lady Aberdeen's campaign was in full swing. Whether or not this latter fact influenced him we do not know, but he no longer involved himself directly in the fight, as he had done, but carried out his routine medical duties, which by 1911 included explaining to the west of Ireland the workings of the National Health Insurance Act. He did, however, give a lecture on sanitation in the Western Districts of Ireland at the Conference on Health, presided over by Lady Aberdeen in Dublin in May 1911, and in it he reiterated his old complaint about Dispensary doctors who spoke nothing but English being appointed to Irish-speaking districts. He said that he:

> … regretted that the Irish-speaking people of his and other districts were regarded as little better than foreigners in their own country because the language was regarded by officials was foreign.
> [Lectures on hens and eggs, and general husbandry] were delivered in English, such was the contempt with which the tongue was regarded by high officials.[26]

This criticism could not be levelled at Lady Aberdeen who had recognised from the beginning the importance of sending Irish-speaking lecturers to certain districts, and with whom the Gaelic League had co-operated in the matter.

With these duties Dr O'Beirne managed to combine his other interests, writing and the theatre. An extremely interesting, well-rounded man with an attractive personality, later in life he was one of the co-founders of the Taibhdhearc Theatre in Galway, an achievement which would alone make him worthy of remembrance. To the end of his life, though, according to

a memoir by his son, Michael, Dr Seumas O'Beirn remembered Lady
Aberdeen and admired her:

> She was always spoken of with great respect because of her work
> against Tuberculosis in Ireland. Nobody thought of her as the Lord
> Lieutenant's' wife, and Lord Aberdeen was not heard of, at all.[27]

A great deal of planning went in to the visits made by the travelling
Exhibition during the two years of its existence. Anna Day, in her history
of Peamount Sanatorium, *The Turn of the Tide*, gives details of the
arrangements:

> These local exhibitions were generally organised by some moving
> spirit in the locality – often the bishop or parish priest, the mayor or
> town clerk, or the chairman of the urban council. The person had to
> get together a few people to talk over the desirability of the
> Exhibition, and get in communication with the central committee in
> Dublin. The central committee had to be assured that the local
> committees would be composed of representative persons, including
> all creeds and sections of the community; that the local medical men
> and the clergy would take part in the movement, and that funds
> would be forthcoming for local expenses; that there would be a
> proper hall, and that the local committee would undertake the
> distribution of literature before the arrival of the Exhibition and
> during its stay, and would provide guides for taking visitors round.
> These matters settled, the question of lecturers had to be organised.
> These were sometimes arranged by the local committees, but more
> often the central committee was asked to provide them. The local
> committee paid the travelling and out-of-pocket expenses and the
> hotel accommodation. The railway companies allowed the lecturers
> and the exhibits to travel at half fare, a concession which made a
> great deal of difference to local committees.[28]

One of the most popular features connected with the Exhibition was the
presence of a lady lecturer who organised special meetings for women
and children. She visited schools and factories, and was warmly
welcomed by nuns and teachers who then set essays for children on the
subject of health. Anna Day estimates that more than five hundred and
forty thousand persons visited the exhibition:

> … more than an eighth of the population of Ireland, and this number
> would have been largely increased if the hundreds who were unable
> to gain admittance to the lectures at most of the places visited had
> been added to it.

The success of the travelling exhibition inspired similar exhibitions in Great Britain, and the Irish one itself visited Edinburgh and Glasgow as well as English and Welsh towns. Ishbel was frantically busy during the months while the caravans were on tour. Marjorie Pentland recalls that:

> ... each place wanted her to come and introduce it, to form their branch of her association, and "with more than her customary energy, and that is saying a good deal," as one paper remarked, she set off from Dublin two or three times a week, leaving by an early train and returning late, or else spending the night with some local magnate. Conservative landlords, Nationalist mayors, priests, sons, north and south, high low, joined in welcoming the WNHA ... [She] carefully mapped out dates and routes, chose exhibits, and awaited telegrams about the van's progress.[29]

The travel to seemingly remote places was made easier by the fact that in those years Ireland had one of the most comprehensive rail systems in Europe but the mental and physical energy can be explained only by the fact of her total commitment to the crusade. At these Association meetings many suggestions were put forth as to how to fight the enemy, but the leading efforts urged were:

1 The establishment of a District Nurse in conjunction with the Queen's Institute (the body established by a previous Vicereine, Lady Dudley);
2 The care of tuberculous patients in their own homes;
3 The care and instruction of young mothers with infants;
4 The provision of school meals for children and the cleaning and heating of schools.

While working for these specific objectives, the Association never lost sight of one of its basic aims – the election of its members to Boards of Guardians and other local bodies, which would give the WNHA some measure of political power. In this respect the Association had only limited success, but it did achieve much in the other areas, notably in the 'care and instruction of young mothers with infants'. This campaign to reduce infantile mortality started with a conference on the subject called by the Dublin branch early in 1908, to which were invited the Masters of the Maternity Hospitals, the doctors of the city dispensaries, and interested health workers. As a result, during the following summer, almost two hundred lectures on the care of infants were given to mothers and older girls throughout the city. In the same year a depôt for pasteurised milk was opened in Sitric Road on the north side of the city of Dublin, and here delicate infants who had been referred by doctors were given a ration every day and were cared for by a doctor and a nurse. The machinery for the pasteurisation had been bought with a generous grant from Mr Nathan Strauss, a wealthy New Yorker who was sympathetic to Lady Aberdeen's crusade.

Something more was needed, however, and it was decided to set up special clubs for mothers and babies on the lines of the one set up by the WNHA in Belfast in the previous year. The first of these Dublin clubs, called St Monica's, opened in June, 1909 in St Augustine Street, in the oldest part of Dublin, south of the Liffey. We have no idea who thought of the name but as St Monica was the mother of the once-wayward St Augustine, it was a neat choice. More clubs followed, each having a doctor and nurse attached. The 'Souvenir Booklet' (1946) of the WNHA gives a full account of their activities.

> Weekly sessions were held, and mothers attended with their babies and had them weighed. The doctors gave them any advice necessary – for many years giving their services free – and the nurses visited the homes to help the mothers to carry out this advice. Lectures on mother-craft, home nursing, sewing and cookery were given by qualified lecturers. Milk in sealed bottles, from tuberculin-tested cows, was distributed to mothers unable to nurse their infants. Milk foods and other nutrients were available at low cost, or, in necessitous cases, free. Infant clothing of suitable pattern was supplied, and at some Clubs, dinners were provided for expectant mothers. Ante-natal, dental, massage and Violet-Ray clinics were instituted. Boot, coal and dental thrift funds were organised with success. Physical drill and folk dancing were taught. Day nurseries were established where possible, and, as far back as 1912, St Monica's Club had a playground attached. In 1916 the first School Medical Clinic in Ireland was opened in conjunction with St Patrick's Club – at that time situated in Whitefriar Street.
>
> During the years 1909-1910 – by all accounts the busiest period in the Association's history – the Dublin Branch carried on an active campaign to have the Notification of Births Act, 1907, extended to the City, and was rewarded for its efforts by having the Act adopted in 1910. Five years later an Emergency Advisory Committee considered how further facilities could be given to the Maternity Section, and brought pressure to bear on the Government to extend the Treasury Grant for Child Welfare Work. The scheme was not accepted in its entirety, but led to the Corporation giving a grant in 1916 to the Association for its Babies' Clubs.[30]

While doctors, nurses and health workers could have nothing but praise for these clubs, and the contribution they were making to infant health, there was a body of opinion in Dublin that disapproved, for political reasons, as a ballad of the day made clear. Called 'The Ringsend Babies Club,' and written in 1910 by a so-called 'local admirer,' it described Lady Aberdeen's efforts as part of a plot to anglicise the infants of Ireland, and their mothers. She had come to Ireland wondering how best to capture the hearts and minds of the locals, so she started by frightening people with talk of microbes that attacked their bodies:

> There were microbes all about us – on our fingers an' our toes
> An' every man had millions of them climbin' up his nose

There was a strong hint that 'Mrs Aberdeen' had invented these microbes, for 'no one had ever seen them' until she came along and even stronger hints that anyone who helped in her campaign did so for advancement.

> Some of them [members] are gone to fill the jobs they nobly won,
> When they sold their Nationality for "butties" an' a bun.

The meetings are described, – tea-drinking, speeches about the glories of Empire, prayers for the royal family and:

> they take the babies from the hampers an' the bags,
> An' wrap them up in Union Jacks, an' coronation flags
> An' comb their hair with curry-combs, an' stuff their ears with silk;
> An' give them half-a-teaspoonful o' disinfected milk;
> An' then they dedicate them to the service o' the Crown,
> An' while they sing "God Save the King" they jig them up an' down,
> They Pasteurize them, sterilize them, steep them in a tub
> An' hang them on a line to dhry – in the Ringsend Babies' Club.[31]

Of soldiers and battles

HE OFFICIAL MEDICAL PROFESSION demonstrated in very obvious ways its approval of Ishbel Aberdeen's efforts on behalf of public health. In 1909 she was elected an honorary member of the British Medical Association – the first woman to be so honoured; the International Medical Society of France awarded her its Médaille d'Honneur, and the Royal Institute of Public Health elected her President at the meeting of its Congress in Dublin in August 1911. At this meeting, reported in the *Irish Times*, the Chairman and retiring President, Sir William H Lever, introduced Lady Aberdeen as a lady who 'had created no barren organised charities' but had introduced into necessary organised charities the voluntary help of those who, like herself, took a high view of their duties, 'and thereby the faults of ordinary charities had been obviated and the charities themselves had become active and vitalised'. He referred to her encouragement of Irish industries, which had 'done much, not only for the prosperity of the people, but for the raising of peasant life,' her responsibility for the publication of 'that valuable book – *Ireland's Crusade Against Consumption*' [sic] and 'her most far-reaching and successful activity, the founding of the WNHA'.[1]

When Lady Aberdeen, who as incoming President had donned the badge and chain of office, addressed the gathering, she expressed her realisation that the honour paid to her was a recognition of the good work done by the WNHA. This work, she emphasised, was an attempt 'to popularise the opinions arrived at by the medical profession, and to get them put into practice'. To this end, she said the Association's efforts were:

> … carried out in close co-operation with the more official section
> of our workers – that is, the district nurses, some forty of whom are
> maintained by the Association, and the women guardians and
> members of District Councils, of whom there are now 158 in
> Ireland.

Having thus diplomatically paid tribute to official health workers, Ishbel then went on to speak of the importance of mobilizing ordinary women in the fight against tuberculosis, using a military metaphor – they were to be 'enlisted ... as active soldiers in the campaign.' However, they needed training, and here she broadened the scope of her speech, and talked of the desirability of educating girls 'in all those subjects which bear on the health of the home'. Women doctors, nurses, official health visitors and sanitary inspectors all receive specialised training for their work, so why should not ordinary women be trained for housewifely duties? This training should not be confined to schools, but could and should be part of a regular University course.

> I believe that the opportunity that such courses would give, would attract many girls to the University who would never think of coming now, and that it would greatly advance the desirable object of girls of the leisured class wishing to follow up their school life by a University course. If once they realised how such studies carried out on University standards would revolutionise the aspect of home life and household management, filling every daily duty with vivid interest, and opening out endless opportunities of carrying on the studies of college years into the region of practical life, and applying them for the benefit both of the individual house, and for social service generally, they would assuredly take up such studies.

If this were done, she continued, it:

> ... would help to abolish the baneful notion that the care of the house, and the service of the house is on a lower plane than other trades and professions, and that there is something menial in their pursuit.

This speech of Lady Aberdeen's, which was reproduced in the September issue of the *Dublin Journal of Medical Science*, 1911, under the heading 'The Sphere of Women in Relation to Public Health,' was a particularly clever one.[2] Not only did it make clear the distinction between doctors, nurses, health workers, and the charitable laity, thus avoiding any danger of stepping on any professional toes, it encouraged women's aspirations towards higher education, while at the same time anticipated any accusation that educated woman would be rendered unfit for domestic duties. The woman would not be lured away from the home but would be educated to be happy there – a neat piece of sophistry.

She returned to the subject later in the year when she delivered an address in University College, Cork, on the last day of October 1911. Ishbel spoke on the subject of domestic science 'to a large audience, chiefly ladies,' as the *Irish Times* put it. Her remarks were largely a repetition of what she had said earlier in Dublin – a University education in domestic science would enable women to carry out their housewifely duties both skillfully and with pleasure. But she spoke openly about the prejudice against further education for women, saying:

> Often and often when girls have wished to pursue the education,
> the foundation of which they have had at school, or when they have
> wished to train themselves for some public positions, they have
> been met with the commonplace remark that woman's place was at
> home, and the desire for development of their natural gifts had been
> treated as a revolt against home duties, and a desire to ignore
> family claims.

There was not an answer to this remark, and she hoped that her audience would take full advantage of the opportunities now being offered to them by the University in the course called 'Sanitary and Domestic Science'.[3]

Praise was heaped on the WNHA, not only at home, but also abroad. A very practical token of recognition of its work was the prize awarded in Washington in 1908 by the International Congress on International Tuberculosis. This was given to the voluntary organisation, which since 1904 had accomplished the most effective work in the fight against tuberculosis, and the WNHA was bracketed with the New York Tuberculosis Association as first prize winners. The Washington Award Committee sent a certificate, signed by ex-President Theodore Roosevelt, and a share of the prize money. Marjorie Pentland said this was to be £200, but Anna Day quotes it as £1,000, while Professor Evans puts it as one thousand dollars – a more likely sum.

The Times ran a long editorial in praise of the work of the WNHA, noting that the death rate in Ireland from tuberculosis had dropped since the Association had begun its work. Professor Alun Evans, in his paper on Lady Aberdeen's health promotion caravans has pointed out that there was some confusion about these figures. According to a Medical Research Council of Ireland Report, by Dr J Deeney (1954), the disease was already waning in Ireland at this time, having peaked in 1902.[4] *The Times,* in its editorial of 1908, said:

> Outsiders have no idea of the hard work, trouble, patience and
> whole-heartedness with which Lady Aberdeen has entered into the
> undertaking.

Ishbel was particularly pleased by this recognition of her efforts and
Marjorie Pentland records that she exulted:

> Aren't the figures splendacious? Just fancy, The Times has a
> special article and leader about us: I can scarcely credit it![5]

Aided by Lady Aberdeen's persuasive powers, American interest in
the work was such that a generous grant from Mr P F Collier, founder of
Collier's Magazine, New York, enabled the WNHA to operate the first
tuberculosis dispensary in Ireland in Charles St, Dublin in 1911 and
maintain it until its takeover by the Dublin Corporation in 1913. Another
generous American gave a grant of £1,000 a year for five years for the
establishment of a 'hospital for consumption' in Dublin, and it was
opened at the Pigeonhouse Road in Dublin in August 1910, bearing the
name of its benefactor, Allan A Ryan.

Not all Lady Aberdeen's enterprises were popular, even among those
whom she might have expected to support her. Official obstructiveness
(a combination of bureaucracy and personal animosity, especially from
Sir Henry Robinson), Nationalist rejection, and Unionist suspicion were
all predictable, but what was most surprising to her, carried away as she
was by her own convictions, and educated in the etiology of tuberculosis,
was the general hostility towards the centres where the disease was to be
treated. This was understandable, based as it was on fear of infection.
Indeed, the very success of spreading the word that tuberculosis was
infectious, rather than hereditary, contributed to public unease.

One of Lady Aberdeen's proposals was to acquire disused coastguard
stations from the Admiralty and use them as institutions where
tuberculosis could be prevented. 'Preventoria,' as they were called, were
based on an idea, as Professor Evans has pointed out:

> ... borrowed from America where a cottage at Lakewood, New
> Jersey, once the home of the President [Theodore Roosevelt] was
> fitted up as an Institution to which was given the name of a
> "Tuberculosis Preventorium for Children."

Professor Evans notes that the *British Medical Journal* hastened to
add that it was in no way responsible for this addition to the medical
terminology.[6] A coastguard's cottage was acquired at Sutton, on the

northern side of Dublin Bay, where an isthmus joins the headland of Howth to the mainland, and the project immediately ran into trouble. The *Irish Times* of May 18th 1909, reports that a deputation from Sutton approached Lady Aberdeen to protest against the establishment of a 'Health Home' there. This deputation included Mrs Andrew Jameson, Father Colohan, the parish priest of Howth, Alderman Bergin, Lady Stokes, Mrs Noel Guinness, Mrs Roper and Andrew Jameson. Mr Jameson read a memorial signed by two hundred residents of the mainly prosperous area, 'protesting against the conversion of the coastguard station into a home for consumptives'. It would depress the value of property, and children would be open to infection. Because of the nature of the building, isolation of the invalids would be impossible, and it would pose a particular danger to the health of the local Christian Brothers, fifteen hundred of them, who regularly walked from Sutton to the Golf Links at Howth. All in all, consumptive patients would be a source of danger.

Lady Aberdeen, replying to the deputation, assured the members that the home in Sutton would be purely preventive. No actively ill patients would be sent there, only people who were, because of their poor circumstances, at risk of developing tuberculosis. Never one to let an educational opportunity pass, she quoted an article from an American journal in which the writer stated that there was less risk of infection from one hundred patients in a sanatorium than there was from two hundred uninstructed consumptives going about the streets. The President of the College of Physicians, Dr Andrew Horne, added that it had long been the practice of physicians in Dublin to send tuberculosis patients to Howth for the pure air that was found there. They stayed in lodging houses there, and were potentially a greater source of infection than patients in a well-regulated institution would be. It sounds as if the meeting was an acrimonious one, and although Lady Aberdeen gave a written guarantee that 'at present' only preventive cases would be sent to Sutton, the deputation was not satisfied and withdrew.[7]

A similar deputation came from Dalkey in August, with the same concerns. The local coastguard station was to be taken over, it was believed, by the WNHA, and equipped as a Health Home. The *Irish Times* reported the meeting in its issue of August 3rd 1909, quoting the members of the Dalkey Urban Council as being totally opposed to the project. It would, said Mr J Judd, leader of the deputation and Vice-

Chairman of the Council, be a most unsuitable place for a 'Health Home'. The north-east wind blew for four or five months in the early part of the year and this would prevent patients taking their much-needed exercise in the open air. Taken all round, Dalkey was thoroughly unsuitable, occupied as it was by 'the best class of people', whose homes had a rateable value of £200 per annum.

Lady Aberdeen said that the Association was 'most anxious to secure the full approval and co-operation of the immediate neighbourhood' at which Mr Judd interrupted to say that that was doubtful. (Mr Judd had previously been quoted in the *Irish Times* of May 20th 1909, as criticising Lady Aberdeen's Health Homes and being sceptical about Her Ladyship's assurances. "Why doesn't she set up one beside the Viceregal Lodge if they are so harmless?" he asked at one of the Council meeting.[8]) Ignoring the interruption, Lady Aberdeen went on to say that coastguard stations were not suitable for advanced cases of tuberculosis, but were preventive only. A few weeks of rest, fresh air and good food would do the patients, especially the children, a world of good and would strengthen their defences against disease. She asked:

> Would you, who live under such favourable conditions yourselves in Dalkey, interfere to prevent this? There are some who are afraid that the anti-tuberculosis crusade is creating a scare injurious to the country.*
> Gentlemen, I appeal to you to counteract this scare. It only exists where people are misinformed ... We must dissipate the scare by showing that the only safe countries to live in are those where measures are being taken to efficiently fight, and ultimately destroy, the power of the foe.

Mr Judd, ignoring this appeal to the deputation's charity, good sense, and innate intelligence, said bluntly 'If you send people in a weak state of health to the coastguard station you will be signing their death

---

*It was rumoured at the time that sales abroad of Irish lace and crochet were affected by the publicity given to the incidence of tuberculosis in Ireland as people, it was said, were afraid of infection. However, a note in the Minute Book of the WNHA, October 1909, reports that Mrs Hamlyn-Byrne, a member of the Executive, read letters from the London stores, Whiteleys and Harrods denying any fall in the sales of either lace or crochet. Maude Wynne, in her book about her father, Sir Michael Morris, Lord Killanin, ex-Chief Justice of Ireland, *An Irishman and his Family*, also referred to the scare 'injurious to the country'. She conceded that Lady Aberdeen did good work, but that 'Ireland appeared to her next door neighbour, England as almost a leper island'.[9]

warrant.' He was told yet again, that no patient would go there who was in any way consumptive and the local Medical Officer of Health, Dr Wright stated firmly that the coastguard station should be used only as a holiday home. Lady Aberdeen asked that if that were the case, would they be satisfied? Dr Wright said 'yes', the councillors agreed, and the deputation withdrew, 'apparently satisfied,' with the explanation said the *Irish Times*.[10]

In the event the Dalkey project never went ahead, although the Sutton Preventorium functioned successfully for several years. A preventorium in Clifden, County Galway, was also established, without, it seems, much opposition from local people, whose houses were not of high rateable value, and who themselves lived mostly in isolation.

Much more vigorous was the opposition to the Sanatorium for actively-ill tuberculosis patients which the WNHA established at Peamount, County Dublin, under its own auspices. The funds required for the sanatorium were hard-earned. Lloyd George, Chancellor of the Exchequer, had brought in a Health Insurance Act in 1911 which allowed for a million and a half pounds for anti-tuberculosis work, and Ishbel wanted a share of it for a sanatorium. Under the terms of the Act, the government undertook to provide beds for tuberculosis patients who were recommended by county councils for treatment. However, there were not enough beds in the country for the expected influx of patients, and in order to provide the much-needed accommodation a grant would be given to any voluntary body that would undertake to provide it. The WNHA, given its past record and the fact that it had recently set up its own 'Sláinte' Insurance Society, asked to be designated as an authorized agency under the Act.

Instead of the help and encouragement the Association quite rightly expected, it met with strong opposition. The chief opponent was Sir Henry Robinson, who as Vice President of the Local Government Board was a very powerful man, and no friend to Ishbel. Sir Henry and Ishbel had had an uneasy relationship over the years, and they had clashed over several matters. He regarded her as an interfering amateur, and she regarded him as an obstructive bureaucrat. He was not a man to be steamrolled, even by someone as imperious as Ishbel, and it was not, apparently, in her nature to use flattery or coaxing or even straightforward diplomacy. When she saw something that needed to be done, then it should be done, in the way which she thought best, and that was it. The major battle between the two opponents is described by Marjorie Pentland, who tells how Ishbel, having lobbied in London for 'her' grant was able to write to her husband on May 20th 1912:

> Had a long and I think successful afternoon at the House.
> Masterman says he sees no difficulties if the Irish L.G.B. are in
> favour. So I have wired Sir Henry Robinson [Chairman of the
> National Insurance Commission] asking him to wire Birrell and
> Masterman if he agrees to our request for £25,000. It may sound a
> lot to ask for but remember if we are to take cases all over Ireland,
> add to the Allan Ryan Hospital, build temporary sanatoria, erect
> and send about shelters, train nurses, provide care and nourishment
> for home patients – it will soon go! Of course, it seemed the worst
> day possible to go to the House; everybody frightfully busy, hot
> weather, people's hair standing up, Home Rule debate, etc, etc.
> However, *Deo gratias*![11]

Ishbel went back to choose sites for the sanatoria, while architects and lawyers drew up plans and deeds which she dared not sign because the Treasury grant never came. Then it was discovered that Sir Henry Robinson had written to the Treasury protesting against a grant being handed over to 'an association of irresponsible women'. Back to Westminster went Ishbel; so did Sir Henry, and on June 20th Ishbel wrote to her husband:

> It was war, open and declared, this morning. I was real sorry for
> Birrell, truly wishing to be nice to me and yet at the same time to
> act up to his instructions from Sir H.R. The latter made no pretence
> of concealing his open hostility and would not give way an inch.
> Masterman, in the chair, was most friendly and supporting. Mr
> Birrell asked me to return at 7 p.m.; by then there had been an
> interview with Mr Lloyd George; they understand that we have
> taken every step in conjunction with the County Councils. Mr
> Birrell is writing to the Councils that we are authorised to do the
> work, that all speed will be made to have the buildings ready by
> October. He authorised the purchase of Peamount to be carried
> through tomorrow! Shall we sing the "Hallelujay Chorus"?[12]

Marjorie Pentland goes on to describe further confrontations between Sir Henry and Lady Aberdeen, as told to her by Sir Arthur Salter, assistant secretary to the National Insurance Commission.

> Whenever a fresh issue arose they knew that come wind come
> weather Lady Aberdeen would certainly arrive from Ireland ready
> for the fray. Sir Arthur well remembers the impression of intense

concentration she conveyed, her ample form firmly seated at one side of the table and at the other Sir Henry Robinson, sharp-witted, lean, wiry; opposite in build, alike in determination. As Sir Arthur watched the combatants, they reminded him of a torpedo destroyer in action against a battleship; or in a more abstract metaphor, of the possible fate of any object – say Birrell – placed at the point of impact between the immovable mass and the irresistible force. Sir Arthur greatly admired the vitality and tenacity displayed by Ishbel during the negotiations; although he claims that as a general rule 'the more reasonable male is likely to see the other side better than a woman with a purpose'.[13]

The WNHA applied for, and received a grant of £2,500. Questions were raised in Parliament by opponents of Lady Aberdeen, a Mr Moore asking: 'Will the Treasury take into consideration the fact that this so-called philanthropic association is run chiefly on political lines by the wife of the Lord Lieutenant?' Despite this, the Association was able to go ahead with its plans for a sanatorium at Peamount, County Dublin and the property was bought at the end of June 1912. Work went ahead on the site to make it suitable for patients, but local opposition was strong, based on the twin fears of infection and a drop in property values. A letter in the *Irish Times* on July 21 1912, from a Justice of the Peace for County Kildare, Edward M Connolly, spoke of the terror which residents of the districts felt when they heard that 'hundreds of the worst cases of consumption in Ireland would be planted in their midst',[14] and there is no doubt that he was voicing what people believed.

Assurances from medical men who supported the scheme that there was no danger of infection were not believed, and on the 22nd July a band of about 50 men, armed with pickaxes, hammers and ropes entered the grounds at Peamount and wrecked one of the newly-built pavilions there, causing about £500 in damage. As they left, triumphant, they threatened to return and do further damage but four men, described as the ringleaders of the mob were arrested and charged with damaging the property. Two of the men were found guilty and were each sentenced to six month's imprisonment. This caused further resentment in the district, and at their weekly meeting the Celbridge Board of Guardians received a deputation protesting against the siting of the sanatorium. For the deputation Captain Connolly, RN and Colonel Claude Lane pointed out that the district was thickly populated, and therefore unsuitable for such an enterprise. They added that the Parish Priest of Celbridge, Father

Dunne, had given permission for his name to be used in the protest. In August 1912, the Celbridge Number One District Council expressed its sympathy with the jailed men by adopting a resolution calling for clemency towards them by the Lord Lieutenant on the grounds that the men 'were misled by the strong resolution of protest passed by public bodies and acted on the impulse of the moment'. A petition signed by many local people was presented to Lord Aberdeen, and on 7th September 1912, he ordered their release from jail.

The *Irish Worker*'s comment on the affair might very well have been quoted as incitement; in the course of a general and vitriolic attack on the medical profession in the issue of 3rd August 1912, it stated:

> Lady Aberdeen, finding that money was to be made available under
> the Insurance Act by providing accommodation for consumptives
> acquired an old residence at Peamount near Lucan, and got a
> foreign firm over to build a small hospital in the grounds.[15]

The *Irish Times*, a month later, in an editorial dealing with what the paper perceived as the public unpopularity of Lord Aberdeen, lamenting the influence of Their Excellencies in Irish public life, singled out Lady Aberdeen's work with the WNHA:

> This organization established by Lady Aberdeen, and driven
> forward by all the force of her commanding personality, has
> become a vast power in the land …This Association, which Lady
> Aberdeen controls absolutely, now exercises large Government
> functions and has the spending of large public funds.[16]

These accusations were wildly far from the truth; not only did Lady Aberdeen never make any money from her activities, she contributed to the funds from her own pocket, as well as tirelessly soliciting private contributions. The trip to America in late 1912, for example, was in order to raise funds for Peamount, because the budget, even with government subsidies did not cover all the running costs. Lord Aberdeen had requested leave of absence in order to accompany his wife on that tour, but the Prime Minister, Asquith, sent him a firm refusal, pointing out that no Viceroy had ever before crossed the Atlantic during his term of office, or put himself so far out of reach.

> From a political point of view, [said Asquith] it seems at least a
> doubtful policy at this stage of the Home Rule controversy for the
> Viceroy to go to the United States where there are so many Irish-
> Americans. I have not heard from the King but I suspect he will

take a similar view.[17]

It is a measure of Ishbel's influence over her husband – and an instance of their mutual lack of political *nous* – that Lord Aberdeen should even contemplate leaving his post on what was, after all, private business, while the country was in a state of crisis over Home Rule and northern Unionist opposition to it.

Peamount was meant, as Anna Day has pointed out in her history of the institution, to provide emergency care for patients recommended for sanatorium benefit by the county insurance committees and for the county councils, while these bodies were carrying out their own permanent arrangement. However, a number of:

> … county councils did not want the expense or responsibility of providing such accommodation and wished to take permanent beds in Peamount. To obtain exclusive use of such beds cost £70 each per year plus £1 per week per patient for maintenance when occupied. The hospital authorities tried to give an even distribution of beds, but counties Kerry and Donegal seemed to need the largest number.
> Instead of being used as a temporary emergency institution, Peamount soon took on the character of a permanent sanatorium, because twelve counties preferred to make an arrangement whereby they could always have a certain number of beds rather than build their own sanatorium. The property was vested in five trustees, nominated by the WNHA, with the approval of the Irish government. The management of the sanatorium was in the hands of the WNHA.[18]

In spite of the early set-back, the work at Peamount was completed in October 1912, and the sanatorium was fully in operation in the following year. The buildings were of timber, and could easily be destroyed (cleansed by fire) if they became impregnated by germs. Single-storey in construction, they consisted of a series of pavilions, open air chalets and shelters, a dining room, a recreation hall, and a home for medical staff.

Arthur Griffith's Nationalist paper, *Sinn Féin*, ever-critical of Lady Aberdeen and her works, said bluntly in 1914, 'Dublin never had need of Peamount' and accused her of 'inventing the tuberculosis scare,' and the 'exploitation of tuberculosis for political purposes'.[19] This vehement denigration of her anti-tuberculosis campaign had started years before when, on January 18th 1908, *Sinn Féin* published verses by Alice L

Milligan, the Nationalist writer, mocking Lady Aberdeen. Entitled 'To a Lady Bountiful,' the poem asked what was the price the Irish nation would have to pay for the charity bestowed by her ladyship.

To A Lady Bountiful
(On reading of her visit to Cork)

You who bring with lavish hand
Gifts to the poor throughout the land,
Before we bid them bless your name
In any town to which you came
Or any dreary country place
In which you showed your smiling face,
Or here where last your bounty's spread,
What are you asking in its stead?

When we hear your voice appealing
For purer air and light, and healing,
We could bless you on our knees,
Combatant of foul disease,
And we could think as forth you ride
Of one who fell by the wayside,
The wounded robber-beaten man
Rescued by the Samaritan,
When none of his own faith and nation
Had pity on his desolation.

But lady, we have heard it said
That where you give, you ask instead
A price more precious far than gold:
Into your hands is honour sold.
Before your feet is homage tendered
And patriot faith to you surrendered,
Therefore we think not of that man
Rescued by the Samaritan.

Our memories picture forth another
Esau when tempted by his brother,
Yielding his God-given birthright up
In base return for food to sup.
Or of that play we think again,
In which the demon merchant men
In famine days brought bags of gold
For which immortal life was sold.

This fable old has meaning new,
And some are false but many true,
And though your gifts be fair to some
Remembering in whose name you come;
We shall not yield their price to you.

Alice L Milligan[20]

A week later the paper published a letter from Mrs Alice Rushton, secretary of the WNHA in reply to the criticisms voiced in Alice Milligan's verses. Introducing the letter the editor said that all the paper's conventions were broken by having a letter sent in reply to a poem. 'We insert it on this occasion,' he said 'but we give notice herewith that none of our poets will again be submitted to such treatment.'

Mrs Rushton went on the attack immediately, pointing out that the appallingly high figures of the death-rate from consumption had always been available to the public and that Miss Milligan and her friends (or indeed anyone else) could have mounted a campaign against the disease. If they had done so she had no doubt they would have commanded much support.

> It would seem, however [she went on] whatever may have been the cause – that this great patriotic duty was overlooked, and that Lady Aberdeen was the first to throw herself warmly into the work of trying to focus public attention on the matter, especially that of the women of Ireland.

The Women's National Health Association came into existence because of Lady Aberdeen's appeal to Irishwomen of all creeds and classes to join her in the campaign against tuberculosis, a highly patriotic undertaking.

> I fail to see [wrote Mrs Rushton] how the "patriot faith" to which Miss Milligan alludes, can be "surrendered" in work that requires patriot faith of the more earnest kind to carry it along. Given that Miss Milligan and those who think with her, have a monopoly of this fine quality, surely it would be more courageous of them to join our Association, and endeavour to permeate it with their "patriot faith" than to hold aloof, and simply criticise.[21]

Editorial comment on Mrs Rushton's letter was predictable.

> The business of the British Lord Lieutenant in Ireland under any government is to keep this country acquiescent in its plunder and oppression in return for £20,000 a year taken out of our pockets,

and the business of his wife is to act as a political souper. Lady Aberdeen's interest in our health ... is part of the game. Her Ladyship has to play it ... but when the Irish people are asked to regard as a philanthropist a foreign lady for whose board and lodging they are compelled to pay, we presume they may shrug their shoulders.[22]

In *Sinn Féin's* issue of the following week, February 1st 1908, a letter appeared from a lady who styled herself a personal friend of Alice Milligan. She objected to Mrs Rushton's charge that Irishwomen had overlooked the 'great national duty' of national health, and opined that Mrs Rushton's twenty-year residence in London must have kept her out of touch with her countrywomen, for otherwise she would have known that there were women who were working at home for the good of their own people, and without 'the patronage of a lady Viceroy'. The type of crusade launched by Her Ladyship would never achieve anything worthwhile because:

> ... those of us who have lived our lives in the country and among the people, know that the only way to help them is to live amongst them as a kindly neighbour, loving them for their own sakes and helping them with our experience, "out of friendship." They won't stand patronising, meddling in their private affairs, or bullying them over their dirty houses, or bad ventilation.

'Banaltra,' as she signed herself, suggested that Mrs Rushton should join with her and others, and:

> ... bring her evident earnestness and energies into the National movement, study the country and the people, and work for the general good on Sinn Féin lines.[23]

In the same issue of the paper, February 1st, Alice Milligan herself had a long article in which she set forth her credentials as a worker for the health of the Irish people, and repudiated the charge that she and her friends neglected the work of a health crusade. She had many friends, priests, young doctors, hospital nurses, lady guardians, members of religious communities, National school teachers who came face to face with disease and suffering, and she herself had once been a school-teacher and a lecturer on hygiene:

> Moreover, I was always the person on the school staff who was appealed to by the girls to organise mountain climbs, expeditions, walks, expeditions to view the sunrise.

Before that, as a schoolgirl she organised games in the open air for the sake of a school friend who 'was threatened with consumption, and needed fresh air and exercise'. Furthermore, she once successfully nursed a friend who was suffering from a lung complaint, and used that experience to advocate benefits of fresh air and cleanliness wherever in Ireland she was carrying out her duties as a Gaelic League lecturer, but she could testify that there already were many such advocates, especially in convent schools and institutions. It was not out of 'petty egotism' that she listed her experiences, but to make it clear to Mrs Rushton that neither she nor her friends were:

> ...impracticable persons who neglect vital questions and preach ancient history, ancient hatreds, and the propaganda of ancient languages.

Miss Milligan accepted that Lady Aberdeen's health crusade was well-intentioned, and although she herself could never, as a matter of honour, join 'any association under Viceregal, royal or any government patronage' she had recommended it 'to young ladies of the Loyalist class in Belfast, and elsewhere', and she would consider it very wrong to try to bar anyone from joining in to condemn them for doing so. However, it was not Lady Aberdeen's philanthropy outside the sphere of politics that was in question, but her behaviour in Ireland, which was, by virtue of her office, entirely political, so that politics and philanthropy were, in her case, inextricably entangled. Miss Milligan went on:

> We understand perfectly well that her mission is one of conciliation. That she seeks to undermine the faith of extreme Nationalism. And in face of this we who desire to preserve the National faith cannot accept for our people gifts or help or healing from her hand.[24]

Miss Milligan's reply to Mrs Rushton was the end of that particular exchange. Lady Aberdeen, through Mrs Rushton, wisely made no further comment but *Sinn Féin* relentlessly kept up its campaign against the Aberdeens until the day of their departure from Ireland. Typical of the *Sinn Féin* attitude and style of attack is an impassioned article in its issue of July 18th 1908, which broadened the criticism to include those who were foolish enough to be taken in by imperialism masquerading as philanthropy. Quoting from a Tipperary paper the writer said:

We find long accounts of the reception of the British lady to whose husband we pay £20,000 a year and expenses for doing nothing in particular. It appears the British lady was received at the Convent, which was "tastefully decorated," with, among other things, the English flag, and a little pupil of the Convent was put forward to read an address to her in which it was states "her kind encouragement was very precious to them". The poor little National School children were put forward to present an address written by some wielder of a facile pen. "We are all pleased and proud to see your Excellency among us today, not only in your own person, but also as the representative of our gracious Queen. We know the interest which you take in the prosperity of our beloved country and all that you are doing at the cost of so much personal exertion and fatigue for the welfare of Ireland. We thank you for the honour you do us by visiting our school and we pray God to bless and reward you for your work for the poor and sick of this land."[25]

Commenting on this loyal and, of its nature, sycophantic, address *Sinn Féin* added:

The amount of gratitude this country can pretend to feel towards the parasites that feed on it is stupendous. What have parents to say? Surely it is their duty to see that their little sons and daughters are not brought up in the ways of the sycophant?

The writer could testify that there already were many such advocates, especially in convent schools and institutions. As a Nationalist paper *Sinn Féin* could do no other than criticise Lady Aberdeen and its insistence that Irish people *themselves* could solve an Irish problem – even though that problem was in large part due to British misrule – was entirely in keeping with the paper's ethos. Looked at from that angle Lady Aberdeen's actions were neither acceptable nor desirable.

Lady Aberdeen's relations with the medical profession, so cordial at first, cooled when differences arose over the implementation of the National Insurance Act of 1911, and some acrimonious correspondence passed between the National Insurance Committee of the Conjoint Committee British Medical Association and Irish Medical Association and the WNHA in the summer of 1912, but agreement was finally reached between the two bodies. In the November issue of *Sláinte* (the magazine of the WNHA) it was reported that there 'was not the slightest hostility' between the National Health Insurance Commissioners and the WNHA.

Lady Aberdeen encountered opposition even within her own Association, when some people objected to the WNHA having anything to do with the Insurance Act, legitimising it, as it were, by setting up an Insurance Society under its aegis. The Act was seen in some quarters as being a political manoeuvre by the wily Lloyd George, and in others as an unwarranted intrusion into the privacy of the individual. The Irish Catholic Church was not in favour, as the burden of insurance costs could be too heavy for farmers and small firms.

A public meeting, organised by the Provisional Committee of the Irish Health Insurance Society, under the auspices of the WNHA was held in Dublin on January 16th, 1911, to explain the provisions of the Insurance Act. Alexander Irwin, LLD, of Coleraine explained what the Act would mean both to employer and employee and what benefits it would bestow, and then, as the *Irish Times* reported next day, the Countess of Aberdeen addressed the meeting. She told those present that some branches of the WNHA had decided not to take part, mainly because they saw the Act as political, but also because they felt 'insurance work is outside our sphere'. However, she must remind them that 'the Act is now the law of the land', and therefore it had to be obeyed. The new Irish Health Insurance Society would be a society totally distinct from the WNHA, and the Association's funds would not be used in its organisation, because she had secured private funding for this purpose. Answering questions from the body of the hall, Dr Irwin told his listeners that:

> ... the maternity benefit has to be spent as the woman wishes, for the reason that, if it was at the disposal of the husband, it might, in some cases, be spent in celebrating the event.[26]

This was indeed, in some eyes, an attack on male and patriarchal rights.

In spite of the opposition within the WNHA (in Queenstown for instance, the branch voted against her, causing the *Cork Examiner* in its report of January 15th to comment that 'Lady Aberdeen had nothing to gain ... the common good is all that she aims at'.[27]) an Insurance Society later called Sláinte, was formed, and was duly rated as an Approved Society for the purposes of the Insurance Act. Lady Aberdeen worked vigorously for this cause, and was supported by her husband, to the extent that literature sent out by her bore the Viceregal frank. This action was severely criticised by political opponents, and the *Belfast Evening*

Telegraph in an editorial on January 9th 1912, quoted the *Daily Express* as saying 'Not for the first time under present auspices the Viceregal Lodge in Dublin has turned itself into an active partisan organisation'.[28]

The *Northern Whig* in its editorial of the 10th January said that Lord Aberdeen was now seen as the representative of the Nationalist Party, 'Since the day he arrived in Dublin he has obeyed the decrees of the Hibernian with the regularity and precision of an automatic machine'. It went on:

> The WNHA is supposed to be non-political, but an attempt is now being made to use it for the purpose of foisting Lloyd George's vexatious schemes upon the Irish people. Unionists throughout Ireland must register a vigorous protest against the meddlesome interference of Lady Aberdeen in this controversial matter.[29]

The editorial concluded by complaining bitterly because the WNHA 'appeal' on behalf of the Insurance Act had been sent out franked with an official stamp. General Unionist perturbation led to an exchange in the House of Commons, reported in the *Irish Times* on March 6th 1912, when a Mr Chambers asked whether the Chief Secretary was aware that the Viceregal frank was used on WNHA envelopes containing:

> ... amongst other matters, a pamphlet known as the "Little Red Book" explaining in a popular way, and from a Liberal standpoint, the main benefits of the National Insurance Act, and will he explain why there has been this expenditure of public money on stationery and postage.[30]

Mr Birrell, in a printed reply, explained that the stationery did not bear the Royal Arms and was not supplied at public expense but in accordance with a custom of long standing in connection with matters of public interest and social or charitable objects His Excellency's frank was used.[31]

The WNHA's nationwide involvement in public charitable work, and its attraction for socially-inclined, charitable and energetic women with time to spare was challenged in the spring of 1911 by the formation of a new body – the United Irishwomen. The name, with its historic overtones, might have suggested a nationalistic or even revolutionary society, but the group was, in fact, composed of women who wanted to improve living standards in rural Ireland and who, as the *Irish Homestead*, the journal of the Irish Agricultural Organisation Society pointed out 'wanted to make Ireland happy'. The IAOS, the governing body of the co-operative movement founded by Sir Horace Plunkett, had always held that the participation of women in the movement and in public life in general was most desirable. Influenced, perhaps by articles and letters in the *Irish Homestead*, a Wexford woman, Mrs Anita Lett, English-born, and well-to-do, held a series of meetings in her locality from 1908 to 1910 with the aim of establishing a society for the betterment of Irish country life. The outcome of these meetings was that a new organisation – christened the United Irishwomen, by Susan L Mitchell, the poet and assistant editor of the *Irish Homestead* – was formed, and Mrs Anita Lett became its first President. Although the United Irishwomen shared many of the aims of the WNHA, such as the education of women, especially in the area of domestic hygiene and child rearing and the provision of nurses in country areas, the organisation was quick to point out that there would be no overlapping and no friction between itself and either the Gaelic League or the WNHA. In any event, as Sir Horace Plunkett argued, the needs of Ireland were so great, that there was room in the country for all such associations.

Plunkett's diaries and letters make it clear that whatever kindly feelings he had once had towards Lady Aberdeen had quite evaporated and that he now felt animosity towards her.

He wrote in his diary:

Fri 30th Sept 1910 (Dublin)

... The "United Irish Women" – about 50 of them met at Plunkett House. I looked in, AE in chair. The organisation is not quite in being. But the idea is to have a women's social & economic movement, a sort of counterpart to the IAOS. I hope it will succeed. Miss Spring Rice & Mrs Pilkington were there.

Fri 28th Nov 1910

[Lady Aberdeen] was furious because at the Plunkett House the United Irishwomen were trying to organise themselves on my terms ... I gave her small satisfaction.

Tues 28 March 1911 (Dublin)

...Long letter to *Irish Times* about the United Irishwomen ...

Wed 29 March 1911

Lady Aberdeen seeing my letter in the Irish Times was exceeding wrath – She made a speech (written carefully & given to the Press) expressing friendship for the United Irishwomen & desire to help them but suggesting that they should be allied with – ie absorbed by the Women's National Health Assocn.

Tues 11th April 1911

Quarterly meeting of IAOs Cttee – good business done. Lady Aberdeen also arrived at Plunkett House with outriders, to meet the United Irishwomen & ask them to "come into the parlour" ie to be absorbed in "affiliated with" was the phrase – the Women's National Health Assocn.

Fri 19th May 1911

... I learned that Lady Aberdeen was working the Press against the U.I. pamphlet.[Plunkett's own pamphlet]. There is a deadly silence in the Dublin papers otherwise inexplicable.

Sat 20th May, 1911

J.G. Healy [editor of *Irish Times*] told me he could not review it [the pamphlet] in the *Irish Times* on account of Lady Arnott's relations with Lady Aberdeen. [Lady Arnott's husband, Sir John, was the proprietor of the *Irish Times*].[32]

Plunkett's letter in the *Irish Times* was inspired by a previous letter (25th March, 1911) by Sir Henry Grattan Bellew on the need for co-operation amongst voluntary organisations in Ireland. In their work 'there must necessarily be some overlapping', and in many cases very opposite means may be adopted by different organisations, whether under official or private management, to reach the same results. Thus, well-intentioned and hard-working people often find themselves in opposition. They squander their energy by attacking one another instead of being more tolerant and realising that all are working towards the same goal. Sir Henry concluded by pointing out that there was room enough and work enough in Ireland for many different organisations, and he called on 'the good and honest workers ... to extend a helping hand to each other'.[33]

In his letter (29th March 1911) Sir Horace Plunkett clarified what Sir

Henry Grattan Bellew had said, and amplified his remarks about the 'organisations that are springing up'. He took it that Sir Henry was referring specifically to the newly-formed United Irishwomen, and he wanted to make it clear that this new group was in no way a threat to existing organisations, the IAOS, the Gaelic League, the Industrial Development Associations or the WNHA. Each group had its own work to do, but they all worked 'to some extent, on parallel lines,' and he outlined the co-operation that existed between them, especially amongst the first three. He went on:

> I come now to the precise aim and function of the United
> Irishwomen. Their service ... is restricted to rural communities. In
> the first place, they will endeavour to induce the country wives and
> daughters to take an active and intelligent part in all those functions
> of the co-operative societies with which women are specially
> competent to deal with. The second governing motive of the United
> Irishwomen will be the desire for better social life in the country.

Neither of these aims could pose any threat to the WNHA; indeed:

> ... any candid supporter of the Women's National Health
> Association will recognise that this two-fold work is helpful to its
> aims, and ... there is no reason why the Health Association and the
> new Association should clash.[34]

The same issue of the *Irish Times* carried a leading article commenting on Sir Horace's letter, and agreeing with the points he had made. The United Irishwomen, a totally non-political body, were trying 'to do on its social side the work which the Irish Agricultural Organisation Society is doing on the economic side'. As for the Women's National Health Association, their work 'in fostering the health of the country was beyond praise' and it has aroused the women to a realisation of the problems which only women can solve. It is obvious that these two societies are working in fields equally important, but perfectly distinct. 'One deals only with the promotion of health; the other, starting where the first leaves off seeks to encourage the development of wealth and happiness.' There was no reason, therefore, why the two groups could not work together, and the writer hoped that 'no jealousy or friction should develop between them'.[35]

Lady Aberdeen reacted immediately. On the evening of the day Plunkett's letter appeared she presided over a WNHA meeting in Pembroke House to inaugurate a 'Babies' Club' for the No 4 South City

Dispensary district, and she made use of the occasion to make a statement about the relations between the United Irishwomen and the WNHA. The *Irish Times* reported her next as saying:

> I am very anxious, that there should be no misunderstanding
> regarding the attitude of the Women's National Health Association
> towards this new organisation.

She had, from the time she first heard of the United Irishwomen, been greatly attracted 'by the ideas put forward by those who were the spokeswomen for the new organisation' and had asked for, and been promised, 'copies of the papers containing the constitution, objects and regulations, as soon as these should be printed'. She understood that these would be available in a few days and she stressed:

> ... meanwhile it has been the earnest desire of the Women's
> National Health Association to devise a scheme whereby the two
> Associations could work together in closest alliance, and which
> would be acceptable to both.

From her reading of Sir Horace Plunkett's letter it was obvious that the projected work of the United Irishwomen in rural districts would be very similar to that already carried out by local branches of the WNHA, and that if both groups were to work independently then there would indeed be 'difficulty and friction'. However, if they were to amalgamate it would be to everyone's benefit, and she had already contacted the executive of the United Irishwomen with a proposal to this effect.[36]

The language of the speech is very mild and the proposal of amalgamation seems quite reasonable but Plunkett, knowing Lady Aberdeen's character, could well have been right when he described her as 'being exceeding wrath', and of planning to absorb the new organisation. It was, after all, encroaching on what she regarded as her territory, active and public good works, and it would lure away some of the soldiers she needed for her crusade. On the other hand, it is possible that the level-headed Ishbel meant exactly what she said and no more, and that she saw in the United Irishwomen's proposed work an unnecessary duplication of her own. However, the refusal of the *Irish Times* to review Plunkett's pamphlet because of the friendship between Lady Aberdeen and Lady Arnott does seem to indicate that Lady Aberdeen was personally aggrieved by the emergence of a new organisation.

Plunkett's correspondence with Lord Monteagle of the Pembroke Charity Fund throws more light on his attitude to Lady Aberdeen and shows that his early respect for her had completely disappeared. In a letter to Lord Monteagle on the 8th April 1910, he refers to money given to 'Lady Aberdeen's TB crusade', and says that it is to be 'distinctly and definitely understood that no more money will be given out of the Fund'.[37] Conversely in another letter to Monteagle on the 16th March 1911, he refers to the United Irishwomen's meeting that took place that day in Plunkett House and adds that he would like to 'give them as much as £500 a year for three years'.[38] Monteagle agreed and on the 18th March, Plunkett wrote thanking him, and added, 'I am convinced these are the right kind of people to do this important work'.[39]

The unspoken message is that Plunkett has infinitely more respect for them than for the WNHA and in a letter to Monteagle three days later, the 21st of March, he says bluntly, 'Better to leave nursing entirely to the Women's National Health Association, and her lot of worshippers and office-seekers'.[40] He uses the same phrase 'worshippers and office-seekers' in his next letter to Monteagle, dated 29th March, and accompanying that day's issue of the *Irish Times*, which published his own letter:

> I send you a copy of to-day's *Irish Times*. You will read between the lines that I am trying to defend the United Irishwomen from what I am afraid is an organised attack upon them by Lady Aberdeen and her entourage of worshippers and office-seekers ... I am convinced the United Irishwomen will be immensely helpful to the Irish Agricultural Organisation Society.

In sending the *Irish Times* of the 30th March to Monteagle, Plunkett expected Monteagle to be amused by Lady Aberdeen's speech and added that:

> ... the United Irishwomen can not be affiliated with the Health Association, but in future I hope there will be no friction, but on the contrary, working relations between them'.[41]

No rivalry between the United Irishwomen and the Women's National Health Association was reported in public, but given human nature, it is more than likely that at local level there was some of that 'friction' that both groups wished to avoid. The social composition of each Association seemed at first to be very similar, but as the years went by the United

Irishwomen established a broader social base, and became identified with rural life in a way which the WNHA never did. The United Irishwomen's organisation had an advantage over the WNHA in that it was solidly backed by the influential and male-dominated IAOS, and this may have been a factor in its initial success.

Both societies survived the change from British rule to Irish Free State, but while the Women's National Health Association slowly declined, the United Irishwomen flourished and in 1935 changed its name to the Irish Countrywomen's Association, a true reflection of its membership. It is now a vigorous and powerful organisation which has revolutionised the lives of women in rural Ireland, and has fully realised the aims of its founders. The ICA has generously honoured the memory of Lady Aberdeen by planting trees in her honour in Herbert Park, Dublin, and by training in *An Grianán*, the ICA's College, foreign student holders of the Lady Aberdeen scholarship awarded by the Associated Countrywomen of the World.

All this, however, was in the future, and in 1911 Lady Aberdeen had more to concern her than the founding of the United Irishwomen. There was the ongoing work of running the WNHA, presiding at its meetings, editing its magazine *Sláinte*, travelling the country to win support for Lloyd George's Insurance Act, the usual round of bazaars, concerts, hospital and school visiting, and, of course, official entertaining, especially that in connection with the royal visit of King George V and Queen Mary in 1911.

For the Coronation itself (where Ishbel wore a gown on which the design was made by the Dublin Metropolitan School, with a girdle of gold worked out in Celtic design, and a veil of Limerick lace) Lady Aberdeen organised a special gift to the Queen from the women of Ireland. This was a gown of fine Irish poplin to be paid for by contributions from all Her Majesty's Irish namesakes, ie Mary, or any of its diminutives or derivatives. Nationalist feeling of outrage at this 'loyal gesture', was expressed anonymously in the ballad 'To the Marys of Ireland,' to be sung to the tune of 'The Wearing of the Green'

To the Marys of Ireland
O, Mary dear, and did you hear our queen is to be crowned?
And to help her buy a hobble skirt the hat is going round.
'Twill be of Irish poplin, trimmed with *disinfected* lace,
To show how warmly and how well she loves the Irish race!

O, I met with Lady Microbe, and she took me by the hand,
And says she, "We want to compliment the Marys of your land;
Our gracious queen is Mary, too, and she is pleased to say
She'll take a tiny gift from them on Coronation Day!"

O Mary dear, you needn't fear your penny or your crown
Will bear disease across the seas to healthy London town;
'Twill be surely disinfected, pasteurised, and washed with care,
To banish all the poison of the tainted Irish air!
Mary darling! do not listen to the vile, disloyal few
Who have said your queen will laugh at you, for sure it isn't true
She'll murmur "Chawming Emerald Isle! so generous and so green,
Its Marys go in rags themselves to decorate their queen!"[42]

Lady Aberdeen also organised an 'Address of Welcome' from the women of Ireland. In a letter the *Irish Times* published on the 9th February 1911, she outlined the scheme, asking for contributions, ranging from ½d to one shilling [5p]. This was to pay for the costs of illumination and binding, and the address would be of entirely Irish workmanship, 'both in design and execution.'[43] *Sinn Féin* saw not only colonialism at work in these schemes of Lady Aberdeen, but personal ambition. Under a cartoon 'The Viceregal Begging Box' on the 18th February 1911, the *Sinn Féin* writer described the proposed gift as a device for the Aberdeens to secure a Marquisate – a device which would be defrayed by contributions of Irish copper. Lady Aberdeen was 'exploiting this country in her family's interests'.[44] The paper threatened to publish the names and addresses of any teacher, lay or religious, who cajoled or coerced pupils into signing and paying their halfpennies. Over the next few months *Sinn Féin* reported rumours of intimidation by employers, workhouse governors and hospital staff. The management of Jacobs' biscuit factory wrote denying that its staff had been forced to sign, but nobody else bothered to contradict *Sinn Féin*.

A group, the 'Nationalist Women of Ireland' was formed to counter Lady Aberdeen's efforts and it held regular meetings, voicing indignation and outrage. In April the paper stated that the WNHA were tricking people into signing the Address – when they came for their penny dinners they were asked to sign their names; they did so, and were then furious when they found out how they had been fooled. In the next month, May, a ballad called 'Mary's Mendicants' was published and read:

They're begging for Queen Mary,
Please hear their plaintive cry.
We a copper crave for Mary,
And the Coronation's nigh.

On the 13th May *Sinn Féin* reported that the Address of Welcome had 'collapsed', because only a small percentage of Irish women had signed it and that was the end of that particular campaign against Lady Aberdeen. Another one, referring to a university appointment – the Degani Affair – over which she was alleged to have used her influence soon followed and continued for months.

Suspicion of Lady Aberdeen, her schemes, and her motives, did not, however, stop people from attending the exhibition *Uí Breasail*, organised by the Women's National Health Association, and held in Ballsbridge for the last week of May and the first week of June 1911. The name, that of the mythical Irish land of content, had been chosen by competition among the members of the Association, and the winner, Mrs T Daly from Fuerty, County Roscommon, had received a prize of £5. The exhibition was, according to the *Irish Times* of May 24th 1911:

> ... on so vast a scale that no one description can be applied to it; there is an Educational Exhibition, a Health Exhibition; the importance of the Department's (DATI) exhibit, coupled with the industrial display makes it almost a National Exhibition. There is a Town Planning Exhibition, itself a feature of the first importance. It is a great Bazaar ... it is a vast Fête, a galaxy of entertainments.

These included singing, instrumental music and step-dancing in the Village Hall, a shooting gallery, golf, putting and croquet, firework displays, band concerts, and cinematograph displays, pony and donkey rides and a Café Chantant where the 'leading professional artistes of Ireland' gave their services. The Café was 'organised by County Dublin ladies' and 'the catering was run by Mrs Egan and Mrs Andettel Jones, helped by a hundred ladies, prettily dressed as Quakers'.[45]

The Health Exhibition included a Food Section where basic information on food values, and simple home cooking was available. Typical diets were drawn up showing:

> ... firstly how a family of five may be fed on an expenditure of 12s 6d [62^1/2p] per week, and secondly, how a less well-to-do family may be more economically, but adequately fed on a corresponding expenditure of 8s 6d [42^1/2p] per week.

Sinn Féin found these suggestions both unrealistic and insulting and, as usual, mounted a personal attack on Lady Aberdeen. The Nationalist periodical, The *Leader*, also took the opportunity to launch a personal attack on Lady Aberdeen. While generally complimentary about the Exhibition, and happy to publish advertisements for it (one featured a drawing of a pretty young lady, with the caption 'Kathleen Ní Houlihan going to *Uí Breasail* in her Dripsey dress') it couldn't resist quoting the Court Circular which reported the presence of the Viceroy and his wife at the Punch and Judy at the Exhibition. The *Leader* commented:

> Her Ladyship is an accomplished hand at "pulling the strings" herself and as for ventriloquism she has no equal among amateurs. Frequently on public platforms she has given exhibitions of her powers, using a "figure head" known as the Lord Lieutenant for her popular entertainment.[46]

Although not everyone thought so at the time (The *Leader* called it 'silly') the most significant section of *Uí Breasail* was the Town Planning Exhibition. The main portion of this Exhibition had been organised by the Royal Institute of British Architects in London in the previous year and since then had been on tour. The WNHA had arranged for it to come to Dublin with its Director, Professor Patrick Geddes, an authority on town planning, and had had an Irish section added to it. The *Irish Times* hailed it with pleasure, pointing out that in an old city like Dublin, with its 'wretched rookeries,' it was essential that a study should be made of 'the methods adopted in other centres to effect improvements that have conduced to the health and social advancements of the citizens'. The WNHA was to be congratulated on its initiative in bringing the Exhibition to Dublin, so that public attention should be drawn to the whole question of housing and town planning which, as the WNHA so often pointed out, was 'at the root of good national health'. Although, as the paper noted, the section dealing with Irish problems had been hastily put together, and was, therefore, incomplete, it was of special interest as it contained 'models lent by the Local Government Board illustrating cottages erected in various parts of the country under the Labourers' Acts'.[47] The writer from The *Leader* was not impressed by these, saying 'I did indeed see a model of a labourer's cottage, furnished in what I should imagine was a faithful imitation of the Viceregal Lodge'.[48]

The Aberdeens had both been campaigning for some time for an improvement in housing in Ireland, and in the previous February the

Viceroy had delivered what was described as 'an impassioned speech' at the annual dinner of the Royal Institute of the Architects of Ireland on the subject of the housing of the poor. On the following day, 28th February 1911, the *Irish Times* editorial commented on his speech, saying that a campaign such as he called for was 'a primary necessity'. Tuberculosis was, said the writer, 'too firmly lodged in tenement houses to be dislodged,' and added that:

> ... the Recorder recently pointed out that not only are these
> tenements for the most part wretchedly unhealthy, but that the rents
> asked for a single room often amount to an extortion on the poor ...
> The last census revealed that one quarter of the population of
> Dublin was living in one-roomed tenements.

Other cities had slum clearance schemes, he pointed out, but not Dublin where 'we lack either the brains to devise them or the money to finance them'.[49] The Exhibition showed that there was no lack of brains, and that there might even be some money available for slum clearance, but although public-spirited people were optimistic about such schemes, there were others who felt less hopeful. At a meeting, 'The Housing of the People,' held on May 29th 1911, under the auspices of the Dublin Citizens Association, and reported next day in the *Irish Times*, Reverend Father Coleman said that, yes, slums were being cleared, but that 'new ones were created every day by poor people, many of whom were very destructive.' Agreeing with him, Reverend Father Fottrell, SJ, said that:

> ... there should be organised inspection of the houses of the
> working classes and some inducement should be given to make
> them keep the house clean'. He suggested that bags of coal would
> be suitable inducements.[50]

Lady Aberdeen was, of course, familiar with the state of housing in Ireland, both urban and rural, through her work with the WNHA, and realised that the anti-tuberculosis campaign could never succeed where people lived in dirt and squalor. At the inaugural meeting of the Town Planning Association, which took place in Dublin on 27th November 1911, Lady Aberdeen, as President, referred in her speech to 'the belief that the housing problem was at the root of many of the worst evils which afflicted the human race in its civilised communities' and expressed her hope that the new Association would do great things for Ireland. Much was already being done by health workers 'both official and unofficial' and by local authorities but much still needed to be done, and she called for 'immediate united and organised action.' When, she said:

> ... they were exhorted to preach the gospel of cleanliness, and found the people they were to preach to had often to carry up every drop of water they used four or five flights of stairs, without light or any other convenience, then they felt the time was ripe for a patriotic movement.

She appealed to:

> ... the people of all classes, all creeds and all parties in Ireland [to organise a scheme] in which all sections of the people could join [and to] take such action as would make their towns and cities and villages fit places for rearing the citizens of [the] country, [places that would meet] not only the physical, but mental, moral and spiritual needs of human beings, with a right to have the opportunity of leading a happy, healthy and useful life'.[51]

Lady Aberdeen's appeal was heeded to the extent that the Town Planning Association did arouse some public interest and was sufficiently active and vigorous to organise an important Exhibition in Dublin in 1914.

We do not know if Ishbel was hurt by criticism from several quarters, but it is fairly safe to assume that she was not devoid of the normal human emotions. However, it was clear that her physical energy was still phenomenal and equally clear that criticism would not deflect her from the paths of righteousness which she felt it her duty to follow.

Sláinte

O N THEIR FIRST SUNDAY back in Ireland in 1906, Lord and Lady Aberdeen attended Divine Service in the Chapel Royal. There they listened to a sermon by Dr Paterson Smyth, Vicar of St Ann's, Dawson Street, and Chaplain to His Excellency. Dr Smyth spoke of the sad state of the city of Dublin and its 'swarming tenements in the slums' where men, women and children led lives of utter misery. He pleaded with the state to do something for those human beings who were condemned to such a terrible existence, because the problem was one that no individual agency could solve. 'Help us all you can,' he begged the Viceroy, knowing even as he spoke, that the King's representative could do no more than add his own voice to that of those begging the Government to 'do something'. However, in his private capacity, Lord Aberdeen was a kind-hearted man, known for his charity, while his wife was a woman who actively campaigned for the betterment of the lives of the poor and the needy.

There was plenty for Ishbel to do in Dublin. The city was in an even worse state than it had been when the Aberdeens were first in office in 1886. Unemployment had been high then, it was even higher now, and the slums had become even more overcrowded and unsafe. Infantile mortality was extremely high, and tuberculosis had joined the other diseases, such as typhoid, typhus, scarlet fever and smallpox, which were known to be the main killers of infants, older children and adults. Ishbel Aberdeen's major campaign was, as we have seen, directed against this 'white plague,' but in the course of her crusade, she found that it was not a foe which could be fought in isolation, but one which had many allies, seen and unseen. As she campaigned she learned about poor housing, lack of hygiene, ignorance, and prejudice, inadequate diet, and deep-down grinding poverty.

A record of what she and her helpers found, not only in Dublin, but throughout Ireland, was kept in *Sláinte*, the magazine of her organisation, the Women's National Health Association and it gives a vivid, though unemphatic, unsensational account of conditions in Ireland in the years immediately preceding the First World War. The name *Sláinte* (good health) was in accord with Ishbel's sympathy with Irish native culturalism. Membership cards for the WNHA were available in Irish or in English and there were occasional articles in Irish in the magazine – which no doubt was a great solace to those who, like the Dublin coal merchant O'Carroll, were prosecuted for having their names inscribed in Irish only on their carts. The magazine first made its appearance early in 1909. The paper was of good quality, and the cover was an attractive shade of blue, emblazoned in bold type with the title, *Sláinte,* and the words 'edited by the Countess of Aberdeen'. In the first number, January 1909, Ishbel as editor, said:

> It may seem a bold thing, at first sight, to introduce a new magazine
> to the favour of the public in these days. But the Chaperone of
> *Sláinte* is a little lady who has a place ready made for her in
> thousands and thousands of homes in Ireland. She has been called
> for by crowds of Irish men, women and children of all ranks and
> conditions of life who, during the last 18 months have been
> crowding the meetings and joining the ranks of the Women's
> National Health Association of Ireland.[1]

Ishbel pointed out that the branches were all isolated from each other and that it was only at headquarters in Dublin that people knew what was going on nationwide, and so, she said, lapsing into that whimsy that sometimes afflicted her and that jars so terribly with her normal briskness:

> … the aid of our little fairy *Sláinte* has been involved, and we hope
> to send her, month by month, in her St Patrick's blue dress, up and
> down the land.

A study of the periodical makes it clear that although a professional was responsible for its layout and the technical business of getting it to the printers (Maunsell and Company of Abbey Street in Dublin) Ishbel herself chose the contents. The editorial notes with which every issue opened were obviously hers, and her voice speaks loudly and clearly through them. Highly practical as ever, she asks members of the Association to try to get more subscribers for the magazine. '*Sláinte* she says, 'cannot hope to compete successfully with Magazines only intended for the amusement of their readers', but she can promise 'to collect and deliver monthly information of great value to all interested in the health of the country', and she promises prizes for those who get the most subscriptions before a certain date. *Sláinte* was never a commercial success, and it is doubtful if it ever broke even. At one of the Association's meetings, the business manager and publisher, Mr Kevin Kenny, of Kenny's Advertising Agency, told the members that now subscribers were badly needed, as the finances were in a bad way, so much so that the Earl and Countess had had to pay £120 a year out of their own pockets to keep the magazine going.

There was quite a good spread of advertising in the paper, not only from firms connected with health products, such as Smith and Sheppard for medical appliances, McLaughlin & Co, for Sanatoria buildings, and various chemists, but from firms with general products – Becker Bros for tea, Field and Co for meat and poultry, Williams and Woods for jams and preserves, and Alex Findlater and Sons for general groceries. Some advertisers rather cleverly linked what they were offering to the campaigns fuelled by Ishbel's enthusiasm. For example, the National Window Cleaning Company announced boldly that 'Life without Light is Death', while a more long-winded one for magic lanterns from T Mann, Opticians, stated that 'The Chief Cause of Intemperance and Emigration is the Dull Monotony of Village Life' and that 'The Remedy is to be found in Entertainment and Social Gatherings'.

Correspondence was to be addressed to the Secretary at the Viceregal Lodge, and it was to here that the WNHA Branch notes were to be sent. Requests for WNHA pamphlets were to be addressed to the Literature Secretary at the same address. The Branch notes, from the 150 branches around the country, were reports on their activities throughout the year, or the month, as the case may be. Some were long-winded and rather soulful, and not, seemingly, to the Editor's taste, as she asked in one of her own Notes, that they be 'short and crisp', and offered a prize for the best report, no more than a paragraph long. No more was heard of this proposal, and the notes continued to vary not only in content, but in style. Space to fill on a page probably accounted for the fact that some of them were not tightly-edited, and conversely, lack of space accounted for the brevity of others.

The Editorial Notes are themselves 'short and crisp', being in the main announcements about forthcoming events, or reports on special meetings, conferences and so forth, but now and again Ishbel's evangelical voice is heard. Calling on all members to work enthusiastically for the cause she points out:

> ...the great thing is to create an interest in health questions and to connect them with bright little illustrated lectures and other entertainments and to make people feel how much more they will get of life if they keep their windows open and their houses clean, and if they will eat nourishing food and practise temperance and self-control in all things.[2]

Unfortunately, this sort of advice was worse than useless in a world where people lived in squalor that was not of their own making, and were unable to afford the food that would nourish them properly. Furthermore, it was exactly the kind of statement that gave ammunition to her enemies who contended that she knew nothing of the realities of Irish life. She followed these crass words in the following month's issue of *Sláinte* (December 1910) with the almost equally futile recommendation that branches should run:

> ... weekly social entertainments [as did the Wexford branch], not to be looked on as money-making only, but as directly promoting good health, by promoting cheerfulness and taking people out of themselves.

There could be some light chat about health matters during the entertainment. Ishbel's ideas of 'light chat' and 'entertainment' may be gleaned from the New Year's Calendar of 1911 sanctioned by her and reproduced in the magazine. This featured good spirits – the Fairy of Fresh Air, The Spirit of Light and The Magicians of Cleanliness and Brightness. If you opened your windows wide they would fly in and would be followed by their sisters – Health, Temperance, Cheerfulness, Perseverance, Happiness and Prosperity. All these benevolent visitors liked a long list of things, including soap and water, pure milk, stirabout, wholemeal bread, freshly-made tea, flowers, well-groomed cows, spick-and-span back yards, dainty cooks, handy husbands, wise fathers and helpful boys and girls. Their enemy, the White Demon, on the other hand, liked nothing better than shut windows, soiled clothes, swarms of fleas, sickly uncared-for cows, hordes of rats, manure heaps at the door, tinned foods, strong drink, family quarrels, hopelessness, ruin and misery.

The White Demon had obviously been defeated in at least one household, for the picture on the calendar showed a charming domestic scene – father, mother, children all working hard in a clean and cosy country kitchen. The caption read 'A Scene from *Uí Breasail*', and the calendars were available at two pence each or at sixpence per dozen.[3] The calendar was based on a play *The Triumph* by Mrs F E Eaton, which was in turn, based upon her own book *The White Demon and How to Fight Him*. The main characters are the good fairies – Fresh Air, Cleanliness, Cheerfulness, etc – who visit the poor cottage where Sheila Murphy and her brother Danny live with their widowed mother. The children's father had died of tuberculosis and their mother was now suffering from the same disease. The fairies transform the cottage and the life of its inhabitants and all ends happily with Mrs Murphy going off to a sanatorium to be cured of her disease and the children given a good grounding in the basics of health and hygiene. It is a spirited, well-written little story chosen by the Board of Education as a reader in the National Schools, but the dramatic possibilities do not seem very great. Ishbel herself wrote a foreword to the book, in a highly whimsical vein, ending with the pronouncement that the fairies were alive, well and active in Ireland.[4] This invocation of supernatural beings was in line with the taste of the times – J M Barrie's *Peter Pan* was at the height of its popularity, A Conan Doyle was entranced by spiritualism, and in Ireland Douglas Hyde, Lady Gregory and W B Yeats all affirmed their belief in the worlds of myth and magic.

Judging by its content, the selection of material for the main part of the magazine was Ishbel's own, and unlike her ill-judged advice and recommendations it shows an awareness of the problems of a health campaign in a world where circumstances militated against its success. Her contacts in the International Council of Women helped her to get articles from Britain, Europe and North America, some of them reprinted from other sources, some original. Her choice reflected her many concerns. Articles on the prevention and treatment of tuberculosis were in the majority but material included articles on street-trading by children, the education of girls for motherhood and the care of children, dental inspection in schools, housing problems, playgroups, the correct feeding of infants, and the importance of hygiene, not only in the home but wherever people might congregate.

Some of these articles were, and are, of general interest. A health crusade by Dr Evans, Medical Officer of Health in Chicago, a report of which was reprinted from *McClure's Magazine* told of the appallingly unhygienic conditions in bakeries in that city where bakers and kitchen workers slept in caverns, 'dirty, begrimed catacombs', which in some cases they shared with pets (in one cellar 16 dogs were found). In the hotels the kitchens were so hot, and so lacking in ventilation that the sweat from the faces of the cooks often dripped into the soup they were stirring. Without having to say so, Ishbel admired Dr Evans' methods of educating the public. Everywhere people were accosted by Dr Evans' advice:

> …warning placards in street cars, daily hints in newspapers in any and every language, short fresh-air articles sent out by Chicago Health Department and Fresh Air Bulletin Boards in factories and department stores.

There were huge posters in every public school room, and children were given smaller versions to take home, where they could translate them into whichever language was spoken by their immigrant parents. These parents were assailed with good advice in the 'Nickel Theatres' which under Dr Evans' influence were properly ventilated and protected by fire regulations and where 'talking machines' gave five-minute health chats, in 'language adapted to the locality'. Ishbel read with interest the comment that the moving picture, the new form of entertainment was 'becoming more and more the great amusement of the masses, and that properly regulated it may have great educational value,'[5] and later there are reports in *Sláinte* of cinematography performances and even a mention of a special health film from the Association. All this was merely a development of what she was already doing with her travelling caravan and magic lantern shows, but the big difference was that Dr Evans had the support of the municipality of Chicago while Ishbel had, at best, limited support from official bodies.

The range of subjects covered in *Sláinte* is to be expected, but the tone of the articles varies somewhat. There are some sickly-sweet stories (one of several by Selma Lägerlof was illustrated by Jack B Yeats) featuring ailing little girls, and then there are robust descriptions of dirt and disease that are not for the fainthearted. An article about the dangers posed by flies described how they fed on sputum, swarmed on a baby's nappy and 'were greedy for dressings from a discharging wound'. It was 'disgusting to read about these things, but reality is disgusting', commented the editor. In a piece entitled 'Uncleanly Habits and the Spread of Consumption,' Dr Octavius Hall, Medical Officer of Health, Devonport, cautioned readers about the abuse of saliva:

> It frequently aids in the cleaning of knives, nurses clean the faces of their infant charges with this misused fluid; breathing into glasses as

an adjunct to polishing them is quite common practice.

Other dirty habits included dropping cutlery or even food on the floor, and then replacing it on the tray, washing dishcloths with hankies and dusters and licking a finger to turn the pages of a book. 'These warnings', read the editorial note, 'are calculated to make the flesh creep'.[6] Equally unsavoury is the description of the dirt commonly found in most classrooms, as described in an article reprinted from the *Edinburgh News* on the cleansing and disinfection of schools. Normal dirt to be found in the classroom, said the article, includes that on shoes 'fouled by streets', scales from skin, 'dried organic secretions from skin, mouth, nose, etc,' dust in hair and clothing, organic dust raised from floors by the movement of children, and 'material blown in from the street'. The situation is especially dangerous when pupils are dirty and in need of a hot bath, and with clothing in a deplorable condition. Children's heads are dirty – some 60% to 80% of them verminous – and they suffer from skin diseases such as impetigo, scabies and ringworm. Eyes and ears are also infected and are discharging purulent matter. Daily cleansing and disinfecting is therefore essential.[7] This description of slum school children in Edinburgh could fit Irish children, especially those in Dublin. One wonders how much good could be done in those circumstances by disinfection, given that it was poverty that led to the sorry condition of the children in the first place. Nevertheless it was right to emphasise the need for official action to clean the premises in which children were forced by law to congregate and where they passed their diseases on to one another.

A letter in *Sláinte* in September 1909 pointed out one of the obvious ways in which infections of the mouth, the throat and the chest could be spread in a schoolroom. 'Tuberculosis,' the writer stated, 'is spread by sucking pencils, especially in schools where pencils are handed out to the children in the morning',[8] collected in the afternoon, and handed out again next morning. The odds are against the child getting back yesterday's pencil, so he is sucking up another's germs. It is impossible to prevent children sucking the end of a pencil, so the only solution is to have each pencil labelled with an individual child's name, and the correspondent tells how this can be simply and cheaply done by means of a piece of light material which can be written upon, attached to the top of the pencil with a clip.

It was an undeniable fact that Irish schools were poorly-equipped and maintained in comparison with those in England and Scotland, and that the grants available were lower than in those areas. An official report published in 1904 showed that the majority of rural Irish schools did not have enough classrooms, and that under Irish rules desks needed to be provided only for a proportion of the attendance, so that some children had to stand for part of the time.[9] An article in *Sláinte* in May 1909, by F North, entitled 'Irish Schools and Health', made disturbing reading. The highest mortality among children, it said, was in the ten to fifteen-year age bracket – the school-going years, and this could be related to the fact that most of the 'State-aided public elementary schools' were dirty and insanitary. Many of them had no proper 'sanitary conveniences', and even where such conveniences did exist they were not kept clean. Some of these buildings were no more than hovels, poorly-ventilated, with low ceilings, so that children breathed 'vitiated air'.[10]

A country chemist, in an article 'Observations from Behind a Counter' published in *Sláinte* in September 1909 said bluntly 'I have frequently seen children seriously injured by school life', and described them as ashy-faced, heavy-eyed, dejected half-starved little souls'. They suffered 'brutal canings' and were 'poisoned and stupefied by long hours in foul air'[11]. The buildings were inadequately heated and in rural areas children often brought a sod of turf each to place on the open fire. Inspectors were quoted as pitying the children who had to work in these conditions, one saying 'it is downright cruelty to have a schoolroom for children so cold that an inspector, even with a heavy overcoat on feels chilled in hands and feet'. Lack of space meant that classes were sometimes held in porches or cloakrooms where wet outer garments were hanging. The cleaning of premises was done by the pupils themselves in rotation, as there was no provision for a cleaning service.

The WNHA campaigned for improvements in the maintenance of the National Schools, and Lady Aberdeen led a deputation to the Irish government to ask for a grant for heating and cleaning of the premises. It was eventually acquired and in May 1911, *Sláinte* published a letter from the Secretary of the INTO thanking Lord and Lady Aberdeen for their help. In the same issue there was a letter from Mr Birrell, the Chief Secretary, saying that Treasury sanction for the grant would never have been got without the help of the Association who had worked in co-operation with the school managers. A small victory for the WNHA, but the war against disease had to be fought on many fronts and the diet of the poor was one of the chief battlegrounds. The children who came to school were in many cases under-nourished, and therefore prone to infection. Some indeed could not come at all – Dr McDonnell told the Dundalk branch in January 1910, that he knew of several children, who were 'unable to attend school for want of clothing or for want of food'. In one instance he remembered where the head of the house was sick for seven weeks and there was absolutely no food in the house. The children could not go to school, and the parents were summoned to court. Fortunately, Dr McDonnell was on the Bench, so they were not fined.

Many of the Association's branches set up a scheme of school dinners so that children would be assured of at least one good meal a day during term time. The *Irish Times*, in an editorial on April 16th 1913, praising the work of the WNHA, noted that 80 to 90 schools were receiving meals from various branches ('for who could expect half-starved children to learn?') and added 'The work which the Association does for the children of Ireland establishes its greatest claim to public support'.[12] Some of the schemes were more elaborate than others – in Clonmel for instance, the local branch of the WNHA provided cheap meals in a dining-room every day from 1 pm to 3.30 pm and these were not confined to school children only. Food could be eaten there or taken away and was sold at prices from a half penny for a small cup of soup, cocoa, tea or coffee, or slice of bread and jam, to fourpence for a full dinner of meat, green vegetables and potatoes, plus pudding. The main course consisted of stews, bacon, sausages, or fish on fast days. Children came in at three o'clock, after school, and soup, jam rolls, and rice pudding were their favourites. Breakfast was also served from 9 am. Meals were given out on production of a ticket, bought at the door.

The food provided by the mid-Antrim branch was less elaborate, but it was consumed on the school premises. Cocoa, sugar and milk were provided by the Branch and children got a hot drink every day, prepared by the mistress in the school, and the clearing up was done by the girls themselves. Each child brought one penny on a Monday morning, and that paid for the week's cocoa. A photograph of some of the children who received these 'cocoa dinners,' taken by Lady Aberdeen, appeared in *Sláinte* in January, 1911. On Valentia Island Lady Fitzgerald, Vice-President of the local WNHA, supplied milk daily to the school during the winter months, and in Carlow the Association opened a milk depôt where milk and soda or plain milk could be had for one penny per half pint glass and soup was available on certain days in winter at one penny per pint.

Shortage of milk during the winter months was a problem nationwide, so much so that a special Viceregal Commission was set up to look into the matter. The Commission was impressed by the way in which the labourers gave their evidence at the Cork sitting. They spoke in:

> ... an extremely intelligent manner, and showed that there was an absolute and immediate necessity to improve the milk supply in the district.

Not only the quantity but the quality of the milk needed to be improved and the Branch Notes in *Sláinte* regularly report calls for the inspection of dairies, the testing of milk and the installation of sterilising and pasteurising plants. There were recommendations now and then that goats' milk be made available, as it was known to be free of tuberculosis. There was, however, a prejudice against goat-keeping in Ireland, as Lady Aberdeen pointed out at the first meeting of the Irish Goat Society (April 16th 1912) which was founded largely through her efforts. Goats needed to be rehabilitated in public favour, she said, because of the careless manner in which they were kept. They were not properly fenced in, strayed, caused damage to plants and trees, and were poor milkers because of neglect. The society aimed to improve the various breeds of goats in Ireland and to educate people, especially cottagers, in the proper management of the animals. As she had previously told the *Evening Herald* (13th April) she herself had:

> ... ten or twelve goats here at the Vice-Regal Lodge ... I once had a goat for one of my children who was delicate, and the animal used to travel about with me wherever I went.[13]

Later that month the *Evening Herald* described the menagerie at the Viceregal Lodge as numbering about one hundred prize dogs and puppies, with thirty cats and kittens in a cattery. There was also a collection of goats – thirteen or fourteen of them, including two billy goats called 'Musket' and 'Charlie' – and their milk was fed to the cats and dogs, supplemented by milk from a Black Dexter cow. In spite of the efforts of the Irish Goat Society, faithfully recorded in *Sláinte*, goat-keeping never became widespread in Ireland, although the breed was strengthened by the introduction of the Toggenburg and Anglo-Nubian strains and the milk yield improved.

Sláinte, April 1912, reported that farm labourers suffered lack of milk when they no longer resided with the farmer as he then felt no obligation to supply it to them. They often had no more than one pint a day during winter months even though there might be five or six children in the family. In industrial centres like Belfast and Newry, children were being reared on tea, so that later on they refused to drink milk. Home baking was a lost art because of the difficulty of getting milk and in rural districts the use of porridge seemed to have died out. One realises, of course, that *Sláinte* magazine was aimed not at the actual sufferers from disease, or those who lived in dirt and squalor often through no fault of their own, but was intended for the enlightenment of the educated, comparatively well-to-do members of the WNHA and their friends. The more knowledge they could acquire the better equipped they would be to help the less fortunate and less articulate members of society to whom they owed a duty of care. They would also be in a position to point out to local authorities how far ahead other countries were in matters of public health.

Ishbel herself made contributions to the magazine from time to time, usually articles about hospitals and institutions she visited abroad, and generally they were written in a brisk, factual style. Her account of a trip to Canada and the United States on the occasion of the1909 Quinquennial meeting of the ICW is mainly reportage on the Congress itself and on visits to hospitals and sanatoria but she did allow herself a few comments on her journey aboard the RMS *Megantic*. 'The arrangements for ocean travelling in these days,' she wrote, 'are such as to remove all difficulty and anxiety, even from the most timid traveller.' She noted that there had been an 'extraordinary improvement' in accommodation for second and third-class passengers. Not only were their sleeping arrangements spacious and comfortable, they now had 'their own Dining Room, Smoking Room and Reading Room'.[14]

The sterner realities of life were still on Ishbel's mind, however, and she reminded readers that there was strict medical supervision of passengers – no one with a disease was allowed to travel, for the health regulations in Canada and the US forbade the entry of any such passenger to the country, and the shipping company was required by law to return that person, free of charge, to the port of embarkation. Furthermore, she wrote, any immigrant who developed a disease within three years of landing in the United States must be brought back home by the shipping company. Under these rules, she added, many were sent back to Ireland suffering from consumption.

Only once, as far as I can discover, did she fall into the fashionable trap of being sentimental about tuberculosis. This was in an account of a meeting she had with a young invalid, Mademoiselle Kamm, who lived in Geneva. A sufferer herself from tuberculosis, she had gathered money for Day Camps where out-patients attending TB Dispensaries could spend the day resting on long chairs in open-air galleries, with a 'bright-faced' nurse in attendance. She had also established a sort of union of invalids, by asking patients to inscribe helpful sentiments in an album, which was then passed around to cheer up others. Ishbel described the young girl as resting in a:

> ... bower of a bedroom, daintily decorated in pink and white, and her whole face suffused with happiness, as I told her that I had that morning seen her 'Galeries' ... actually used by patients. "Oh, Madame," she said "tell them how happy I am; show them my photograph and tell them that there is nothing like working for others, and that I die rejoicing in the thought that by God's blessing this enemy of the human race is to be driven out of the world through the people of all countries working together for God and humanity."[15]

The photograph accompanying the article shows an extremely pretty young girl lying amid flowers on a be-frilled bed, beaming out at readers. The comparison that comes to mind, anachronistic as it is, is with the popular image of St Thérèse of Liseux, another sufferer from TB, whose inner steel has been so glazed over with sentimentality as almost to disguise it.

The treatment of tuberculosis sufferers in sanatoria was dealt with in many articles and the views expressed by writers give an insight into the thinking of the times. Ishbel herself said at the opening of the Allan A Ryan Home in August 1910, that she wanted the place to be 'a "home" and as little as an institution as possible', and the message of goodwill received from Dr Hermann Biggs, Medical Adviser of the Board of Health of New York City expressed the same hope. 'Institutions,' he said 'should be so attractive that people would want to go there.' Optimism was a large factor in recovery, so patients should be encouraged to believe in a cure, and they must be ready to co-operate in their treatment and accept that it was for their benefit. Dr Biggs was a fervent believer in the curative properties of fresh air.

> I have no doubt that if the Irish peasantry should leave their homes and live in open sheds, in a decade most of the tuberculosis would

have disappeared from among them.

In his sanatorium at Otisville, New York, patients must sleep on open porches out of doors under all conditions. The temperature sometimes fell to ten or fifteen degrees below zero but there were never any cases of pneumonia. Too much rest was bad for patients, he had found, so now it was a matter of policy to set convalescents to work. They were employed as 'nurses, orderlies, helpers, gardeners and waiters' (but not as cooks) and this kept down the maintenance costs of the institution.[16]

Work was also advocated in an article in *Sláinte*, in September 1910, on 'Tuberculosis among the Working Classes' which described the running of the Sanatorium at Benenden in Kent, where, once patients showed an improvement in health, they were 'set to work and developed muscles instead of fat'.[17] This made life more interesting for them and most people were grateful to have an occupation. Not everyone would be happy with this régime, it seems, because in the course of a WNHA Council meeting reported in *Sláinte* in June 1913, Lady Aberdeen said that:

> ... it would be a good thing if local branches before sending patients
> up to Peamount would impress upon them that it was part of the
> treatment that they should do some work, so that when they were
> asked to work in the Sanatorium they would not think it *infra dig*.[18]

Therapeutic though it undoubtedly was, there was an element of moralising in this insistence upon work based upon the Victorian and Edwardian horror of the undeserving poor, and the fear that honest working men might be corrupted by idleness and unaccustomed luxury. This fear is actually spelled out in an article in *Sláinte*, March 1910, entitled 'The Financial Factor in the Crusade against Consumption' by Alexander Walker, MD. The author is critical of the building and maintenance costs of sanatoria 'for the poorer classes'. The first sanatoria were intended for wealthier people, 'and in those, architecture, appointments and dietary were suited for people of fastidious tastes and delicate appetites'. Those running sanatoria for poorer people unconsciously imitated this treatment, with the result that the present methods of construction were wrong and unnecessarily expensive. There was no need to use stone or brick. 'All that is needed,' he writes, 'is protection from rain and cold winds' and new techniques meant that a building could last thirty years, which was quite long enough. He then lists the advantages of inexpensive structures. They:

1 can be begun on a small scale, and extended as needed;
2 allow for easy segregation according to sex, class, and stage of disease, so should be châlets not blocks;
3 afford greater opportunities for patients to adapt themselves to rural life and for learning trades. Patients, he points out, are not 'cured,' the disease is merely 'arrested,' so it would be foolish to return to the city for a year or more;
4 are more "home-like" and far more to the taste of the poor. Here he adds that 'a life of luxury and idleness has the worst influence on those who must return to humble conditions of life'.

None of these advantages could be found, says Dr Walker:

> ... in a palatial building with its endless corridors, its well-kept gardens, handsome furnishings and its large staff of nurses and patients. [Running costs were very high in such a building, for] the more imposing the structure, the greater is the cost of maintenance. A large staff, more numerous and possibly higher-paid servants, a more pretentious style of living and a more dainty dietary naturally accompany residence in a building of imposing appearance.[19]

Practical and moral arguments were, therefore, in favour of simple treatment and accommodation for the sick poor. The question of suitable surroundings for those of the lower classes who were to be treated for tuberculosis had already been addressed by Dr Parsons, Physician to the Royal National Hospital for Consumption in Ireland, in a lecture on the occasion of the Exhibition of 1907 and reprinted in the second volume of *Ireland's Crusade Against Tuberculosis*, edited by Lady Aberdeen. He quoted a German doctor as disapproving of verandas or open-air galleries in private sanatoria because patients might chat about social, religious or political questions, 'which prevent rest and raise the temperature'. He went on:

> These objections, forcible as they doubtless are in sanatoria for the wealthier classes, do not carry so much weight in sanatoria for the poor, where all belong to the same social class, and the majority to the same religion.[20]

It was quite safe so, given the unthinking homogeneity of the lower classes, to allow them to associate on open-air verandas and galleries, and Irish sanatoria were designed accordingly.

The daily regimen of a sanatorium was described in an article 'The

Control of Tuberculosis at Rotherham', also in the March 1910 issue of *Sláinte*. A typical day started at 6.30 am when the patient was given a pint of milk. Breakfast was at 8.45 am and consisted of porridge, bacon and bread, with jam or butter and a pint of tea. At 11 am another pint of milk was consumed, and at 12.45 pm. came lunch – roast pork, vegetables, milk pudding and half a pint of milk. At three o'clock there was another pint of milk, and at 5.30 pm the patient was given tea, bread and butter, jam, or, three times weekly, eggs. At 8 pm there was bread and the last pint of milk of the day. Once a week the patients received fresh fruit or fresh vegetables. In the intervals between eating and drinking there were medical inspections, and some carefully graded recreation but patients were advised that:

> health must rank before amusement. Games which engender heat or excitement are to be avoided, and the reading and writing of letters must be restricted to the forenoon.

There was to be no singing except as advised, and no smoking except by permission. Conversation was to be cautious. 'Don't talk about your symptoms to anyone but your doctor', patients were told, 'and never talk to other patients about their symptoms.[21] Conversation of any kind had to cease at 8.30 pm, and then the lights went out.

An account of life in Peamount Sanatorium was given by a 'Nurse/Patient' in *Sláinte*, December 1913, and although it gave no details of the regimen the impression it conveyed was of a peaceful and caring place. The writer described the charm of the rural surroundings, the sound of the birds in the early summer mornings and the scent of new-mown hay, while within the buildings the 'kind and conscientious staff' saw to the patients' every needs. She kept to herself for the first few days but then realised that 'Life still held Duty for me' and settled into the routine of the place. 'It would be hard' she wrote, 'for anyone to be lonely or unhappy for long at Peamount' because of the friendliness and real kindness of the staff. Lady Aberdeen was a frequent visitor, and the writer praised her tact in giving her 'some small WNHA work' to do while she was ill. She noted, too, that the Countess was popular with the patients, because of her 'ready sympathy,' and 'the kind word she had for all'. The article is illustrated with photographs of Peamount, including one of the little Church, where the Nurse/Patient found an aura of deep spirituality and a sense of 'Our Lord's presence' when she attended Sunday Mass there.[22]

Lady Aberdeen's crusade against tuberculosis emphasised the importance of a healthy diet, but ignorance of food values was widespread. The country pharmacist who wrote about the appalling conditions in rural schools (*Sláinte*, September 1909) was worried by the way in which young mothers fed their children. 'Hardly a day passes,' he wrote, 'but some poor distracted creature comes to me about her baby which she has nearly killed with kindness.' He was glad to see that the WNHA was providing pamphlets telling people how to eat properly, but he asked the Association to have them illustrated and use them to tell mothers what *not* to give babies, ie 'bread, bacon, potatoes, cornflour, tea, etc'. He also asked for them to be made simpler, pointing out that ordinary people didn't understand what 'starchy' meant, never mind 'farinaceous'. A sample food budget for a family of seven – five children, mother and father – promising sound nutrition at a cost of 8/- [40p] per week was published in *Sláinte* in April 1909 and prompted a typically savage comment from *Sinn Féin*. Headed 'A Herring or Two Eggs for Herself,' it read:

> *Sláinte*, one of Lady Aberdeen's latest ventures, had an epoch-making article recently on "A Family Budget at 8s a week". No danger of the experiment being tried at the Castle. Here is a piece of information: An average herring contains more nourishment than two eggs!
> But "Herself", it is to be presumed, has no ambition to go on a herring diet.[23]

A more cogent criticism was made in a letter by a reader in the June issue of *Sláinte*, who pointed out that at the prices currently being charged for staples such as flour, oatmeal, milk, potatoes, etc, there was no hope of buying food for a family of seven for 8/- per week. She took issue too with the contention that the family could make do with four ounces of tea and one pound of sugar per week. In his less than convincing reply, Dr E Coey Bigger, author of the original article, queried the prices the correspondent had quoted and suggested that there was overcharging in her district. His prices, he said, were average ones, and in any event 'the principal object of the article was to show how to obtain the best nutritive value for the least money. Prices were mentioned only for purposes of comparison. Furthermore, tea was never intended for children, and sugar should be kept to a minimum. *Sláinte* published recipes for cheap nourishing food, using vegetables, oatmeal, eggs, the cheapest cuts of meat such as belly of pork, scrag end of mutton, rabbit and neck of lamb. The *Sláinte* recipes were usually straightforward and the quantities were sufficient for normal appetites, but an occasional daintiness crept in. A recipe for an 'Economical Dish of Eggs and Cheese for Four People,' published in *Sláinte*, September 1914, called for two eggs, two ounces of cheese and one slice of bread, all of which a hungry man could down in minutes. At the *Uí Breasail* Exhibition in 1911 there were lectures and working demonstrations. By then the suggested family budget had gone up by 6d, to 8s.6d [42¹/₂p] per week, but this too was found by correspondents to *Sláinte* to be inadequate. Considering that the people who read the magazine and who wrote letters on the subject of feeding families on a very limited income, were not those to whom the advice was primarily directed, their negative reaction was an interesting and important one. If they, relatively well-to-do, educated, free from emotional constraints, and capable of devising theoretically-adequate dietary programmes, found the proposed budgets unrealistic and therefore unworkable, what use were these budgets to people without their background and advantages?

The WNHA was on more secure ground when it dealt with the feeding of infants. The Nathan Strauss Pasteurised Milk Depôt in Dublin provided pure milk for babies and the infantile mortality in the area showed a drop as more mothers availed of the service. Doctors and nurses in the district gave out books of 'milk tickets' to poor mothers and they not only received the daily allowance of pasteurised milk for their babies but were given general advice on health, hygiene and the proper feeding of young children. It was recognised by the Association that 'breast was best', (a conviction shared by the medical officer at Guinness's Brewery, who gave out free milk to the employees only if the mothers were unable to breast-feed) but as it was not always possible for mothers to feed their infants naturally, then pasteurised cows' milk was the next best thing. It was necessary to instruct the mothers in how best to bottle-feed their babies, and the nation-wide Babies' Clubs run by the Association followed the same pattern as that set up in the Nathan Strauss Depôt. Mothers were shown how to sterilise bottles and the use of the 'feeding tube,' a long rubber appliance leading directly from a milk vessel into the baby's mouth was absolutely forbidden. The sale of this item, which it was impossible to disinfect, was illegal in France and in some of the states of the USA, and one of the recommendations of the Viceregal Commission on the Supply of Milk was that it should be illegal in Ireland also.

A glimpse of what ignorant mothers might be giving to their children is revealed in the illustrations in *Sláinte*, September 1910. These are captioned 'Don't Give Baby a Taste of Everything You Have Yourself' and show a table laden with beer, bread, tinned salmon, tinned pineapple, potatoes and cucumber. Advice on hygiene is given, 'Don't Stand Milk Basin Near the Sink,' and the picture shows flies over the uncovered milk, cockroaches on the wall and the floor, and mice on the ground and on the draining board. Presumably this is what the ladies of the Association found in some of the houses they visited – a state of affairs that would either have defeated them or encouraged them to greater efforts. It was emphasised in several reports that 'ignorance, not want of affection in mothers' was at 'the root of most of the evils'.

These household visitations were not always welcome, as was acknowledged now and then in the Branch notes. The secretary of the Mullingar Branch, referring to the work of the District Nurse, reminded members of the Association in her report in February 1910, that there was 'a natural prejudice of the poor afflicted against a person invading their homes to do them good,'[24] and in a report in *Sláinte* in January 1911, the secretary of the newly-formed Mullacash Branch emphasised the importance of educating young people in health matters. She wrote:

> The older women have settled convictions and resent (very
> naturally) any attempt to change them. They very strongly repudiate
> any right to enter their homes, and find fault with their management
> of them.[25]

It would seem that some, at least, of the energetic members of the Association were sensitive and tactful in their dealings with the poor, and aware that their efforts would not always be welcome, an attitude far removed from that attributed to them by their critics. Ideally, members would, as the Secretary of the Tullamore Branch said in her report (*Sláinte* March 1910), be expected 'to keep a friendly unofficial eye on matters affecting the health and sanitation of the district within their notice'.[26] The Londonderry Branch report, published in April 1910, indicated how members should behave. 'We work quietly and unostentatiously in the homes of the people and in the schools that are open to our visitors,' wrote the Secretary, adding that members conveyed 'in friendly fashion plain rules for healthy living' and that they dispensed sympathy as well as, 'at times, much-needed nourishment'.[27]

Sometimes the work of a local branch came up against the deep-rooted snobbery of a small community, as Lady Edith Gordon, native Kerrywoman and Nationalist sympathiser, found when she worked with the Killorglin branch of the WNHA. In her memoir *The Winds of Time*, she recalls how 'no crusade was ever started with more resolute determination'. The Committee 'impartially recruited from Catholics and Protestants' worked with enthusiasm, campaigning for public hygiene, the appointment of a District Nurse, and the establishment of an Infant Welfare Centre. In one of the principal streets of the town there were no sanitary arrangements; in another, the only access to the back yards of the houses was through the house itself, so that the 'cows, ponies and donkeys, had to be led through the living rooms and shops from the stables to the street'. The initial enthusiasm eventually faded away, and the question of 'social precedence' caused the closure of the Infant Welfare Centre. Families living in a more exclusive street in the town did not wish to mix with families from a less desirable area, and so on, right down to the poorest of the poor. 'You'd never know who you'd be mixing with' was the cry, so the babies were kept at home. Edith Gordon concludes her account:

> ... we came at last to the melancholy conclusion that since nothing we said would ever make any impression in Killorglin we might as well cease from our efforts and close the branch.[28]

Many of the reports referred to the help given to the branches by the clergy of all denominations – 'were it not for the help given by the local clergy we never would have made such progress', ran the Dundalk report of 1909 – and in many cases the Roman Catholic parish priest or curate in the district was either in the chair or spoke words of encouragement to the meeting – unlike Edith Gordon's curate who 'sarcastically remarked of the Killorglin WNHA Committee that "not half of them have their own necks washed".' The nuns, too, were generally enthusiastic, and co-operated with the WNHA in setting up the Guild of Good Health among the schoolgirls. Boys' Battalions which were also set up to teach boys the rudiments of hygiene and the importance of fresh air and exercise do not appear to have had the same co-operation and encouragement but this may have been due to the popular belief that these matters were more properly for women and young girls.

Persuading sufferers from TB to go to a sanatorium took a great deal of tactful perseverance because of the old fear of the workhouse, with its connotations of pauperism. Patients had to be convinced that the new sanatoria were very different places and furthermore, that there was a reasonable chance of a cure. Unfortunately, some cases were so far advanced before treatment in a sanatorium that the mortality rate was perceived as being very high and people quite naturally concluded that being sent to a sanatorium was a death sentence. The practice of sending incurable cases to a sanatorium was criticised by Dr Hanley, the Medical Superintendent of Peamount,* saying that:

> … to send people from far away to Peamount in almost a dying condition is a cruelty to them and to their friends and it is also very unfair to the Institution, inasmuch as it is depressing to the other patients, and it is not possible that anything could be done to help them. We are doing our very best.[29]

He had recently had to take in two men who were actually dying, and all he could do for them was to send for a priest to give them the last rites. Dr Hanley said there should be a shelter where these advanced cases could be sent where they could be cared for in their last moments, and where they would not be a danger to their family and friends.

When patients were persuaded to go to a sanatorium with a reasonable hope of a cure (what Lady Aberdeen described as 'economically cured', that is with a prospect of being fit for future employment), very often they were beset by worries about their family at home and how they would cope in the absence of what was often the sole breadwinner. A further worry was a long-term one – would they be able to get work in the future? This was a very real problem, and Lady Aberdeen had seen it as such from the beginning. In many cases men and women were unfit to return to their previous employment, as conditions there were unhealthy and therefore unsuitable. Light work, preferably in the open air or in well-ventilated premises would be ideal, but although Lady Aberdeen lobbied vigorously for a suitable scheme, and canvassed individuals and groups to provide work for ex-patients, the results were disappointing. Opportunities were few, and in any case TB was a stigma; the more so now that it was known

---

* Dr Hanley's appointment in 1913 had caused much controversy for it had been alleged that the disqualification of the previously-appointed Dr McGrath to the post had been unfair. Lady Aberdeen had played a large part in the appointment of Dr Hanley and she had been accused of favouritism.

to be infectious. Lady Aberdeen was reported in *Sláinte*, October 1910, as having been very distressed when she learned that, following on the visit of the travelling Health Exhibition to Killeaden the family and friends of a girl known to be a sufferer from consumption were shunned for fear of infection. She added that a woman's rightful place was at sick beds, no matter what illness, and there she would learn how to guard against it.

The fear of infection was widespread and well-founded as instanced by the report made by Dr Colohan, Medical Officer of Health for Galway, to a branch meeting of the WNHA. He told his listeners that patients in the Galway Hospital were 'complaining about having to lie side by side with consumptive patients and were refusing to use their cups and plates'. He added that he would do the same himself. Employers, even if they had work suitable for ex-patients were reluctant to take them on, and employees did not wish to mix with them. This problem, in spite of continuing efforts down through the years, was not solved until modern drugs offered a complete cure for tuberculosis and former sufferers were no longer seen as a health hazard.

The other worry, however, regarding patients' families at home could, to some extent, be eased. Many branches of the WNHA had what was called the Samaritan Committee, a group whose function it was to alleviate distress in the homes of the poor. They helped out in every possible way, providing clothes, shoes, food, bedding and furniture and were sometimes able to get work for healthy younger members of the family. Holidays for children were arranged by them, and they advised on the care of the TB sufferer when he or she returned, emphasising the need for strict hygiene and isolation where needed and where possible. This work was done in conjunction with the District Nurses, and in Dublin, the Tuberculosis Nurses, and other charitable organisations such as the St Vincent de Paul Society, the Social Service Guild and the Strangers' Friend Society.

At the fifth annual meeting of the Central Dublin Branch of the WNHA, in January 1913, Lady Aberdeen, who was presiding, was quoted in *Sláinte*'s, February issue as having told the members that the Association had offered its services on the proposed Care Committees to look after the welfare of the families of patients in sanatoria. She had pointed out to the Commissioner that the Association was expert in the problems posed by TB, and that the Samaritan Committees had for years looked after families in the homes of sufferers. The treatment of a man or woman in a sanatorium would be useless, she stressed, if food, nourishment, clothes, separate bedrooms and beds could not be included in the treatment. 'What use is it,' she asked, 'sending them to sanatoria, if we do not look to the family?' Dr Prudence Gaffikin, attending physician at Peamount, emphasised the importance of relieving patients' minds about home conditions:

> If they are not peaceful, we are wasting our money. We might as
> well pour water on stones and expect things to grow on them as to
> give food and medicine to patients who are breaking their hearts.[30]

Distribution of food, clothing, blankets and good advice was helpful, of course, and eased the immediate distress of many poor people, but the insoluble problem was that of accommodation. There was nothing the ladies of the Samaritan Committees, the Tuberculosis Nurses, the Dispensary doctors or anyone else could do about the poor housing conditions, especially in Dublin and other large cities and towns. The Association was well aware of this and the frustration felt by its members was vented in a speech by Lady Aberdeen in her role as President of the newly-formed Housing and Town Planning Association to a Conference of delegates in October 22nd, and reported in the November issue of *Sláinte*. She asked:

> What is the point of spending money fighting TB if sufferers come
> 'back from sanatoriums to crowded, unhealthy dwellings? What's
> the use of rescuing children if their mothers have to live in
> overcrowded contaminated dwellings?[31]

That indeed was the question, but it could not be answered by the WNHA nor by any voluntary body. It was a matter for the state.

Of houses, health and more

B Y MID-1913 IT WAS clear to Ishbel Aberdeen that her crusade against tuberculosis was being fought by her loyal troops of the WNHA with vigour and determination and that battles were being won every day against ignorance and apathy. These were only minor victories, however, and the war would never be won until the twin obstacles of poverty and bad housing were overcome. There was nothing she could do about poverty apart from ameliorating some of its worst effects in individual cases. Even her successful craft industries could help no more than relatively few people. But there was, perhaps, a chance that she could do something about the housing situation. Admittedly the *Irish Times* had referred to her lack of progress in this field, saying in an article lauding the work of the WNHA, on April 16th 1912, that while 'the housing question lies at root of health movement [it is] … the one area where the Association has had little success',[1] but she was determined to attack the problem.

It was a problem that had been a source of worry to concerned persons for many years. Official reports regularly spoke of the dreadful conditions under which the poor of Ireland existed, not only in urban areas but in rural ones too. As Lady Aberdeen pointed out in her speech to the *Housing and Town Planning Association* in October 1912, the:

> …poets' and idealists' idea of escape from the towns [was] a fallacy
> … [there was] overcrowding and insanitary houses in country
> districts.

She knew what she was talking about, not only from personal visits to villages and provincial towns but from the information gleaned from the notes sent to her by local branches of the WNHA. These spoke of insanitary houses, and small cottages where windows could not be opened, damp dwellings, over-crowded and in a bad state of repair. The ladies of the Association, and their medical and clerical supporters, did their best with cottage improvement schemes – prizes for the best-kept home and the most productive garden, for example – but they could not, on their own, tackle the basic problem. Mrs Balfour may have spoken for many at the March meeting of Drogheda Branch of the WNHA in 1909, when referring to a proposal that a sanatorium be built, she suggested that better housing was a greater need.

The provincial towns and villages began to lag behind rural housing, but some energetic local authorities showed spirit and initiative, as was evidenced in the case of Roscrea, County Tipperary. In an article published in *Sláinte*, October 1911, Thomas Doody, Clerk of Roscrea Number One Rural District Council, described what had been done in the town. He started by saying that while the housing of the labourer had been improved greatly – according to the latest report 35,409 cottages had been built for him, and more were to come – people living in villages and small towns were not so lucky. In Roscrea, which was, he contended, typical of many other Irish towns, there were slum houses where there was:

> ... no pure air, no clear light, no adequate arrangement for the separation of the sexes, no sanitary convenience of any kind, no drainage. Darkness, dampness, dirt and dust ... everywhere, all creating a feeling of despondency and despair.

Spurred on by Lady Aberdeen's TB Exhibition when it visited Roscrea, the Council had decided to co-operate with Her Ladyship and the WNHA in their campaign against TB, and to remove the source of so much disease and misery. The worst of the slum cottages were knocked down and new ones were built that were fit for people to live in. Each cottage cost £160 and it was immediately rented out at one shilling and seven pence [about 8p] per week. Everyone was pleased with the arrangement, and there were plans for further slum clearance and new building.[2]

A very specific description of sub-standard dwellings in rural areas was given by Mr T J Byrne, ARIBA, Surveyor to the South Dublin Rural District Council in a paper read at the Health Conference and reported in *Sláinte*, October 1911. He spoke of the 'shanties' he had seen:

> ... four-walled structures on plan, walls without foundation or damp course, or even dry or mortar binding to the stone. The enclosed space (in the better class) no more than 14' x 10', and from 5' 7" high along the walls, 5' - 6' from one end to the other, and a wooden or sacking screen dividing space for beds from common living (and often sleeping as well) room.

Interestingly, Mr Byrne was not content merely to hold a utilitarian view of rehousing – it was not enough to build cottages that were adequate in the functional sense, he was concerned with aesthetic and social values. Too many of the cottages being built were undistinguished in design, and they were scattered haphazardly about the countryside instead of being grouped together in a more friendly fashion. He felt too that enough use was not being made of Irish building materials, which were eminently suitable for the purpose and were readily available.[3]

Housing in the country was substandard, but it was in Dublin that the worst overcrowding in the worst surroundings was to be seen. Slum conditions there have been well documented by social historians working from contemporary statistics, and Joseph V O'Brien in his book, *Dear Dirty Dublin*, gives a vivid picture of what tenement life was like. These mouldering, once-elegant houses, some owned by members of the Dublin Corporation, had 'cracked walls, leaky roofs, rickety stairs, broken windows and worm-eaten floors'. Water supplies often consisted of one tap in a back yard, and sanitation was almost non-existent. The open doorways allowed free access to unlit hallways at night, and these spaces, reeking with urine, excreta, vomit and alcoholic fumes were open to prostitutes, criminals and derelicts. According to the census of 1911 there were over 21,000 Dublin families living in one-room tenements, with 60% of the rooms containing more than three persons.

O'Brien goes into details and tells of one family that had two rooms and a closet, 'but the family consisted of husband, wife, wife's mother and seven children aged between one year and seventeen'. In another instance three families, ten persons in all, lived in a room that was an entrance to another crowded room where parents and seven children slept in straw on the floor, without any covering. In yet another, a husband, wife, her brother, and seven children (one of whom was dying of TB) were living in one room. Poverty in all cases was extreme, and furniture, crockery and general household effects were rudimentary and makeshift. A broken bedstead, a stool, a zinc bucket, a can, mugs and jam jars for drinking were often the only items found in these rooms.[4] One of these habitations was brought to the attention of the public by an editorial in the *Irish Times* on September 19th, 1913, which described how William O'Leary, his wife and six children, aged between one and thirteen years, lived with O'Leary's brother and his consumptive child in one room in Marlborough Street. William and his brother Patrick were charged with assault during the riots which took place in the city and it was at their trial that details of their living conditions emerged. These slums were, thundered the *Irish Times* 'a physical danger, a moral degradation, a grave social peril for us all' but what was to be done about them?[5]

In these conditions how could sufferers from TB be isolated from their families? There simply wasn't the space, the ventilation, or the minimum of equipment that was needed for even semi-isolation. In spite of these drawbacks the tuberculosis nurses employed by the WNHA found that families were very co-operative, even those who, because of poverty, lived in the cheapest accommodation, the top back of a tenement.

> Considering difficulties caused by illness, lack of sanitary appliances, absence of water supply or disposal of rubbish, rooms are kept in fairly cleanly condition. The Nurses' instructions about disposal of sputum, opening windows etc, are received in a kindly manner and the people do their best to carry them out.[6]

Nevertheless there were sad stories of children dying of TB while their healthy younger brothers and sisters slept underneath the bed, and one particularly gruesome report told of a man coughing his lungs out in the room where his wife was making black puddings for sale. Obviously the Dublin housing problem could not be solved piecemeal – what was needed was a complete reform of housing policy and a break-up of the tenement system. Dublin Corporation, according to Mary E Daly in her work, *Dublin, the Deposed Capital*, 'at no stage evinced any strong hostility to tenement landlords'.[7] A comprehensive building programme would have had beneficial effects 'not least the provision of employment at a period when there was widespread unemployment, especially among building workers and general labourers', but the financial burden was too great for a mere local authority. Some slum clearance had been done, but it was a slow business – Ormond Market, for instance, 'a rookery of tenements and ruinous sites' had been listed as unhealthy in 1876, yet it remained a derelict waste ground until Lady Aberdeen persuaded the Corporation to lease it to her. With the support of well-wishers and the expert help of two gardeners, Miss Tuke and Miss Geddes, the site was transformed into a garden playground. A similar transformation took place in Augustine St where St Monica's playground adjoined the Babies' Club there. In Ormond Market a boys' camp was set up in September 1912, by Lady Aberdeen. Here boys between 14 and 18 years of age, who had suitable references and who were in good health could stay every night from 6 pm on. Bed cost one penny, as did breakfast, or a hot bath.

A cold bath or shower was free.

Dublin Corporation was jolted out of inactivity by a tragedy that occurred on the 2nd September, 1913, when two houses in Church St, numbers 66 and 67, collapsed in the late evening, killing seven people. The death toll would have been higher if the occupants (46 members of eleven families) had all been in bed. Many of them were, fortunately for them, enjoying themselves at an entertainment in the nearby Father Mathew Hall and escaped the collapse that killed three adults, two youths and two small children. The landlady of the premises said that she had made repairs that satisfied the Corporation, and that she had never been told that the buildings were dangerous. Critics of the Corporation, notably the *Irish Times*, renewed their calls for a comprehensive policy of slum clearance, and noted that the current industrial unrest could be linked to the degrading conditions in which the Dublin workers lived. The paper called for a Viceregal Commission on Housing, and were supported in this plea by the WNHA. In the event, what the Chief Secretary, Augustine Birrell, set up was a committee appointed by the Local Government Board to look into the whole question of housing in the city. 'The Dublin Housing Inquiry', the published record of the inquiry is, as Joseph V O'Brien points out:

> ... one of the most important social documents in the history of
> modern Dublin, delineating in great detail the living conditions,
> housing, rents and wages of the working classes of the city in the
> closing years of direct British rule.[8]

It has proved a valuable source of material for social historians, but its immediate impact was negligible. The overall recommendations did not commit the government to any new expenditure and Dublin Corporation was left with its major problem – finance – unsolved. The *Leader* suggested on 6th December 1913, that the difficulty of acquiring land for building could be overcome by using some of the unoccupied land in the Phoenix Park – Crown property – for housing but this was not taken seriously.

The time was now right for Lady Aberdeen to act. First she led a deputation of WNHA members to the Chief Secretary, Mr Birrell, at the Castle, to underline the close connection between housing and health. She proferred to him the Association's resolution which emphasised the:

> ...urgent need for better housing of the working classes in cities and
> in towns, the present conditions being a menace to the health of our
> people, and a reproach to civilisation.

As she reasonably pointed out, the finance needed for a new programme was beyond the scope of private and local enterprise, so government funding was needed. Public health was, after all, an imperial matter, as well as being of local importance, and she reminded Birrell that a deputation from the Association of Local Authorities had been with him the previous week, with the same request. Assistance was needed if they were to build 'comfortable and sanitary houses for the working classes at rent within their means'. Dublin was not the only area where conditions were bad; there was overcrowding in Limerick city; in Athy the houses had half an inch of water on their floors; in Castlecomer thirteen people were found living in one room; in Newbridge tenants paid high rents for totally inadequate housing, and in Tralee patients returned from the sanatorium to 'terrible hovels'. Mr Birrell was sympathetic, and expressed a hope that something would be done, although he could give no promises. He would, however, pass the matter on 'to more authoritative quarters'.

Lady Aberdeen now took more positive action. She would show how a city should look and how its inhabitants should be housed. At the *Uí Breasail* fête of 1911, one of the major attractions was the Cities and Town Planning Exhibition, which had been brought over to Dublin at the Aberdeens' own expense. It later toured the country as a Health and Housing Exhibition and although the *Irish Worker* sneered at it as 'farcical nonsense and tomfoolery'[9], it was well received in places as far apart as Belmullet and Cork. It inspired the founding of a Civics Institute and the Housing and Town Planning Association, of which Lady Aberdeen was President, and the creation of the Garden Playgrounds in Ormond Market and St Augustine Street. At a meeting of the Housing and Town Planning Association in early January, 1914, and reported in the *Irish Times,* the President informed them that they were going to stage a Civic Exhibition in Dublin in the following summer. She obviously had little faith in Birrell's influence in Westminster, and may have wondered if indeed he would exert himself to push the matter forward. She looked at the situation realistically, saying:

> Between the conviction that the present condition must not continue, and that something must be done, and the embodiment of the ideal we are reaching after, there is a mighty gulf, which at the present moment looks very black and which it will need all our courage and perseverance and patriotism to span.

An Exhibition, she went on, would help clear minds and concentrate efforts towards the housing of the people and the reconstruction of Irish towns and cities. Lady Aberdeen then listed what could be shown at a Civic Exhibition, as had been seen in other countries – housing, roads, sanitation, heating, lighting, water, food and milk supplies, and transport, especially facilities for workers who had to travel to their places of employment. Equally important were elegant public buildings, open spaces, playgrounds, recreational and educational facilities, art galleries, libraries and museums, while special attention must be paid to the needs of children, the sick and the aged. It was, she granted, a big project, and the time was short, but public opinion was on their side, and in any event it could be broken up into sections, with responsibilities allocated to various committees. Nothing less than the whole reconstruction of Dublin would do if the city was to thrive in the future, and she proposed that a Civic Survey be carried out, adding that His Excellency, the Lord Lieutenant felt so strongly on the subject that he was offering a prize of £500 for the best Civic Plan 'with the special object of furnishing adequate and convenient housing for working classes round the city'. The adjudication of this prize would be made by a selected committee of experts with international reputations.[10]

It was agreed to hold the exhibition and a site was obtained in the old Linenhall barracks, in Henrietta Street, on the north side of the city, in the midst of an area of extreme poverty. Work went feverishly ahead to have everything ready for the opening on July 15th 1914, and Lady Aberdeen threw her energies into organising and publicising the event. She was scheduled to attend a meeting of the International Council of Women in Rome in June but would be back in time for the opening, and had no doubt that her carefully-chosen committee would have everything under control. She herself persuaded the American Mr Gordon Selfridge, the king of shopkeepers, and a valuable old acquaintance since the days of the Chicago Fair in 1893 when he had helped in the sale of Irish goods, to visit Dublin in June and to give a lecture on 'The Romance of Commerce'. Tickets for the talk in the Mansion House cost 2/6 (12½p) each, (proceeds to the Exhibition Committee) and a large number of people attended.

Preparations were well advanced, and the Exhibition looked as if it would open on time, but the political unrest in Ireland was causing unease, so much so that on the 6th July Lady Aberdeen sent a letter to

British newspapers emphasising that it was quite safe to come to Ireland. The Belfast City Council, however, refused to send a representative to the opening ceremony in the Linenhall Barracks, because 'in the unsettled state of the country an official visit might be misinterpreted'.

The *Irish Times* in its editorial of the 15th July welcomed the opening of the Exhibition, saying that the organisers deserved credit for their courage. 'They have chosen a time,' said the writer 'when men's minds are grievously troubled about politics, and the nations' destinies are in the melting pot,' but whatever society might yet emerge in Ireland would have need of their vision and encouragement. There was a goodly gathering of important people at the official opening on July 15th, including municipal representatives from all over Ireland. A Civic Pageant starting from the Mansion House at 1.15 pm was cheered on its way through the city, as was the Lord Lieutenant's party, escorted by the Fifth Royal Irish Lancers. Mr Birrell presented a golden key to Her Excellency, and an address praising her for her efforts on behalf of the people of Dublin:

> You are not likely to be forgotten in this city for your devotion,
> unfaltering, persistent, restless, ever-working for the welfare, the
> health and the prosperity of the Irish people.[11]

Birrell was no admirer of Lady Aberdeen or her husband but he was constrained by politeness and by custom to speak with unctuous flattery. At the time of the labour unrest – the great lock-out in October 1913 – Birrell wrote to Prime Minister Asquith complaining:

> … the Aberdeens are back and fussing about, attending deputations
> which are waiting *on me*. They can't be left out of anything for a
> moment. It is a capital disaster their being here at this critical time,
> but as I have no suggestion to make I ought not to send this
> agonized cry of acute misery[12].

The tributes paid to her Ladyship by the executive sub-committee of the Exhibition were more relevant and possibly more sincere. They commended her 'tact, judgement, business capacity, patience and kindness,' qualities which she always seemed to display when dealing with fellow-workers and subordinates, but most of which were lacking in her dealings with bureaucrats. Photographs of the occasion show her smiling contentedly, graciously accepting tributes and applause, and newspaper reports describe her as wearing a blue Wedgewood poplin gown, and a black hat trimmed with some feathers, ribbons and plumes.

Visitors to the Exhibition could travel there by tram – a service ran on a circular route from the south quays to the north, stopping at the entrance. Price of entry was six pence and once inside the ten-acre site, the public could gaze at pictures of Dublin showing its beauties as well as its black spots – the slums. Exhibits of housing projects in English, Scottish and Continental cities showed what was done elsewhere – that of Liverpool judged to be the most impressive and there were plans and models of cottages, as well as lectures in the Summer School of Civics under the direction of Professor Geddes, the town-planning expert. The various government departments, including the Land Commission, the Registry Office, the Congested District Board and the Department of Agriculture and Technical Instruction all had stands and there were demonstrations of poultry-rearing and bee-keeping. The Women's National Health Association showed what a hygienically-correct home should look like, and how the sick should be cared for. In the Industrial Section there was a keen demand for samples of jellies made by White, Tomkins and Courage, and porridge made from their oatmeal was also popular – although not as popular as the samples of cakes and biscuits from the nearby Jacob's stand.

In keeping with the spirit of the Exhibition the firm of Dockrells (builders' providers) showed models of ideal homes, and the Anglo-American Oil Company proved that their stoves were suitable both for heating the home and cooking all meals. Visitors interested in Arts and Crafts marvelled at the replica of the Ardagh Chalice made by the firm of jewellers, Hopkins and Hopkins, and on view at their stand. Then they admired the display of fine craft work in the King's Inns which had been arranged under the direction of W G Strickland, the Art historian. Here they could see a magnificent collection of eighteenth- and early nineteenth-century Irish silver (on loan from the National Gallery) as well as examples of internationally-famous Irish printing and book binding. There were practical cookery demonstrations and the boys of the Industrial Schools demonstrated the techniques of carpentry, tailoring and wire mattress-making.

Out of doors there were agricultural demonstrations, including the manuring of the land, and one of the major exhibits from Belfast was a municipal abattoir. The Dublin Corporation showed the latest methods of gas and electric street lighting and one of the most spectacular exhibits was their 'electric water fountain' which was illuminated at night. In the Child Welfare Section there were free medical and dental inspections of school children, which led Dr Prudence Gaffikin of the WNHA later to report in *Sláinte* (January 1915) that the majority of the youngsters examined suffered from malnutrition, defective sight, bad teeth and a general tendency to weakness of the chest.[13] There were, however, enough hand-picked, healthy children available to give a display of folk dancing, a new enthusiasm of Lady Aberdeen's, who had, the previous year, brought over from America Miss Elizabeth Burchenal, a leading light in the folk dance movement. The activity had proved popular in some Dublin schools, and a grand rally was held in the Phoenix Park, at the Civil Service Cricket Ground. One thousand two hundred children took part, and music was provided by the band of the West Kent Regiment.

Concerts and cinematograph programmes were held every half hour in the Hall of the Civic Exhibition (capacity 600) and the band in the Old Temple Gardens, lent by the King's Inns for the occasion, played musical selections throughout the day. There was a Punch and Judy Show, merry-go-rounds, a switchback railway, sailing boats and the usual side shows and the tea gardens served light meals all afternoon (1,000 of them served one Wednesday) under the direction of ladies from the WNHA branches in Terenure, Rathgar and Clondalkin. A local and immediate benefit to some of the poor citizens of Dublin came at the closing of the Exhibition. As it was being dismantled local residents invaded the premises and made off with certain items. Sir Patrick Abercrombie, winner of the town planning prize, recalled some years later that the Countess of Aberdeen had to stand helplessly by, 'as an enormous flock of people ... began, one by one, to remove the chairs and tables and carry them off home'.[14]

The Civic Exhibition was a success, and attracted 80,000 paying visitors during the six weeks of its run from mid-July to the end of August, although its popularity was somewhat affected by the outbreak of war between Britain and Germany on August 4th. The *Irish Times* pointed out in its editorial of 15th August:

> Theory is a very different thing from practice, and practice [Town Planning] must mean a large expenditure of money. The Exhibition will not give us this money.[15]

However, it hoped that the Exhibition would awaken public opinion – a hope that was dashed by the events of the years to come. Lord

Aberdeen's prize of £500 was awarded to Patrick Abercrombie for his Town Plan, 'Dublin of the Future,' but his scheme was never put into practice by the new native government.

Criticisms of the Exhibition came from the usual quarters, although Arthur Griffith's comments in *Sinn Féin* were surprisingly restrained, confined merely to a few words at the end of a review of a book on the history of the Linen Hall Barracks:

> We wish the Civic Exhibition every success. But ... may it not be
> that at present we hear too much of the slums of Dublin, and too
> little of the cause that made them slums?[16]

The same issue of the periodical (July 28th) carried a good-sized advertisement for the Exhibition, and there were no exhortations to the faithful not to attend or not to support the event. The *Leader*, which had once referred to Patrick Geddes as the 'Scotch crank,' was surprisingly enthusiastic about the Exhibition. Geddes was now the 'Scotch gentleman' who was running a school of civics in connection with the Exhibition. The writer believed that young men who take a real interest in public affairs, and perhaps, more particularly young priests, would be well advised to attend these courses.[17] On the 22nd August a longer article described the Exhibition in detail, with praise for the Artane Industrial School's 'tip-top exhibit' of furniture, tin-ware, boots, etc, the hair mattresses made by the girls from the Merrion School for the Blind and the tea and scones served by the orphan girls in the care of the Sisters of Charity. The correspondent greatly enjoyed the butter making competition where 'twenty rosy-cheeked, blooming girls, still in their teens' were at work, and was full of admiration for the section describing 'Practical Help for the Care of the Young'. There were doctors, dentists and nurses there, all giving demonstrations and the writer recommended that free tickets be given to priests to distribute 'where they would do most good'. The priests' influence 'would make for good attendance and results'. The article concluded with a strong recommendation to readers that they should attend what was an important and stimulating exhibition.[18]

The *Irish Worker*, the paper edited by the labour leader, Jim Larkin, was more critical, and in the issue of July 18th a piece appeared mocking the civil leaders and politicians who supported the show, describing the crowd assembling outside the Mansion House for the Civic Pageant as:

> ... policemen, ex-policemen, publicans, pawnbrokers, politicians,

patriots, pugilists, bookmakers, shebeen-keepers and vendors of adulterated milk.[19]

The procession itself, it said, was more like a funeral than a pageant. This jocose piece was followed on August 1st by 'An Open Letter to Lady Aberdeen' which was a bitter attack upon Her Ladyship, accusing her of callousness and hypocrisy. The writer had visited the Exhibition, 'with one object in view, the Child's Welfare Section' and what she saw there were 'very silly, very vulgar, very useless placards' that sickened her. Unlike Lady Aberdeen, she said, she cared personally for the babies in the slums – to her their fate was not simply a matter of theory, but 'a heartrending experience'. There was no point in Lady Aberdeen 'prating to the middle and upper classes of the improvidence and ignorance of the poor', while she did nothing to help the mothers and babies of the slums. During the lock-Out, or as Lady Aberdeen's friend, W Martin Murphy, called it, the "Strike", mothers and babies were starving and dying of hunger, and she did nothing to save them. Their blood was on her hands, because she was in a position to help, but stood by and said nothing.

> One and all of us, we are sick and tired of you and your cant and we heartily wish we had heard the last of it. Pottering and fooling with the most obvious of symptoms, whilst ignoring the big ugly festering wounds that are the roots of the disease can do nothing but mischief ... The cure cannot be attained by paid officials of middle class or aristocratic societies; your ignorance is too great, your inspiration too mean.[20]

As far as one can gather, the Aberdeens did not intervene personally in the labour disputes that lasted throughout 1913, culminating in the great lock-out that began in August and lasted until the end of January, 1914.* This disrupted the business of the city and caused appalling misery among the working classes who suffered through a winter, cold, hungry and, in some cases, homeless when they were evicted for non-payment of rent. There were riots, baton-charges and at least five people were killed in the street disturbances. Feelings ran high in the city and class hatreds were inflamed. Earlier labour disturbances in Dublin had been brought to the

---

* In his book *The Chief Secretary, Augustine Birrell in Ireland*, Leon O'Broin quotes a friend, G C Duggan, as telling him that Aberdeen put pressure on the Under Secretary, James Dougherty, to invite the labour leader to see him in the Castle, and that Larkin at once made himself at home there, stretching out on the sofa, and filling the air with smoke from his pipe.[21]

Lord-Lieutenant and the Castle for settlement, and it was widely believed that Lady Aberdeen had entertained Jim Larkin to tea in July 1908 in an attempt to settle the coal strike. A street ballad satirising the so-called stinginess of the Aberdeens contained the line: 'They split the ha'penny buns in two when Larkin comes to tea'. There is no mention in the Aberdeen reminiscences of this unusual social meeting, but Larkin himself in an editorial in the *Irish Worker* of April 5th 1913, refers to a meeting with the Lord-Lieutenant in November 1909 when Aberdeen's 'good philanthropic lady presided over the tea-table in the Viceregal Lodge'[22] and in the following week's issue he again mentions the meeting 'in Lady Aberdeen's boudoir'.[22] Larkin was vitriolic about both Aberdeens, and in the later editorial he accuses them of being overpaid idlers. He goes on to charge them with hypocrisy and asks them why, if 8/6 [42½p] per week is enough for a family of five to live upon, as stated by the WNHA, they themselves do not live at that standard and thereby save the workers of Ireland a great deal of money.[23]

During the months of terrible distress in Dublin, 1913-1914, the Samaritan Committees of the WNHA were busier than they had ever been and there were so many calls on their charity that it was difficult to cope with them all. Typical of many reports was that from the Central Dublin Committee which told of 98 weekly grocery deliveries, 280 separate food parcels and 169 garments given out, as well as extra bedlinen and blankets and coal. At Christmas Lord and Lady Aberdeen sent clothes and plum puddings which were distributed at a Christmas party. Lady Aberdeen's own contribution to the alleviation of distress was the opening of the *Sláinte* restaurant in Ormond Street. Here mutton broth could be had at one penny for half a pint and cooked meat and hot potatoes could be taken away for twopence and threepence per portion. Rice pudding with currants was very popular with children, who could buy it for a ha'penny or one penny. They could also get tea, coffee, milk or cocoa, with bread and jam for one ha'penny, but the restaurant manager reported that 'tea, regrettably, was still more popular than anything else, among children of the working class'. A full three-course dinner was available for six pence and was bought by 'regular customers drawn from different grades of society'. However, the manager noted, 'during the present deplorable strike a large number of tickets for free meals have been distributed to mothers and children affected'.

The charge that Lady Aberdeen was callously unconcerned by the effects of the labour troubles was no more than a piece of anti-establishment propaganda, as was the implication that she knew nothing of the realities of slum life. Nevertheless, her stated purpose in opening the restaurant, as quoted in *Sláinte*, January 1914, does sound altogether too lofty for the circumstances of the time. She had instituted the restaurant, it was said:

> ... so that women and children of the working classes may obtain wholesome and nourishing food under elevating, and above all, cheerful conditions when it is not possible for them conveniently to do so in their own homes. They may thus be encouraged when their own circumstances may more happily allow, to make their homes brighter and better for their husbands and children by devoting more care and thought both to the choice and selection, from its nutritive qualities, in the purchase of food, and to the preparation and service of it.[24]

One can readily see how such sentiments, with their barely concealed criticisms of the 'ignorant and feckless poor' who needed guidance from their betters, would antagonise many people, and blind them to the practical value of the work Lady Aberdeen and her Association were doing.

The Civic Exhibition of July-August 1914 was Lady Aberdeen's biggest and most public project in the period 1912-1914, while her day-to-day work went on at its usual frantic pace. Official activities connected with her husband's position had to be carried out, and she had to play her part as hostess at functions in the Castle and in the Viceregal Lodge. Drawing-rooms, State Dinners, Balls, functions of every description had to be graced by her presence, and she had to dress suitably for the occasion or risk being accused of rudeness. Fortunately, she had never lost her interest in fashion, and she continued to support Irish industries. Reports of her dress on public occasions almost always included mention of Irish poplin, tweed, linen, crochet or lace or embroidery done by the Royal Irish School of Art Needlework.

In addition to the big State occasions there were regular dinners on a smaller scale in the Viceregal Lodge for local worthies. These dinners were not to Augustine Birrell's taste – he described them in his reminiscences, *Things Past Redress*, as 'ordeals,' where:

> ...Divines of the various Protestant persuasions, doctors of medicine, intrepid surgeons, men of the law, skillful dentists and

perfumers and others whose special "lines" were sometimes easy, sometimes hard to discern.[25]

Guests at these dinner parties included people such as Lord and Lady Dunsany, Lord and Lady Carrick, Sir Nugent and Lady Everard, Sir William Thompson (the Registrar-General), and Lord and Lady Pirrie, all close friends of the Aberdeens. Violet Asquith in a letter to a friend (16th November 1912) described the 'social entertainments' there as 'very heavily-impregnated with duty and almost impossible to leaven'.[26] At least, if they were official functions the food arrived more or less on time, for when the Aberdeens were dining informally meals were much later. Maurice Headlam remembered that:

> ...one drawback ...to staying with the Aberdeens was the late hours
> – dinner was nominally at 8.30 but they would not appear till about
> nine o'clock. Then they went round the circle, saying a few words to
> each guest – for there were always guests in addition to the house
> party – and it was 9.15 or later before one set down to dinner.[27]

Katherine Tynan Hinkson, the writer, and a great and gushing admirer of Lady Aberdeen, referred in her memoirs *The Years of the Shadow*, to the haphazard arrangements for dining in the Lord Lieutenant's residence saying:

> Even if you were kept up to the small hours at the Viceregal Lodge,
> even if dinner was postponed till eleven o'clock one never minded.
> One was steeped in an atmosphere of warm comfort and kindness.[28]

Lady Edith Gordon was more specific in her recollections of visits to the Lodge, commenting in passing that as the Liberal Viceroy was ostracised by Unionist Ireland, the Aberdeens were spared having to spend time with people with whom they had nothing in common. 'The Lodge,' she wrote, 'was a delightful house to stay in.' Meals, however, were erratic:

> Dinner was seldom before 11 pm and often very much later. At the
> end of a strenuous day devoted to distant sanatoria and milk depôts,
> there were generally meetings to be attended in the evening, lasting
> until one's usual bedtime, but the most thoughtful of the ADCs
> invariably sent, on these occasions, soup and poached eggs to one's
> bedroom to sustain one between tea and the midnight meal.[29]

Lady Gordon pointed out that Lady Aberdeen was:

> ...capable not only of existing without food, but without sleep,

being frequently found by a house maid at sunrise, seated in her evening dress at her writing table.

Not the easiest of women to deal with, one imagines, and Marjorie Pentland admits as much when she quotes Miss Lucy Gwynn, first registrar of women students at Trinity College, Dublin as saying to her:

> Lady Aberdeen's own power of work was so amazing that she did not always realize when with others the flesh was weaker than the desire to help was strong; she would sit up till the small hours rather than leave anything unfinished, while her companions were too weary to think of anything but bed.[30]

Her energy was more than physical, it was fuelled by an inner compulsion to be up and doing, and it may perhaps have derived from a need to keep at bay her own private sorrows. The longing for her beloved son Archie must have always been there, and it was better to fill the lonely watches of the night with work than to give in to grief.

Marjorie Pentland ventures a cautious criticism of her mother's social manner when she goes on to say that although:

> ... she had an easy playfulness with children, a happy touch with the young, could laugh merrily over any discomfiture to herself, yet she felt out of her element in light conversation. She could not abide any hint of flippant gossip, any jokes about worthy people or serious matters.[31]

No wonder Birrell found the dinners tedious, for he was a man of outstanding intellectual quality, whose 'cultivated and independent personality,' according to his biographer, Leon O'Broin, 'was illumined by flashes of humourous declamation.' He 'persistently saw the funny side of public affairs and human behaviour,' an attitude not shared by many people, and certainly not by Lady Aberdeen. Violet Asquith records a conversation between Lady Aberdeen and Birrell in which he makes fun of one of the WNHA's workers. Lady Aberdeen described her as a very 'able woman ... ' only to be interrupted by Birrell saying 'The ugliest woman I ever saw – the very ugliest.' Lady Aberdeen (smiling rather bewilderedly) put " most efficient". Birrell – "Oh that face!"[32] Hardly an example of sparkling wit and humour, more a manifestation of Birrell's weariness with the Aberdeens and their worthiness that left no room for light conversation.

Overseas visitors came to Dublin and were entertained by the

Aberdeens with the correct amount of pomp and ceremony according to their office. One of those who stayed at the Viceregal Lodge was Mr Mackenzie King, Canadian ex-Minister of Labour, and later to become Prime Minister, who was greatly impressed by the working boys' camp in the old Ormond Market, and the children's playgrounds on waste spaces. When he returned home, he wrote to Dublin, according to Pentland, for more information about the scheme, 'in case something of the kind could be attempted in Canadian cities'.

A more important visitor in the summer of 1912 was Prime Minister Asquith who came over with other Liberal leaders at the request of John Redmond, leader of the Irish party, in order that he might see for himself the strength of Home Rule feeling in Dublin. Those who attended the public meeting which Asquith addressed in the Theatre Royal applauded him heartily, but a group of Suffragettes from England attempted to set the theatre on fire and caused some commotion. The following evening, their leader, Mary Leigh, hurled a hatchet at Asquith as he rode in an open carriage through the streets of Dublin. Fortunately for all involved it missed and Mary Leigh was later arrested and sentenced to five years' penal servitude. This harsh sentence was later suspended and Mary Leigh released because of ill health. On that visit the Prime Minister stayed with Birrell in the Chief Secretary's Lodge in the Phoenix Park, but when he came a second time in July 1914 he stayed with the Aberdeens and performed the opening ceremony for the Children's Pavilion at Peamount.

Over the years 1912-1914 there were small but vocal expressions of suffragism and women were sent to jail and in some cases forcibly fed. Appeals to the Lord Lieutenant often resulted in clemency, and in a letter from the Secretary of the Irish Women's Franchise League in respect of the release from prison of the leading Irish suffragette, Mrs Sheehy-Skeffington, the writer refers to Lord Aberdeen's personal intervention in the case being 'as it always has been, in the direction of humanity'. In this instance, following a phone call from Mrs Skeffington's doctor telling of the prisoner's ill-health, Lady Aberdeen had interceded with her husband. Dr Elizabeth Tennant in her letter describing the phone call, said that 'apart from any political or social aspect of the case Her Excellency as the "first woman" in the land, was most sympathetic towards one of her sex,' but this act of humanity gave a correspondent to the *Irish Times* an excuse to grumble about Lady Aberdeen's influence over her husband and her supposed interference in government affairs.

The Aberdeens were heckled by suffragettes on occasion but ignored these public protests. The society magazine *Truth* in its account of the Viceregal visit to the Horse Show in August 1913 said approvingly of Lady Aberdeen that she was 'a militant of peace and beneficence from whom the other kind of "militant" might learn a lesson', but it is safe to assume that while Lady Aberdeen deprecated the violent methods used by militants, she had never changed her original view that women were entitled to the vote and should have it. If she read the *Leader* she would not have been amused by that paper's contempt for what it called the 'sufferers' and its crude cartoons and verses implying that what these women really wanted were husbands whom they could nag. One wonders too, what she thought of the paper's policy statement of June 16th 1914 'Our view is that women who are units in the economic world should have votes,'[33] that is, women who managed, or controlled businesses or owned property, or even earned their own living, as in Belfast or Derry. No mention there of married women whose economic security came from their husbands.

Lady Aberdeen, as always, combined her duties as Viceregal hostess with her own active charitable and social work. There were innumerable WNHA meetings at local and at national level, involving a great deal of travel. There were the usual charity bazaars, fetes and sales of work to be opened and as the *Ladies' Field* said in its issue of 12th March, 1912:

> Her Excellency is back and taking up 101 engagements. There is no lady in society who leads such a busy life as Lady Aberdeen, and no charity ever appeals to her in vain to help, either by attending or patronising entertainments or meetings, or to give assistance in other ways.[34]

Then there were visits to Peamount, the editing of the magazine *Sláinte*, the writing of papers and speeches for conferences, but this was not enough. Always eager for something new to do, she held a 'House Castle Party' as the *Irish Independent* called it, to celebrate May Day 1913. This was in accord with John Ruskin's desire to revive old May Day customs in England, and Lady Aberdeen suggested they have a May Queen and Court, such as she had instituted in Canada. Miss Mabel Poë was selected as Queen and twelve counsellors were appointed to guide her during the year of her reign. It was an all-female party, the girls wearing white dresses, sashes of St Patrick's blue, and carrying wands of fresh flowers. Her Excellency cautioned that 'the May Queen should lead in doing good in public, as well as in private, life,' and the *Evening Herald*, describing the function, said 'If Her Ladyship can imbue our society girls with her own high ideals, it will be the greatest thing she has done for our country'.[35] A rather less formal May Day celebration was held in the playground at Ormond Market, where children danced round a maypole and then they, with their parents, were given milk and cakes.

The revival of May Day customs never caught on, but Lady Aberdeen's other new enterprise of that year seemed to have staying power, and would probably have survived if it had not been for the Great War. This was the Welcoming Club and Information Bureau, set up in 2 Ely Place, for the convenience of foreign visitors to Ireland. It was opened formally on August 30th, 1913, by the eminent English Jesuit preacher, Father Bernard Vaughan, and Lady Aberdeen said at the ceremony that the idea had really originated with the auxiliars of the National Health Association in the United States. Those good friends whose generosity had helped establish the pasteurised Milk Depôt, the P F Collier Dispensary and the Home at Sutton, had expressed a wish to have a permanent tie with Ireland that would be of benefit to Irish people returning home from the States. Too often these returned emigrants, or their families, came back to their homeland and were confused and bewildered by the changes that had taken place over the years. The Centre would be a place of welcome for them, and the staff would help them find the information they needed. It would also be of use in other ways, finding suitable accommodation for instance, places to eat, advice on business and commercial life, and the handling of letters and parcels. This forerunner of Tourist Advice Bureaux was a novelty, and a very useful one, and gives an insight into Lady Aberdeen's essentially international outlook. Concerned as she was with local and national problems, she never forgot that there was another world outside Ireland – nor did she forget that the wider world could, and did, help solve local problems.

All this activity could not hide from Lady Aberdeen the fact that she and her husband were constantly under attack from their old critics, Nationalist and Unionist alike. In those years, 1912-1914, the political situation became ever more fraught. Home Rule was by then a distinct possibility and the Aberdeens, open supporters of the measure, grew even more unpopular in Unionist circles, particularly in the north of Ireland, where visits from the Viceroy were not welcome. The *Ulster Guardian* in its issue of January 13th 1912, reported that:

... it has for some time been the fashion in ultra-loyal circles to insult the King's representative in Ireland. The health of the Lord Lieutenant has been omitted from the toast list at Unionist and even non-political functions.[36]

The *Northern Whig* had earlier in the same month announced that Lord Aberdeen had:

... forfeited the respect of Ulstermen [because] since the day when he arrived in Dublin he has obeyed the decrees of the Hibernian with the regularity and precision of an automaton.

The article went on to accuse Lady Aberdeen of 'meddlesome interference' in the matter of the Insurance Act, using her association which was 'supposed to be non-political' in an attempt to 'foist Lloyd George's vexatious schemes upon the Irish people'.[37] *The Ulster Guardian* in its comments on the matter, defended Lady Aberdeen's 'harmless, sensible proposal' that the WNHA branches should organise themselves into an Insurance Society, and described her as:

... a gracious lady who has preached no politics but those of social service, and whose sole offence is that her private political views do not square with those of a particular corner of Ireland.

The *Irish Times* in an editorial on September 3rd 1912, dealing with what it described as the 'public unpopularity' of Lord Aberdeen, made obvious by an unenthusiastic reception at the Horse Show, said disingenuously that it wasn't their Excellencies' Home Rule sympathies that were alienating people, but their 'demoralising effect' on the conduct of official life. They had shown personal favouritism in the making of appointments, and Lady Aberdeen's interference in these matters was to be deplored.[38] A letter in response to this charge, from a Mr John Walker, refutes it and praises the Aberdeen's court for its purity, – morally, socially, and officially. A more robust comment was made in the *Freeman's Journal* editorial of September 4th, pointing out that loyalists had always given trouble to Liberal Viceroys, and that an 'Orange clique' was 'out to get Lord Aberdeen'. The *Irish Times* was now nothing more than 'the mouthpiece of the old gang'. Appointments were now made on merit, not on sectarian lines, and all that Lady Aberdeen did was to 'cut through red tape'.[39] The *Irish Independent* praised His Excellency for having had:

...the temerity to go outside the beaten track and make

appointments from a class rigorously and unfairly excluded in the past either on the grounds of religion or politics.[40]

These appointments obviously did upset certain people, and there is no way of knowing whether or not they were based on merit, or indeed whether the Lord Lieutenant and his wife had as much power as was implied by the criticism and comments. What is certain, however, is that relations between Lady Aberdeen and the all-powerful Vice President of the Local Government Board, Sir Henry Robinson were, as we have seen, very poor. Sir Henry himself in his autobiography, *Memories: Wise and Otherwise*, refers to his 'constant disputes' with her saying that the beginning of all his trouble with her was over Local Government Board appointments, and goes on:

> We had two vacancies for medical inspectors, the appointments of which were made by the Local Government Board; the Lord Lieutenant had no responsibility for them, and no other Lord Lieutenant had ever interfered in such cases. I had discussed the appointments with Mr Birrell, and we selected four applicants as possessing the qualifications we required, and Birrell left the final selection to me. I had not the least idea the Aberdeens were interested in the matter till I was just about to sign the warrants, when I received an urgent summons to attend at the Lodge to see Lord Aberdeen. He referred to the vacant posts, and said that Lady Aberdeen had great experience in public health matters and considered Drs A and B as the most suitable persons to fill the vacancies, and desired that they should be appointed at once. While he was speaking, Lady Aberdeen was walking up and down the garden outside the windows with Sir William Thomson, awaiting my reply. I said that Dr A had no hospital experience, and that Dr B was very bad-tempered, and that the board preferred Drs C and D, who possessed the exact qualifications they required. Lord Aberdeen went out to the garden to see Lady Aberdeen and came back very much upset, and said that Lady Aberdeen was still convinced that Drs A and B were the most suitable, and regretted to differ from me. I then asked if she knew Drs C and D and was informed that she did not; whereupon I pointed out that she was not, therefore, in a position to decide that Drs A and B were more suitable. I also explained that the appointments were made by the Local Government Board, and that the Lord Lieutenant had no functions in the matter. Lord Aberdeen then said he would telegraph to Birrell. Shortly after I got back to the office, a mounted orderly came with a message from Lady Aberdeen withdrawing Dr B and substituting Dr X. I heard nothing from Birrell on the subject, and on the following

day appointed Drs C and D.
I wrote to Lady Aberdeen explaining why I was compelled to take this course, but she made no reply, and from this time forth the Aberdeens' dislike and mistrust of me became, I am informed, a perfect obsession with them.[41]

This account would seem to make it clear that in the case of Local Government appointments their Excellencies had no say in the matter, however hard they pushed.

Nationalist criticisms of the Aberdeens came not, as we know, from the members of the Parliamentary Party (whose leader, John Redmond, had cordial relations with the Viceroy and his wife) but from the republican, or separatist element, and were voiced in Arthur Griffith's paper *Sinn Féin*, and D P Moran's the *Leader*. Both publications had kept up a steady stream of complaints from the time the Aberdeens arrived in Ireland but they became more frequent and more forceful as the years went on. Some were only minor gibes such as *Sinn Féin*'s sneer in May 1913, at a prize donated by Lord Aberdeen for a singing competition in the Royal Irish Academy of Music. His offer of a 'little brooch' was deemed by the correspondent to have cost ten shillings [50p] out of his salary of £20,000 per annum. This was in the same vein as the previous comment, made in January 1913, on the advertising of Persian kittens for sale at the Viceregal Lodge. Hardly surprising, said the paper, as the Lodge had already been used as a shop to dispose of surplus garden produce.

More serious and more hurtful (and quite untrue) was the accusation in March of that year that Lady Aberdeen had engaged in sharp practice over the transfer of the P F Collier Dispensary to Dublin Corporation in 1912 and that she had made money on the deal. 'Dublin never had need of Peamount', added the writer, ignoring the fact that the sanatorium wasn't large enough to accommodate all those who did need and desire treatment. From the beginning *Sinn Féin* had refused to believe that Ireland had a major health problem with tuberculosis and accused Lady Aberdeen ('Lady Microbe' as she had been christened) of inventing the whole thing in order to make herself important. 'The lady had no sooner set her foot on the Irish shore than she set up a story that Ireland was reeking with TB!', was how an article put it in March, 1914, adding:

England has sent no cleverer political agent into Ireland in our time. We have no doubt that a thousand sentimentalists, and ten thousand job-hunters and tuft-hunters will rise as one worm to declare that

> when Lady Aberdeen invented the TB scare about Ireland she was
> filled with love for Ireland.[42]

Arthur Griffith could hardly have believed that the high death rate from tuberculosis was an 'invention' of Lady Aberdeen's, and the crudity of the repeated attacks does not redound to his credit. Jokes about microbes come more suitably from unlettered, unthinking people, always ready with a laugh and an easy sneer, than from an educated man professing high principles, but in a war of propaganda the easiest weapon to use is taken up.

The straightforward and crude attacks on the Aberdeens in the *Irish Worker* seem paradoxically, less offensive than those of *Sinn Féin*. They reek of honest class hatred, undiluted by any admixture of fair play, and are admirable in the vigour of their prose, if not in their content. Expressing pleasure on Wexford Corporation's refusal to present an address to Lady Aberdeen when she visited that city in July 1913, the *Irish Worker's* correspondent dismissed her ladyship as:

> ...nothing but a busybody going round at the country's expense,
> preaching about consumption to such an extent that we are held up
> to odium all over the world as a plague-ridden nation.[43]

Typical of content and style is the paper's 'Open Letter' to Lord Aberdeen in April 1913. It is heavily sarcastic, 'I have fumigated the room, burned the bed-clothes, disinfected the pen, pasteurised the milk, so after all these pains I feel safe in addressing you', and goes on to talk about the poverty in Dublin and the current strike, which Aberdeen as done nothing to settle, but has handed over the government of Ireland to the Army. Next comes an attack on Lady Aberdeen's ill-judged pronouncement that a family of five could feed itself on eight shillings and sixpence per week – the Lord Lieutenant must have a very healthy bank account by now, considering what 'a paragon of thrift her Ladyship is' on the salary he draws. 'We have listened to this "tomfoolery" too long,' says the writer, as he lists old 'scandals', the National University of Ireland appointment, 'the Peamount scandal, the Castle Jewels scandal and the Microbe Scandal,' and concludes by asking bluntly 'Where are the Crown Jewels?' [44]

The Aberdeens at this stage, when their unpopularity in certain quarters was increasing daily, were without the comfort and support of their surviving children. The sickly Haddo was in Aberdeen, Dudley was still involved in engineering in Glasgow, and Marjorie, who had always been close to her mother, was far away in Madras, where her husband Sinclair, Lord Pentland, was governor. The absence of the Sinclair grandchildren was a particular regret as Lady Aberdeen had always had a great rapport with young children. Her work for poorer children was activated by genuine concern and affection and unlike many people who do good in a remote, though still effective, way she got personally involved and didn't shrink from physical contact. There are stories told of her romping with slum children at the special Viceregal parties, and even if the children had been carefully screened and cleaned up before being allowed into the grounds, they were still a different species.

The worsening political situation in Ireland caused by the imminence of Home Rule and the determination of Ulster Unionists meant that events in Europe were overshadowed by domestic anxieties, but when war came in August 1914, the focus shifted away from national to international affairs. The third Home Rule Bill which had finally been passed was put into abeyance until the end of the war, which everyone thought could not be long delayed, and Ireland got ready to join the conflict. The Irish Parliamentary Party assured Westminster of its support, and called on patriotic Irishmen to aid Britain in its fight against the German aggressor. Belgium had been invaded and its right as a small nation had been violated. Irishmen were to see this fight for rights as their own and were to enlist in what was presented as a moral crusade.

There was work to be done at home as well as in the trenches in France and Belgium, and Lady Aberdeen turned to face this new challenge. As early as August 10th she called a meeting to discuss work for the Red Cross and pressurised the Department of Agriculture and Technical Instruction to set up a training scheme for voluntary nurses (VADS). She also proposed a scheme to equip Dublin Castle as a Red Cross hospital for wounded soldiers. This was eventually done in spite of bureaucratic opposition, and the State Rooms were turned into hospital wards (in one of which the wounded James Connolly, one of the leaders of the 1916 rebellion, lay before his execution). Unfortunately, it was the Red Cross which was to prove the cause of her greatest unpopularity with her critics on every side. As patron of the British Red Cross Society in Ireland she wanted people of all political persuasion to join it, and sent a letter to all the newspapers asking for members. With her letter of the 20th September to Brayden, editor of the *Freeman's Journal* she added a private note, emphatically not for publication, asking that her letter be given a prominent place in the newspaper, because, she said:

> I'm afraid there is a bit of a plot among the Unionists to capture the Red Cross Society in Ireland and run it in such a way from London and through County Lieutenants and Deputy Lieutenants that it will be unacceptable to the Irish Volunteer people, etc. You will understand, I am sure. I believe that ultimately we may be able to have an Irish Red Cross Society directly under the War Office without the intermediary of the British Red Cross.

She added a postscript praising a recent editorial of Brayden's on the subject of Home rule:

> May we exchange heartiest congratulations with you on the consummation of our hopes and on the part you have played in bringing them about.

Brayden did as Lady Aberdeen asked and published the appeal for Red Cross volunteers, but her private note disappeared (it may never even have been seen by the editor) and a copy of it was handed to Arthur Griffith, editor of *Sinn Féin*. He printed a facsimile of it in his paper on October 17th and it also appeared in the *Irish Worker*. Griffith affected to believe that this private note, with its congratulatory remarks on Brayden's recent editorial spoke 'in trumpet tones that the curse of a British-kept press' was upon Ireland, 'the worst curse that could happen to a nation struggling towards freedom', while James Larkin said that the note gave 'a fair index of the relations between the *Freeman's Journal* and the Castle'. He pointed out that, the paper 'was being run with the money of the United Irish League' and wondered what 'the men of America' thought of 'the manner in which the money they subscribe is being expended'.

Larkin's and Griffiths' comments could be ignored, but not those of the directors of the British Red Cross Society in Ireland. They asked Lady Aberdeen to disavow the letter, which of course she could not do. The disagreement between her and the Red Cross became public knowledge, and the *Irish Times* in an editorial on the 31st October severely rebuked Lady Aberdeen for her accusation of a 'Unionist' plot to make political capital out of the sacred work of the Red Cross Society. It was disgraceful that such an allegation be made by 'the wife of the one man whose strict duty and high privilege it is to strand aloof from party politics'. Augustine Birrell in a letter to Lady Aberdeen said consolingly that the 'scandalous article' in the *Irish Times* was the 'parting kick of the jackass' and that it was unlikely there would be very much more made of it – 'a few grumblings and bumblings and perhaps a Question in Parliament'.[45] He put the whole furore down to Unionist jealousy and advised her to make no comment about the forthcoming changes in the Irish Government, especially those affecting the Aberdeens.

In fact, a letter from Asquith (8th October) was already on its way to Lord Aberdeen, pointing out that on the 5th December 1914, he would have been Viceroy for nine years, 'a term which considerably exceeds in duration that of any Viceroy since the Union'. Asquith gratefully acknowledged the 'conspicuous service' Lord and Lady Aberdeen had given 'in circumstances of exceptional difficulty', but he proposed that their work should now come to an end. The obvious thing for Aberdeen now to do was to offer his resignation and to go gracefully, but both he and Lady Aberdeen resisted the pressure. The news had come as a shock to them, according to Marjorie Pentland, for Asquith had been staying with them in September and had said nothing about a change:

> ... the war, they were told on the highest authority would be over in
> a few months, and then – for Home Rule was now law – A. [Lord
> Aberdeen] at last would be able to hand over to a Governor-General
> for the Dominion of Ireland. It seemed clear to them they would be
> settled there for the duration.

Lord Aberdeen wrote to the Prime Minister pleading to be allowed stay on, and Asquith in a letter to his friend Venetia Stanley told her that his daughter Violet had had an emotional letter from Lady Aberdeen, in which she referred to the engagement that existed between her late son Archie and Violet asking, 'How can your father wreck such havoc upon Archie's parents?' This unfair appeal had no more effect than had Aberdeen's pleas, and the decision stood.

For Lady Aberdeen in particular their dismissal was a stunning blow, and she obviously said as much in a letter to Margaret MacNeill, one of her devoted helpers in the WNHA (and sister of John MacNeill, President of the Irish Volunteers) because MacNeill's letter of consolation refers to her friend being 'troubled and wearied' by what had happened. The letter goes on:

> You have worked day and night for a country you have loved and
> for a country that has loved you, no matter what stupid, or
> malignant or disappointed persons may have said.[46]

Other friends rallied round the Aberdeens, and protests were made against their dismissal, but all that was achieved was an extension of office until February 1915. Birrell, announcing this, told Lady Aberdeen in a letter on the 2nd December that the Government couldn't and wouldn't go back on its decision, and that nine years was quite long enough for any Viceroy. Furthermore, the King had made it plain that he would not create a new Irish Dukedom for their benefit, but would, however, confer a Marquisate on Aberdeen. This letter was signed 'Yours Affectionately' – a fine piece of hypocrisy, given what Birrell wrote to Sir Matthew Nathan, the new Under-Secretary on 22nd December:

> I think it would have been too cruel to refuse His Excellency a
> "single ostentatious feather" as Bacon calls such things, with which
> to glorify his sunset.[47]

When the question of a suitable title for the Marquis and Marchioness arose they indicated that they would like the style of 'Aberdeen and Tara', in recognition of their Irish connection. This proved to be an unpopular choice. The *Irish Times* in a third leader on the 18th January 1915, said sarcastically that the 'little hill [of Tara] hitherto unknown' would now 'be fragrant with memories of the Viceregal Office' and Alice Stopford Green, a fervently Nationalist historian, wrote in a letter to *The Times*:

> The Irish people give no consent to this outrage on their history and
> offence to their feelings … Lord Aberdeen's action shows that no
> appeal can lie from Ireland either to his historic imagination or his
> good taste.

However, in his farewell address to the departing Viceroy and his wife, the Nationalist Lord Mayor of Dublin said to them:

> Your new honour is rooted in the cherished seat of our ancient kings
> and heroes. Teamhair or Tara means a pleasant prospect – may it be
> a pleasant prospect on your lives.

One wonders just how 'outraged' the Irish public actually were. An even more significant comment was made by Alice Milligan, the Nationalist writer, when she wrote in the *Freeman's Journal*, 22nd January 1915, that the couple's choice of title:

> … was certainly meant as an expression of sympathy with Irish
> ideals and aspirations … [and] to perpetuate the memory of the fact
> that for a generation of political life they have worked for the
> restoration of a form of National Independence to Ireland and to

give a pledge that in severing their connection with the government of this country they are still sympathetic with its aspirations.[48]

This was a generous tribute from a woman who had been a fierce and vocal critic of Lady Aberdeen in the past and had written disparagingly of her work. However, the matter was settled when King George V wrote to Aberdeen saying that he had not originally realised how closely Tara was 'associated with the ancient history and traditions of Ireland' but that 'numerous communications, including some from Irish men of both political parties as well as by letters in the Press' had shown him that it would offend the national susceptibilities of the warm-hearted people of Ireland were Aberdeen to take the style of Tara.[49]

A compromise was reached, for having consulted experts on Gaelic history, among them George Sigerson and Dr Michael Cox, the Aberdeens chose the title 'Temair,' a variant of the Irish name of Tara. There was still some aggrieved muttering about this choice, but from then on their Excellencies were known as the Marquis and Marchioness of Aberdeen and Temair. Sir Henry Robinson tells a story of a man who believed that 'Temair' was in fact 'Temeraire' and assumed it was a tribute to Lady Aberdeen's fight for the health of the nation. In his subconscious association of the 'Fighting Temeraire' with Lady Aberdeen there is a poignancy, not remarked upon by Sir Henry, in that Turner's painting shows the ship at the end of her glorious career. So it was with Lady Aberdeen's gallant struggle in Ireland. The last tributes were paid, the final illuminated addresses were presented and the good-byes were said.

The state departure took place on February 15th 1915, with the usual pomp and ceremony, and this time, unlike the day in 1886, there was no prospect of a return in glory. Some were glad to see Lady Aberdeen go, notably the *Irish Times* which in an editorial on 13th February that dutifully praised her 'conspicuous devotion and energy' in social service, hinted not too subtly, that she had secured preferment for those who shared her interests in 'sanitation and charity'. She had failed to shine as a hostess, and during the past nine years the Castle had been a very gloomy place, as 'Their Excellencies had showed small inclination towards social gaiety'.[50] The *Freeman's Journal*, naturally enough, took a different view. Speaking of the 'spite' manifested against the Aberdeens because he was 'a Gladstone man' the editorial admired the 'cheery courtesy' with which they had out-faced their critics. Lady Aberdeen's 'well-inspired activity' led 'the war in Ireland against the plague that dogged so many homes and lives'. She had had to struggle:

> ...against misunderstanding and misrepresentation, against the
> obstruction of misguided critics and the more sinister opposition of
> narrow bureaucrats.[51]

One of the most senior bureaucrats with whom Lady Aberdeen had had many a battle, Sir Henry Robinson, wrote spitefully of the departure in his book of memories, saying that there 'was no crowd in the streets and no demonstration whatsoever,' a description which is contradicted by photographic evidence. As the procession made its way through the streets Lady Aberdeen snapped away with her little Kodak camera and the photography (askew and ill-focused) shows a large crowd gathered to say farewell. If there was no demonstration, that was understandable. What could be said but 'Goodbye' to a couple who had been there for nine years, who most certainly would not be coming again, and who may have already, to the assembled crowds, seemed to belong to another world, another era, and one which was coming to an end?

An enduring legacy

THE MARQUIS AND MARCHIONESS of Aberdeen and Temair, as they now were, left Ireland in February 1915, but they both, especially Ishbel, retained their connections with a land which they loved, and with whose fortunes they identified. Politically, they were powerless to do anything to influence government policy, and they believed that their removal contributed to the events that took place in Ireland after their departure. It was a measure of their kindly egotism that they saw themselves as such important players on the national stage and were unaware that, directed by powerful sentiments of separatism, much more significant actors had appeared in the spotlight.

The Irish Parliamentary Party split into constitutionalists and separatists, and its leader, John Redmond, who had managed to extract the Home Rule Bill from Prime Minister Asquith, was side-lined by extreme elements in the party. These, influenced by the ultra-nationalistic Irish Republican Brotherhood (the direct descendants of nineteenth century Fenians) made common cause with Arthur Griffith's Sinn Féin and James Connolly's Citizen Army. The result was a Rising in Dublin in 1916, which was quickly subdued and its leaders (including Connolly) executed. This apparent failure was, however, a success. The revulsion caused by the executions was widespread, and the deaths of the leaders provided new examples of heroic martyrdom. Old resentments and half-buried feelings of patriotism surfaced, were harnessed by the ultra-nationalist groups, and led eventually, after five years (including two of Anglo-Irish warfare) to the establishment of an Irish Free State in 1921.

This was a world in which the Aberdeens could not be expected to take part, but Ishbel maintained her close links with Ireland almost to the day of her death in 1939. Immediately following their departure (or 'expulsion,' as they saw it) from Ireland in 1915 the Earl and Countess travelled to America on a fund-raising mission for their Irish charitable causes. They had hoped that their target of £20,000 would be achieved in six months, but in fact, they spent over two years in the States. It was not as easy to extract money from Irish-American millionaires as it used to be, because there were so many other causes competing for the money, not least anti-British ones. The money was collected, and was handed over to the Women's National Health Association for the groups most in need of it. Peamount sanatorium was one of the main beneficiaries, and its work expanded as a result. The after-care of TB patients, which Lady Aberdeen saw as so important a feature in the fight against the disease, was intensified by the setting-up of the Peamount After Care Guild in October 1918, and a Village Settlement was established in the sanatorium in 1929. This development was inspired by a visit made in 1916 by Lady Aberdeen to Papworth in England, where patients in the TB sanatorium were involved in light industry. The first hostel at the Peamount Settlement was founded with money bequeathed to Lady Aberdeen by an Irish emigrant to America, Mrs Sharpe. While Lady Aberdeen was visiting the United States in 1917 Mrs Sharpe had heard of her mission and had asked Lady Aberdeen to visit her. During the visit Mrs Sharpe, on learning more about the work of the WNHA, asked if the Aberdeens, would, after her death, administer her estate for the benefit of the poor of Ireland. This was duly done, and the first Peamount hostel was named the Annie Sharpe hostel after its benefactor. Other money from the estate was used for various enterprises of the WNHA.

The personal fortune of the Aberdeens declined in more ways than one after they left Ireland. Although they were lucky enough not to lose a son in the Great War, they knew the anguish of worry about Dudley's fate as an officer in the Gordon Highlanders. He was wounded twice but survived, unlike the sons of many of their friends and acquaintances. Wartime taxes depleted their wealth, and the original great land holding in Scotland was reduced to a fraction of its former size. Indeed, the story of the Aberdeen finances is one of gradual decline from the time John Gordon inherited the estate in 1872, caused, it would seem by mismanagement. It could certainly not be attributed to riotous living, although the entertaining which of necessity accompanied the Aberdeens' official positions, first in Edinburgh, (where Lord Aberdeen was High Commissioner to the Church of Scotland) then in Canada and later in Ireland, did strain their resources. It does, then, seem unfair that the couple were, throughout their public lives, accused of being living examples of the stereotypical tight-fisted Scots. In Ireland particular pleasure was taken in quoting a parody of the popular ballad 'The

Wearing of the Green' which alluded to the Aberdeens' supposed meanness. The Viceregal entertainments were contrasted with those of their predecessors:

Those were the days of open court, both plentiful and free,
No niggardly hand supplied the board, or Spenser's Faerie Queene,
Another type of hostess stands, the Lady Aberdeen
When bidden to Viceregal feasts, with second sight I see,
One hand that missed the claret cup, and brewed the tepid tea
That spreads the butter thin and spare, and sliced the buns in two
And brought the sandwiches "en bloc" that were no longer new.

Ishbel, in fact, was particularly generous, not only to organisations but to individuals. Edith Gordon, in her memoir of life in Ireland, *The Winds of Time*, recalled for example, how when Lady Aberdeen came to Kerry, she took her to:

... one of the most poverty-stricken regions ... where human beings, pigs and chickens lived in distressing proximity. In every cottage we entered she left an amazingly generous contribution.

In 1920 the Aberdeens turned over the estate to George, Lord Haddo, and moved to a smaller house in Deeside, called Cromar. Aberdeen, who was then 73, retired from public life and with Ishbel, ten years younger, settled down to country life. Ishbel, however, still vigorous in mind and body, continued with her charitable works, and also with her involvement in the International Council of Women. She had been President of the International Council from 1893 until 1898 and again from 1904 until 1914. Because of the war the organisation lapsed until 1920 when it reconvened and Ishbel played a significant part in bringing members of nations who had once been enemies close together in the bonds of sisterhood. She was re-elected President in 1922 and remained in office until her retirement in 1936. The office entailed a great deal of travelling, and this, added to the five or six visits she made every year to Ireland, meant that there was no danger that she would become bored. She loved meeting new people and was stimulated by her contacts with the intelligent, outspoken and well-educated women from all over the world whom she met through the ICW.

A new interest for both the Aberdeens proved to be the writing of their memoirs. Their joint recollections appeared in 1925 as a two-volume book *We Twa* – a bland account of their career 'resolving' as their daughter, Marjorie Pentland, said, 'not to complain of or criticise anybody who had done them harm'. As a result the book lacks sparkle and very little of Ishbel's personality shines through. The same criticism applies to the sequel *More Cracks with 'We Twa'*, published in 1929 but Ishbel's later memoir *Musings of a Scottish Granny* published in 1936, is slightly more animated. It may have been financial pressures that caused her to write that book and to turn to journalism, in 1935, when a series of articles by her appeared in the *Sunday Post* in February and March. They are slight pieces, of little interest except in so far as they bear upon her early life, and the world which she then inhabited.

Lord Aberdeen predeceased his wife in 1934 and his death meant that she had to give up her home at Cromar and move into a house in the city of Aberdeen. He had been a kindly and supportive husband – indeed, without his help Ishbel could not have achieved what she did achieve – and she missed him greatly. Her children and grandchildren tried to fill the void left in her life and there was a steady stream of visitors (including the Canadian Prime Minister Mackenzie King) to her new home, but, in what seems uncharacteristic behaviour, she looked for solace in spiritualism and séances. Ishbel was realistic enough, nevertheless, to see that a new conflict was brewing in Europe, and was appalled by Hitler's 'unbelievable inhumanities not only to Jews but to Protestants and Catholics as well'. She died in April 1939, aged 82, only a few months before her country again went to war against Germany.

The *Irish Times* reported the death of 'Ishbel, Marchioness of Aberdeen and Temair' in its issue of the 19th April 1939 under the headline 'A Great Friend of Ireland'. Tribute was paid to her 'unceasing work on behalf of the poor', and her crusade against tuberculosis. 'A splendid monument of her work in this connection remains in the Peamount Sanatorium', said the writer, 'which she was instrumental in establishing'.

That certainly was Lady Aberdeen's tangible legacy, and since that tribute was paid in 1939, much has changed at Peamount. In the new independent State the fight against tuberculosis continued, and country-wide campaigns were waged. In the first twenty or so years the emphasis was on the provision of new sanatoria and extra beds in existing ones. Then in 1946 the move to prevention of the disease led to the establishment of mass X-ray units and a nation-wide vaccination scheme (BCG). In 1948 the new Minister for Health in a Coalition government, Dr Noel Browne, himself a one-time TB patient, instituted a major hospital building programme, and several very large sanatoria were built.

In his anti-TB campaign Dr Browne was fortunate to have the support of Dr James Deeny, Secretary of the Department of Health, (whose mother had been a member of the WNHA) a uniquely valuable person, a senior civil servant with vision and energy. As it happened, the large new sanatoria proved considerably more than adequate for their original purpose, for the advent of new drugs in the late 'forties and early 'fifties resulted in a decrease in the deaths from TB and these hospitals are now used for other purposes. Peamount was a subsidiary of the WNHA until that body wound up its affairs in 1955. A board of management then took over and in 1962 the word 'sanatorium' was dropped and the new name registered as Peamount Hospital Incorporated. The hospital, its farm and industries, is now under the control of the Eastern Health Board, and is used for the treatment of diseases of the chest. The number of TB cases has fallen nationally (although there has been an alarming rise world-wide in cases of the disease) but chronic bronchitis, emphysema and lung cancer are on the increase and Peamount is ideally suited for the treatment of these respiratory ailments. A unit for the mentally-handicapped which was established in 1962 has expanded, and residents there are trained to carry out simple industrial work such as making cardboard boxes and packaging. The farm continues to provide wholesome food for patients and staff, including milk from its dairy herd and vegetables from the kitchen gardens but a crop raised in earlier days is now no longer encouraged in this country. Anita Day, in her history of Peamount, *The Turn of the Tide*, tells of an early scheme for the growing and drying of tobacco at Peamount. 'A big shed in the garden was used as the drying shed', she records, and here the work was undertaken by female workers. This scheme' she goes on, 'was probably encouraged by a report in the *Evening Telegraph* in 1912 of a cure for tuberculosis.' No tobacco is now grown or dried at Peamount. In the main house at Peamount, which is the administrative centre, there is a plaque in the hallway commemorating Lady Aberdeen.

What legacy, apart from the obvious one of Peamount, did Ishbel Aberdeen leave to the country which she loved so well? Very little that can be measured in material terms, it is true, but how can one measure what influence she exercised as an educator? That was her main rôle, and the process of education is a very slow and lengthy one. Her hard work encouraging Irish industries at least had tangible results in the short term and it also affected the way Irish people looked on their own heritage of craftsmanship and helped awaken their national pride, so that her influence has been relatively easy to assess by historians of the Irish arts and crafts movement. The work for public health was another matter, because of its emphasis on education. The WNHA did obvious good works, saving the lives of infants, nursing invalids back to health, or easing the last days of the dying, feeding hungry schoolchildren, helping breadwinners get work, providing shoes and clothing for the needy, while all the time alerting people to the dangers of TB. The good works might in time be forgotten, or even resented by a new and nationalistic generation, but who is to know what effects the teaching might have had on individuals throughout Ireland? It is not too fanciful to imagine a bored young girl being lectured by a WNHA member on the importance of hygiene in the home, and then years later, remembering those precepts and putting them into practice.

Official bodies were challenged by Lady Aberdeen to deal with the problems of dirt, disease, over-crowding, bad housing and sub-standard schooling, and in time all these challenges were met to a greater or lesser extent. She was not alone, of course, in calling for better social services, and the temper of the times was such that welcome changes would have come about anyway, but Lady Aberdeen's crusade kept these problems in the public eye and helped to form public opinion. A measure of her importance in this area is the dislike of her openly expressed by Sir Henry Robinson, Vice-President of the Local Government Board. She was more than an irritant – an amateur trespassing on the territory of the bureaucrat – because she persisted with her demands and refused to be overawed by the powerful males of the Civil Service. Robinson's remark quoted earlier about the WNHA 'a bunch of irresponsible women' is revealing and sums up certain contemporary attitudes.

Lady Aberdeen was, as we have seen, no Suffragette, but she did believe that women should, as the first step towards playing a decisive part in public life, be granted the vote. While for various reasons she never campaigned for this cause, and could never be claimed as a champion of 'women's rights' (a phrase which we know she detested), she nevertheless, in her own way contributed to the emancipation of women in its fullest sense. First, by her example, she showed that a woman could be a person in her own right in public life, not merely as an appendage to an important man. It *did* take courage to address public meetings, especially when you remember that like most women of her generation she had been brought up to be submissive and retiring, using her feminine influence in the home and nowhere else. The fact that Ishbel was well-to-do and well-connected was not entirely an advantage – by stepping into the public arena, especially the political one when she worked for the Liberal party, she exposed herself to the possible criticism of family and friends, and the members of her own class who might consider her behaviour at the very least unsuitable. Her sister-in-law and beloved friend, Fanny Tweedmouth, was one of a group of English society women who signed a petition against the granting of women's rights. Fortunately, Ishbel was not constricted by the boundaries of class and was able to reach out to women from different and less privileged backgrounds. Her obvious sincerity and passionate commitment to her causes was allied to a firm belief that women, in spite of the many obstacles placed by society and by custom in their way, could and would eventually take an active part in public life in every country in the world.

Ishbel's was not the only voice proclaiming this belief during the latter years of the nineteenth century and the beginning of the twentieth century – after all, in Ireland alone there were many redoubtable women including Jenny Wyse Power and Hannah Sheehy-Skeffington and the glamorous Maud Gonne McBride and Countess Markievicz who were speaking out on their sisters' behalf – but her voice was an unusual one. It came from the very heart of the Establishment and it preached heresy, namely that women were capable of running their own affairs and could do so better than men had done to date, a statement that carried with it the clear implication that the 'misgovernment' of Ireland was largely due to male inefficiency. (She had quite openly made the same charge earlier at the WNHA founding meeting in Belfast in 1907.) She emphasised the fact that child care, home-making and the nursing of the sick were traditionally regarded as female concerns, so was it not reasonable that women should gain control, financial and otherwise, in these areas? And should they not be properly educated the better to carry out what Ishbel always regarded as their 'duties' in society? The good sense of these proposals was what made them so subversive and earned Ishbel great animosity in official circles. It must be granted too that her personality, as far as one can judge, was no help in dealings with bureaucrats. She was no diplomat, and was impatient with the niceties of negotiation. She saw a problem, saw how it could be solved and did not understand why this could not be done immediately.

If the organisation which Lady Aberdeen had founded, the Women's National Health Association, had retained its early hold on the hearts, minds and energies of women around Ireland and had expanded to become a strong and vigorous nationwide group of women, then she would be well-remembered today. That did not happen, mainly because of the establishment of the United Irishwomen, the society that later became the Irish Countrywomen's Association. A contributing factor in the WNHA's decline may have been the fact that its magazine *Sláinte*, which had been an excellent way of keeping isolated country branches in touch with one another and with the National Executive in Dublin, ceased publication in 1915. The Aberdeens had by then left the country and were having a difficult time raising money in America, so there were good reasons for its closure – the departure of the editor, Lady Aberdeen, and the probable withdrawal of the Aberdeen subvention.

In spite of what both organisations said at the time there was no place in Irish life, especially in rural Ireland, for two such groups, and the WNHA lost out to its rival. It continued its social work concentrating in the main on Peamount Sanatorium and its After-Care Guild, but while many admirable women gave their time and their energies to the Association none of them made the same impact on the public consciousness that Lady Aberdeen had done. That may have been in part due to her personality. Born to command, and although excellent at delegation, she overshadowed her fellow workers to such an extent that no real successor to her ever emerged. Another reason for the decline of the WNHA was the obvious one – many of its original aims had been achieved, and public bodies were now carrying on its works.

The memory of Lady Aberdeen is not officially revered and historical accounts of the era in which she served the people of Ireland make scant mention of her, but here and there in individual hearts she is not forgotten, in spite of the years of official neglect. When I was researching this study of Ishbel Aberdeen's work in Ireland I appealed, through the newspapers, for any original letters or diaries that might be available. The response was good, and while no original documents appeared, several correspondents shared with me family recollections of Lady Aberdeen. One of the first responses came from a man whose grandfather had been coachman to the Aberdeens in Scotland and in Canada, whose father had been born on the Haddo House estate and had later worked for Peamount Sanatorium. Chris Keddie, who turned out to be a neighbour of mine appeared on my doorstep one evening bringing with him mementoes of the Aberdeens and many family memories. They were all fond and happy ones, and he emphasised that the Aberdeens were extremely good and generous employers. He was astonished to hear that anyone should have ever thought otherwise and told me about expensive gifts made to his grandfather and to his father, silver and china that are still in the family. A Dublin doctor sent me an anecdote which his father, who was a boy in Ballyshannon in the early nineteen hundreds, used to tell about Lady Aberdeen. When she visited the town some time around then she preached the benefits of fresh air, especially at night. However, his father recalled, when she stayed in the local hotel she insisted that her bedroom windows would be, in his words 'sealed and shuttered at night'. It may not have been, commented my correspondent, that she was failing to practise what she preached, but that she 'was afraid of the Green Lady or the Goblin Child, said to have frequented Lower Main Street from 1700 onwards'. Nice to think of Ishbel Aberdeen being afraid of ghosts, when no human ever seemed to frighten her, and interesting when we remember that later in life she turned to spiritualism.

An instance of Lady Aberdeen's kindness and helpfulness was told to me by a lady from Kilkenny who remembers her father speaking of her with great warmth. He was on the Committee of the Irish National Teachers' Organisation which was to hold its annual Congress in Kilkenny in 1912, and its first with a woman president, Miss M Mahon. When, late in the day, it became necessary to find a principal speaker, he, greatly daring, approached "the highest in the land". Ishbel accepted at once and, happy to have a platform for her views, gave a speech which dealt mainly with the problem of sub-standard school building. In these 'neither teachers nor schoolchildren [had] any chance of health', and the 'weekly teaching of hygiene must be looked on as a farce or a satire'.

A woman from County Roscommon is another who grew up hearing nothing but good of Lady Aberdeen, as her mother, Anita McCarthy, worked with her in the WNHA and remembered her not only with admiration but with real affection for her genuine kindness. She also saw her as "a source of inspiration and a stabilising influence in her own life". From an elderly lady in Dublin came an account of Lady Aberdeen's generosity to her father, Patrick Doherty, who travelled to Chicago from Glencolumcille in County Donegal in 1893 to display his skills as a weaver at the World's Fair. He spent six months there, and when he had finished he was given two presents of heavy brass, a tall crucifix and a shaving mirror on a stand. Both are highly ornate and valuable pieces and are still in the possession of the clan in Donegal.

Many others wrote to me telling me of newspaper cuttings, scrapbooks, and photographs of the Lady Aberdeen that had been in their family home for years – an indication that some people were sufficiently interested to make a record of her progress. A truly touching and poignant letter came from a woman in Scotland telling the story of her little sister Maggie, who spent two years in the Allan Ryan Home in Dublin and died there in 1912. The family story was a tragic one, and only too common at the time. Mother and father died within a year of one another and four little girls were left orphaned in 1910. The eldest was fifteen, and the youngest was three. They were split up, the eldest going to an uncle and aunt in New York, another to relatives in Essex, and the third to an aunt and uncle in Sligo. Maggie was already suffering from TB, and was sent to Dublin. She had but one relative to visit her, a young connection by marriage, who was working in Dublin at the time. Her sister, now 89 years of age, recalled how Lady Aberdeen visited the child regularly and after her death sent prayer leaflets and a letter of sympathy to the uncle in Sligo. My correspondent very kindly sent me a photo-copy of the letter. It is black-edged, headed Vice Regal Lodge Dublin, February 9 1912, and reads:

Will you allow His Excellency and myself to offer you and your family our sincerest sympathy in the loss of the small little maiden whom you have committed to our care for the past year at the Allan A. Ryan.

She won the love of all by her brightness, cleverness and by her charming disposition. We grieve that her case was one which was beyond the power of medical science to save. I believe she was truly happy whilst at the Hospital and I know that Miss Brennan and the nurses tried to do everything in their power to brighten her life and to soothe her last days.

It is a comfort to think of the dear child being now beyond the reach of suffering and arriving to her parents.

Your constant attention to her was greatly prized by her and also by all her friends, including

Yours very faithfully
Ishbel Aberdeen

It is a letter that says more than the conventional words of condolence and it reveals the essential kindness of Ishbel Aberdeen's nature. More than that, it makes it very clear that to her a cause was not an abstraction, it was all to do with individuals who suffered. In many cases, this suffering was unnecessary for it could have been prevented. That, in essence, was what she tried to do in her crusade in Ireland. It was a noble effort and she deserves to be remembered for it with admiration and respect.

References

CHAPTER 1

1   *United Ireland*, Sat Feb 27th 1886.
2. 'The Aberdeen Romance', *Irish Eclesiastical Record*, Father N Walsh, SJ, November 1897.
3. *We Twa*, Lord and Lady Aberdeen, Reminiscences of Lord and Lady Aberdeen, 2 vols, London, 1925, Vol 1, p 109.
4. *A Bonnie Fechter*, Marjorie Pentland, London, 1952, p 21
5. *Charley Gordon*, Charles Chenevix Trench, London, 1978, p 137.
6. *We Twa*, Vol 11, p 5.
7. *Onward and Upward*, Ed James Drummond 1891-'96 Extracts, from magazine of Onward and Upward Association, Aberdeen, 1983.
8. *We Twa*, Vol 11, p 2
9. *The Recollections of Mary Alice Young* 1996, p 45 Mid-Antrim Historical Group.
10. Lady Aberdeen, Notes for Opening of Farmworkers' Evening Classes at Tarves, 1879, H H Coll.
11. Pentland, p 39
12. *Natural Law and the Spiritual World*, Henry Drummond, Preface p xx.
13   ibid, p 84.
14. Pentland, p 221
15. ibid p 222
16. *Mid-Victorian Britain*, Geoffrey Best, London, 1971 p 136.
17. *Ishbel and the Empire*, Quoted by Doris French, Toronto and Oxford, 1988, p 73
18. *Gladstone*, Roy Jenkins, London, 1995, p 28
19. ibid p 835.
20. Pentland, p 42.
21. ibid p 45.
22. *We Twa*, Vol 11, p 91.
23. Pentland, p 56.

CHAPTER 2

1. *A Bonnie Fechter*, Marjorie Pentland, p 56
2. *Gladstone and the Irish Nation*, Hammond, London, 1938, p 81.
3. *Dublin Castle and the Irish People*, R Barry O'Brien, London 1912, p 15
4. *Irish Times*, 18th January, 1886, Letters from John P Prendergast.
5. Pentland, p 55
6. ibid p 56.
7. ibid p 57

8.   *Dublin Evening Mail*, 20th February 1886.
9.   *Irish Times* 20th February, 1886.
10. *Drama in Muslin*, George Moore,Belfast, 1992, p 142.
11. ibid p 134.
12. *Every Woman's Encyclopedia*, London, 1913, p 217.
13. *Modern Society*, 9/3/1907.
14. *Dublin, the Deposed Capital*, Mary E Daly, Cork, 1984, p 15
15. *Dear Dirty Dublin*, Joseph V O'Brien, Los Angeles 1982, p 29.
16. Arnold White, Letter, 22/2/1886, HHC.
17. Arnold White, Letter, 9/3/1886, HHC.
18. *United Ireland*, 20/3/1996
19. TD Sullivan, Letter, 3/8/1886,
20. *Irish Times*, 29/3/1886.
21. ibid 24/5/1886.
22. Pentland, p 60.
23. *Guide to Irish Exhibits*, Women's Industries Section of the Edinburgh
     Exhibition, Lady Aberdeen, Edinburgh, p 9. 1886.
24. *The Arts and Crafts Movement in Ireland*, Paul Larmour, Belfast, 1992,
     p 49.
25. 'Nuns in Nineteenth Century Ireland', *Women, Power and Consciousness*,
     Caitriona Clear, Eds Mary Cullen and Maria Luddy, Dublin 1995, p 37.
26. R Barry O'Brien, p 16.
27. *Irish Times*, 6/4/1886.
28. ibid 24/4/1886, p 6.
29. ibid 21/4/1886, p 6.
30. *Valentine McClutchy*, William Carleton, Dublin, 1845, p 83.
31. *Freeman's Journal*, 20/2/1886.
32. ibid 15/6/1886.
33. *We Twa*, Lord and Lady Aberdeen, Vol 1, p 263.
34. ibid Vol 1 pp 267-8
35. Pentland, p 64.

CHAPTER 3
1.   *A Bonnie Fechter*, Marjory Pentland, p 65
2.   ibid p 67.
3.   ibid p 65.
4.   ibid p 71.
5.   ibid p 72.
6.   ibid p 80.
7.   ibid p 83.
8.   *Ishbel and the Empire*, Doris French, p 87.
9.   Pentland, p 79.
10. ibid p 90.
11. ibid p 93.

12. ibid p 93.
13. ibid p 94
14. *The Lady of the House*, 15/9/1891.
15. Pentland, p 95.
16. Horace Plunkett, Diary, 20/1/1892.
17. Introduction to World's Fair Brochure, Ishbel, Lady Aberdeen, Chicago, 1893, p 23.
18. *Irish Times*, 15/5/1893.
19. *Guide to Irish Industrial Village*, Ishbel, Lady Aberdeen, 1893, Chicago World's Fair, pp 10-15 Chicago.
20. Pentland, p 104.
21. Plunkett Diary 7/10/1893.
22. Pentland, p 98.
23. Plunkett Diary 26/8/1891.
24. Ibid 2/4/1892.
25. Ibid, 7/10/1893.
26. Ibid, 16/10/1893.
27. Ibid, 18/8/1892.
28. *Irish Times* 6/6/1893.
29. Davy Stephens - 'Davy's Kolumn', *Kingstown Monthly*. July 1894.
30. Parish Priest of Killybegs, Co Donegal, 15/7/1893, HHC.
31. *We Twa*, Lord and Lady Aberdeen, Vol 11, p 149, London.
32. ibid, Vol 1, pp 318-9.
33. Pentland, p 102.
34. *We Twa*, Vol 1, p 320.
35. Pentland, p 110
36. *Ishbel and the Empire*, French, p 137.
37. ibid p 177.
38. Lecture to Catholic Young Women's Literary Association of Toronto – May 31, 1895, Lady Aberdeen. Introduction by Archbishop John Walsh (no publisher), dated Oct 1895.
39. 'Woman's Mission and Woman's Clubs', Grover, Cleveland, *Ladies' Home Journal,* May 1905, quoted in *The Woman Movement: Feminism in the United States and England.* Wm L O'Neill, London and New York, 1969.
40. Pentland, p 75.
41. ibid p 79.
42. Lady Aberdeen, Letter to John Morley, May, 1889, HH Coll.
43. "   "   , Fourth Quinquennial Meeting of IWC, p 221.
44. Canadian Journal, Lady Aberdeen, 11/3/1897.

CHAPTER 4
1. *Freeman's Journal*, 5/2/1906
2. Editorial, *Irish Times*, 5/2/1906.
3. *Irish Times*, 5/2/1906.

4. *TheLeprechaun*, January 1906.
5. *Irish Times*, 8/3/1906.
6. Lady Alice Howard Diary, 21/3/1906.
7. ibid 20/2/1906.
8. ibid 21/2/1906.
9. ibid 1/3/1906.
10. *Dublin of Yesterday*, Page L Dickinson, p 14.
11. ibid p 17.
12. Lady Arnott, Letter (nd) HH Coll.
13. *To All and Singular*, Neville Wilkinson, London, 1925, pp 195-6.
14. *The Brimming River*, RF Brooke, London, 1948, p 98.
15. *Irish Reminiscences*, Maurice Headlam, London, 1948, p 41.
16. 'The Irish Social Ladder', *Irish Life*, November 1912.
17. *Irish Times*, 20/2/1912.
18. ibid 21/2/1912
19. ibid 22.2.1912, p 5.
20. ibid 24/4/1912.
21. ibid 26/4/1912.
22. ibid 27.4.1912.
23. *Freeman's Journal*, 27/4/1912.
24. Horace Plunkett, Diary, 10/2/1904.
25. Lady Aberdeen, Letter to Henry Campbell-Bannermann, 5/1/1906, MSS No. 41, 210, BL.
26. *Irish Independent*, 3/5/1912.
27. *Irish Times*, 6.3.1907.
28. *The Leader*, 2/2/1907.
29. *Irish Times*, 6/5/1907.
30. ibid 7/5/1907.
31. *The Leader*, 22/6/1907.
32. *Sinn Féin*, 11/5/1907.
33. *Dublin Historical Record*, FE Dixon, 1973, p 145.
34. *A Handbook of Irish Life and Industry*, Lady Aberdeen, Dublin 1907.
35. *Irish Times*, 11/7/1907.
36. *The Leader*, 27/6/1907.
37. Wilkinson, p 197.
38. *Irish Times*, 16/3/1909.
39. Lady Aberdeen - Letter to Sir Henry Campbell-Bannermann, 30/5/1907, MSS No. 41, 210 BL.
40. Wilkinson, p 200.

CHAPTER 5
1. *Memories, Wise and Otherwise*, Sir Henry Robinson, London, 1923, p 222.
2. *London Mail*, November 1912, (Quoted in *TheVicious Circle* by Francis Bamford and Viola Bankes, London, 1965, p 190.

3. The Voice of Banba, Dublin Ballad, Brian O'Higgins, Dublin 1931.
4. *Irish Times*, 1905, 6/8/1905
5. *Lantern Slides, The Diaries and Letters of Violet Bonham Carter*, Eds Mark Bonham Carter and Mark Pottle, London, 1996, p 97.
6. ibid p 190.
7 Memorial Volume – Archie Gordon, Christmas 1910, (Published privately), p 31.
8. *Lantern Slides* p 204.
9. ibid p 206.
10. ibid p 96.
11. ibid p 218.
12. ibid p 344.
13. ibid p 369.
14. ibid p 285.
15. ibid p 301.

CHAPTER 6

1. *Crown Magazine* 12/7/1906.
2. *Irish Times*, 22/3/1906.
3. *Irish Times*, 7/6/1906.
4. *Labour Leader*, 16/6/1906.
5. *Onlooker*, June 1906.
6. *Report of International Women's Council Quinquennial*, 1909, Toronto,1909
7. *The Greatest Story Never Told*, Frank Ryan, Bromsgrove, England, 1992, p 5.
8. *Illness as Metaphor*, Susan Sontag, London, 1983, p 43.
9. Programme Notes for performance of *La Traviata* by English National Opera at Coliseum, London, 1988/89.
10. *Sinn Féin*, 8/6/1911.
11. 'The Countess of Aberdeen's Health Promotion Caravan', Professor Alun Evans, *Journal of the Irish Colleges of Physicians and Surgeons*, July, 1995, p 212.
12. *A Bonnie Fechter*, Marjorie Pentland, p 159.
13. Booklet, Dublin, nd.
14. 'What Women Can Do', *The Kerryman* 30/3/1907.
15. *The Northern Whig* 19.2.1907.
16. *Irish Times* 12/10/1907.
17. *Evening Telegraph* 30/8/1907.
18. *Irish Times* 30/10/1907.
19. *Ireland's Crusade against Tuberculosis*, 3 vols, Dublin 1908. VolIII p 121.
20. *Strabane Weekly News* 5/12/1908.
21. *The Fermanagh Herald* 28/11/1908.
22. Prof Evans, p 214.

23. *Freeman's Journal* 7/11/1907.
24. *An Claidheamh Soluis*, 2/11/1908.
25. *Ireland's Crusade Against Tuberculosis*, Lady Aberdeen, Preface, Vol 1, 1908, p 3.
26. *Irish Times* , 3/5/1911.
27. Micheal O'Beirn, *Memorial of Seamus O'Beirn*, (Private typescript)
28. *The Turn of the Tide*, Anna Day, Dublin 1987, pp 16-17.
29. Pentland, p 160.
30. *Souvenir Booklet of WNHA*, Dublin 1946.
31. *Voice of Banba*, Ballad, ed Brian O'Higgins, Dublin 1931, pp 28, 29.

CHAPTER 7

1. *Irish Times*, 16/8/1911.
2. 'The Sphere of Women in Relation to Public Health', Lady Aberdeen, *Dublin Journal of Medical Science*, September 1911.
3. *Irish Times*, 31/10/1911.
4. 'The Countess of Aberdeen's Health Promotion Caravans', *Journal of the Irish Colleges of Physicians*, July, 1995, Professor Alun Evans, p 212.
5. *A Bonnie Fechter* Marjorie Pentland, p 162.
6. ibid p 212.
7. *Irish Times* 18/5/1909.
8. ibid 20/5/1909
9. *An Irishman and His Family*, Maude Wynne, London, p 208.
10. *Irish Times*, 3/8/1909.
11. Pentland, p 169,
12. ibid pp 169-170.
13. ibid p 170.
14. *Irish Times*, 21/7/1912.
15. *Irish Worker* 3/8/1912.
16. *Irish Times*, 3/9/1912.
17. Letter from H H Asquith HHC 26/11/1912.
18. *The Turn of the Tide*, Anna Day, p 28.
19. *Sinn Féin*, 22/3/1914.
20. 'To A Lady Bountiful', Sinn Féin, 18/1/1908.
21. *Sinn Féin*, 25.1.1908.
22. ibid 25/1/1908.
23. ibid 1/2/1908.
24. ibid 1/2/1908.
25. ibid 18/7/1908.
26. *Irish Times* 16/1/1911.
27. *Cork Examiner* 15/1/1911.
28. *Daily Express*, quoted in Belfast Evening Telegraph 9/1/1912.
29. *TheNorthern Whig* 10/1/1912.
30. *Irish Times* 6/3/1912.

31. *Irish Times* 6/3/1912.
32. Diary of Sir Horace Plunkett 30/9/1910 - 20/5/1911.
33. *Irish Times* 25/3/1911.
34. ibid 29/3/1911.
35. ibid Editorial 29/3/1911.
36. ibid 30/3/1911.
37. Horace Plunkett, Letter to Lord Monteagle 8/4/1910.
38. Ibid 16/3/1911.
39. Ibid 18/3/1911
40. Ibid 21/3/1911.
41. Ibid 30/3/1911.
42. *Voice of Banba*, Ballad, p 51.
43. *Irish Times*, 9/2/1911.
44. *Sinn Féin*, 18/2/1911.
45. *Irish Times*, 24/5/1911.
46. *The Leader* 10/6/1911.
47. *Irish Times* 24/5/1911.
48. *The Leader* 3/6/1911.
49. *Irish Times* 28/2/1911.
50. Ibid 30/2/1911.
51. Ibid 28/11/1911.

CHAPTER 8

1. *Sláinte*, Lady Aberdeen, Editorial, Jan. 1909.
2. Editorial Notes, Lady Aberdeen, November 1910.
3. *Sláinte*, New Year's Calendar, 1911.
4. *The White Demon and How to Fight Him*, Mrs FE Eaton, Dublin 1909.
5. Reprint from McClure's Magazine, Dr Evans, *Sláinte*, December 1910.
6. 'Uncleanly Habits and the Spread of Consumption', Dr Octavian Hill, *Sláinte*, January 1911.
7. Reprint from Edinburgh News, Sláinte, April, 1910.
8. *Sláinte*, September 1909.
9. *Report of Mr FH Dale, His Majesty's Inspector of Schools, Board of Education Primary Education in Ireland*, 1904, Parliamentary Papers, (cd 1981.)
10. 'Irish Schools and Health', F. North, *Sláinte*, May 1909.
11. 'Observations from Behind a Counter' *Sláinte*, September 1909.
12. *Irish Times*, 16/4/1913.
13. *Evening Herald*, 13/4/1912.
14. *Sláinte*, Report on Quinquennial Meeting of ICW, Lady Aberdeen Sept. 1910.
15. *Sláinte*, September 1910.
16. 'Message of Goodwill from Dr Herman Biggs', *Sláinte*, June 1913.
17. 'Tuberculosis among the Working Classes', *Sláinte*, Sept 1910.

18. *Sláinte*, June 1913.
19. 'The Financial Factor in the Crusade Against Consumption', Alexander Walker, M.D., *Sláinte*, March 1910.
20. *Ireland's Crusade Against Tuberculosis*, Vol 11, p 3.
21. 'The Control of Tuberculosis at Rotherham', *Sláinte*, March 1910.
22. *Sláinte*, December 1913.
23. *Sinn Féin*, 1/5/1909.
24. *Sláinte*, February, 1910.
25. ibid January 1911.
26. ibid March 1910.
27. ibid April 1910.
28. *The Winds of Time*, Lady Edith Gordon, p 164.
29. *Sláinte*, January, 1914.
30. *Sláinte*, February, 1913.
31. *Sláinte*, November, 1912.

CHAPTER 9
1. *Irish Times*, February 1913.
2. *Sláinte*, October 1911.
3. *Sláinte*, October 1911.
4. *Dear Dirty Dublin*, Joseph V. O'Brien, pp 136-7.
5. Editorial, *Irish Times*, 9/9/1913.
6. *Sláinte*, March 1910.
7. *Dublin, the Deposed Capital*, Mary E Daly p 289.
8. O'Brien, p 151.
9. *Irish Worker* 12/4/1913.
10. *Irish Times*, Jan. 1914.
11. Ibid 15/7/1914.
12. Birrell Letter, quoted in *The Chief Secretary, Augustine Birrell in Ireland* Leon Ó Broin, London, 1969. p 127.
13. *Sláinte*, January 1913.
14. Pentland, p 123.
15. *Irish Times*, 15.8.1914.
16. *Sinn Féin*, 28/7/1914.
17. *The Leader* 1/8/1914.
18. *The Leader* 22/8/1914.
19. *Irish Worker* 18/7/1914.
20. *Irish Worker* 1/8/1914.
21. *The Chief Secretary, Augustine Birrell in Ireland*, Leon Ó Broin, p 127.
22. *Irish Worker* 5/4/1913.
23. ibid 12/4/1913.
24. *Sláinte*, January 1914.
25. *Things Past Redress*, Augustine Birrell, London, 1935, p 198.
26. *Lantern Slides* Violet Bonham Carter, p 344.

27. *Irish Reminiscences*, Maurice Headlam, p 40.
28. *The Years of the Shadow*, Katherine Tynan Hinkson.
29. *The Winds of Time*, Lady Edith Gordon, p 91.
30. *A Bonnie Fechte*r, Marjory Pentland, p 242.
31. ibid p 243.
32. *Lantern Slides*, Violet Bonham Carter, p 218.
33. *The Leader* , 16/6/1914.
34. *The Ladies' Field*, 12/3/1912.
35. *Evening Herald*, 2/5/1913.
36. *Ulster Guardian*, 13/1/1912.
37. *Northern Whig*, 10/1/1912.
38. *Irish Times*, 3/9/1912.
39. *Freeman's Journal*, 4/9/1912.
40. *Irish Independent* 4/9/1912.
41. *Memories, Wise and Otherwise*, Sir Henry Robinson, pp 226-7.
42. *Sinn Féin*, 1/3/1914.
43. *Irish Worker*, 26th July, 1913.
44. *Irish Worker*, 19th April, 1913.
45. Augustine Birrell quoted by Leon Ó Broin, p 129.
46. Letter from Margaret MacNeill, H.H.C. (Pentland, pp 178-9).
47. *Birrell* Leon O'Broin, p 131.
48. *Freeman's Journal*, 22/1/1915.
49. Letter from George V, 22/1/1915, HHC.
50. *Irish Times*, 13/2/1915.
51. *Freeman's Journal*, 13/1/1915.

$\mathscr{B}ibliography$

ABBREVIATIONS:
- **BL**   British Library
- **BNL**   British Newspaper Library
- **HHC**   Haddo House Collection
- **NLI**   National Library of Ireland
- **Pt**   Peamount Hospital

Aberdeen, Ishbel, Countess of (later Marchioness) Aberdeen and Temair
Articles in *Sunday Post*, Feb-March 1935 **BNL**
"My Stage Fright as a Débutante"
"My Wonderful Years in the Highlands"
"Why I love Rotten Row"
"My Honeymoon Adventure"
"A Great Day in My Life"
"A Ticklish Job for Lord Aberdeen"
"My Greatest Friend"
"The Perfect Marriage"
"My Brother and Lady Fanny"

The Canadian Journal of Lady Aberdeen 1893-1898 John T Saywell (ed.)
    Toronto, 1960.
Through Canada with a Kodak, Edinburgh, 1893
"Why I am a Politician" – *The Gentlewoman*, August 1892 **BL**
Guide to Irish Industrial Village Chicago World's Fair, Chicago
(ed) *Archie Gordon, A Memorial Volume* (Printed privately, Dublin? 1910)
(ed) *Guide to Irish Exhibits at the Edinburgh International Exhibition*, Dublin
    1886.
(ed) *Ireland's Crusade against Tuberculosis*, 3 vols, Dublin, 1908, 1893
(ed) *Report of Transactions of the Fourth Quinquennial Meeting of the
    International Council of Women* held at Toronto, June 1909
(ed) *Handbook of Irish Life and Industry*, Dublin 1907
(ed) *Sláinte* Magazine 1909-1915 Dublin (Journal of Women's National Health
    Association) **Pt**
"The Sphere of Women in Relation to Public Health", *Dublin Journal of Medical
    Science*, Sept 1911.

With Lord Aberdeen: *We Twa, Reminiscences of Lord and Lady Aberdeen*, 2 vols,
    London, 1936.
Musings of a Scottish Granny, London, 1936

Biographies of Lady Aberdeen
French, Doris, *Ishbel and the Empire*, Toronto and Oxford 1988
Pentland, Marjorie, *A Bonnie Fechter*, London, 1952.

Letters
From Lady Aberdeen to

Henry Campbell-Bannermann,
MSS No. 41, 210 **BL**

John Morley, **HHC**

To Lord and Lady Aberdeen – various correspondents including
Herbert Asquith, Augustine Birrell,
King George V. **HHC**

About Lady Aberdeen

Horace Plunkett,
MSS 13, 414 **NLI**

Diary References

Lady Alice Howard, MSS 3,600 - 3,625
Sir Horace Plunkett (photocopy **NLI**,
original in Plunkett Foundation Oxford).

Material relating to Women's National Health Association
Minute Books of WNHA1907-1915,Dublin **Pt**
WNHA pamphlet (nd) **Pt**
Souvenir Booklet of WNHA, Dublin 1946 **NLI**

Books
Anderson, R A *With Sir Horace Plunkett in Ireland*, London, 1935.

Bamford, Francis and Bankes, Viola *The Vicious Circle*, London 1965
Barrington, Ruth *Health, Medicine and Politics in Ireland*, Dublin, 1987
Beckett, J C *The Anglo-Irish Tradition*, London 1976
Bence-Jones Mark *The Twilight of the Ascendancy*, London, 1987
Berman, Marjorie Katz *John Morley and Ireland*, Ann Arbor, 1981
Best, Geoffrey *Mid-Victorian Britain*, London, 1971
Birrell, Augustine *Things Past Redress* London, 1935
Bonham-Carter, Mark and Pottle, Mark (eds) *Lantern Slides, Diaries and Letters of Violet Bonham Carter*, London, 1996
Bolger, Patrick *The Irish Co-Operative Movement*, Dublin, 1977
Bourke, Joanna "The Health Caravan", Domestic Education and Female Labor in Rural Ireland, 1890-1914, *Eire-Ireland*, Winter, 1989
Gordon-Bowe, Nicola (ed) *Art and the National Dream* Dublin 1993
Brooke, R F *The Brimming River*, London, 1961
Brown, Noel *Against the Tide*, Dublin 1986

Cameron, Sir Charles *How the Poor Live*, Dublin 1904

Clear, Caitriona *Nuns in Nineteenth-Century Ireland*, Dublin 1993

Connolly, S J (ed) *The Oxford Companion to Irish History*, Oxford, 1998

Coyne, Wm (ed) *Ireland, Industrial and Agricultural*, Dublin 1902

Cullen, L M *An Economic History of Ireland since 1660*, London and Worcester, 1987

Cullen, Mary and Luddy, Maria *Women, Power and Consciousness in Nineteenth-Century Ireland*, Dublin 1995

Daly, Mary E *Dublin, the Deposed Capital, A Social and Economic History 1860-1914*, Cork, 1984

Day, Anna *The Turn of the Tide, The Story of Peamount*, Dublin 1987

Deeny, James *To Cure and to Care*, Dublin, 1989

Donnehy, Wm F (ed) *Record of Irish International Exhibition 1907*, Dublin 1907

Digby, Margaret *Horace Plunkett An Anglo-American-Irishman*, Oxford 1949

Dixon, F E "Dublin Exhibitions (11)", *Dublin Historical Record*, September 1973

Donajorodzki, A P (ed) *Social Control in Nineteenth Century Britain*, London 1977

Drummond, Henry *Natural Law in the Spiritual World*, London 1884

Eaton, F E *The White Demon and How to Fight Him*, Dublin 1909

Evans, Professor Alun "The Countess of Aberdeen's Health Promotion Caravans", *Journal of the Irish College of Physicians and Surgeons*, Dublin, July 1995

Foster, R F *Modern Ireland 1600-1972*, London, 1988

Farmar, Tony *Ordinary Lives*, Dublin, 1991

Fingall, Countess of *Seventy Years Young* (as told to Pamela Hinkson), Dublin, 1937

Gordon, Lady Edith *The Winds of Time*, London, 1934

Gordon Bowe, Nicola (ed) *Art and the National Dream*, Dublin 1993

Gourvish, T R and O'Day, Alan (eds) *Later Victorian Britain 1867-1900*, London, 1988

Gray, Tony *Ireland this Century*, London 1984

Hammond, G L *Gladstone and the Irish Nation*, London 1938

Hinkson, Pamela Tynan *The Middle Years*, London 1913

The Years of the Shadow, London 1919

Hollis, Patricia, *Women in Public, The Women's Movement, 1850-1900* London, 1979

Hoppen, K Theodore *Ireland since 1800, Conflict and Conformity*, London and New York, 1989

Inglis, Brian *The Diseases of Civilization,* London, 1981

Jenkins, Roy *Gladstone,* London, 1995
Johnston, Sheila Turner *Alice, A Biography of Alice Milligan,* Omagh, 1994
Kee, Robert *The Green Flag,* London, 1972

Larmour, Paul *The Art and Crafts Movement in Ireland,* Belfast, 1992
Lee, Joseph *The Modernisation of Irish Society,* 1848-1918, Dublin 1973
Luddy, Maria *Women in Ireland 1800-1918,* Cork 1995
  Women and Philanthropy in Nineteenth Century Ireland, 1997
  with Murphy, Cliona (eds) *Studies in Irish Women's History in the Nineteenth Century,* Dublin 1989
Lyons, F S L *Ireland Since the Famine,* London, 1971

McDowell, R B *The Irish Administration, 1801-1941,* London, 1964
McNamara, Sarah *Those Intrepid United Irishwomen,* Limerick 1995
Maguire, J B *Dublin Castle, A Historical Background and Guide,* Dublin, 1971
Marreco, Anne *The Rebel Countess,* London 1967
Micks, William L *An Account of the Congested District Board, 1891-1923,* Dublin 1925
Moore, George *A Drama in Muslin,* Belfast, 1992
Morley, John *Recollections,* 2 vols, London, 1917

O'Beirne, J W *A History of the Phoenix Park,* Dublin, (nd)
O'Beirn, Michael 'Memoir of Seamus O'Beirn' (typescript, nd)
O'Brien, Joseph V *Dear Dirty Dublin,* Los Angeles, 1982
O'Brien, R Barry *Dublin Castle and the Irish People,* London 1912
Ó Broin, Leon *Augustine Birrell, The Chief Secretary in Ireland,* London, 1969
  No Man's Man, Biography of Joseph Brennan, Dublin 1982
O'Céirín, Cyril and Kit *Women of Ireland, A Biographical Dictionary,* Galway, 1996
Ó Cléirigh, Nellie "Lady Aberdeen and the Irish Connection" *Dublin Historical Record,* December 1985.
Ó Faolain, Seán *Constance Markievicz,* London 1934
O'Higgins, Brian (ed) *The Voice of Banba,* Dublin 1931
O'Neill, Wm L (ed) *The Woman Movement, Feminism in the United States and England,* London and New York, 1969

Plunkett, Sir Horace, Pilkington, Ellice and Russell, George William *The United Irishwomen,* Dublin 1911
Pountney, David Programme Notes for performance of *La Traviata* by English National Opera, London 1988/9
Prunty, Jacinta *Dublin Slums,* Dublin 1998

Robinson, Sir Henry *Memories, Wise and Otherwise*, London, 1923
Robinson, Lennox *Curtain Up*, London, 1942
Rolleston, C H *T W Rolleston, Portrait of an Irishman*, London, 1939

Sheehy, Jeanne *The Rediscovery of Ireland's Past*, Dublin 1980
Smith, George Adam *The Life of Henry Drummond*, London, 1899
Sontag, Susan *Illness as Metaphor*, London 1983

Tallon, Donal *Report on Work of Mansion House Committee, 1898*, Dublin 1898
Trench, Charles Chenevix *Charley Gordon*, London 1978

Valiulis, Maryann Gialanella and O'Dowd, Mary *Women and Irish History*,
    Dublin 1997

West, Trevor *Horace Plunkett, Co-Operation and Politics*, Gerrards Cross Bucks
    and Washington, DC, 1986
Wilkinson, Henry S *The Eve of Home Rule, Impressions of Ireland in 1886*,
    London 1886.
Wilkinson, Sir Neville *To All and Singular*, London, 1925
Wynne, Maude *An Irishman and His Family*, London 1937

Young, Mary Alice *Recollections*, Antrim, 1996

Newspapers
United Ireland Feb-Sep 1886 **NLI**
Irish Times Feb-Sep 1886 **NLI**
Irish Independent Feb 1905-Jan 1915 **NLI**
Freeman's Journal Feb 1905-Jan 1915 **NLI**

Individual articles from Newspapers all from Scrapbooks in Peamount

Strabane Weekly News	*The Onlooker*
Ulster Guardian	*The Kerryman*
Fermanagh Herald	*Irish Life*
Evening Telegraph	*The Lady of the House*
Evening Herald	*Modern Society*
The Ladies Field	*Cork Examiner*
The Northern Whig	*Belfast Telegraph*
Crown Magazine	*Truth*

Miscellaneous

Official Catalogue of Civic Exhibition, in Ireland 1914, Dublin.

Irish Home Industries Association *Catalogue of Goods on Exhibition at Depôt*, Dawson St. March 1888 and

Report of Executive Committee for year ending March 1888

Report of Mr F H Dale, His Majesty's Inspector of Schools (Pamphlet) **NLI**

Board of Education, on Primary Education in Ireland, 1904, Parliamentary Papers (cd 1981) **NLI**

Some Irish Industries, Dublin 1897 (*Irish Homestead*, Pamphlet) **NLI**

The Vice-Royalty of Ireland and the Viceregal Court, Historically Vindicated John P Prendergast, Dublin 1886 (Pamphlet) **NLI**

Index